Dummies 101™ Word For Windows® 95

The Word 95 Screen

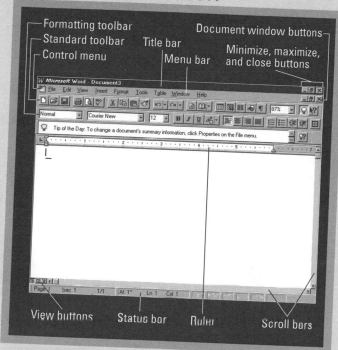

Formatting toolbar
Standard toolbar
Control menu
Title bar
Menu bar
Document window buttons
Minimize, maximize, and close buttons

View buttons   Status bar   Ruler   Scroll bars

The Basics

▶ **Starting Word 95:** Click the Start button, choose Programs, choose Microsoft Office, and choose Microsoft Word.

▶ **Exiting Word 6:** Choose File⇨Exit or click the Close button.

▶ **Creating a new document:** Choose File⇨New, press Ctrl+N, or click the New button.

▶ **Saving a document:** Choose File⇨Save, find the folder in which you want to save the document, enter a new document name in the File name box, and click the Save button.

▶ **Opening a document:** Choose File⇨Open, press Ctrl+O, or click the Open button; find the folder the document is in; select the document that you want to open; and then click the Open button or press Enter.

▶ **Closing a document:** Click the Save button, choose File⇨Save, or press Ctrl+S to save the document one last time, and then choose File⇨Close.

Text Formatting

▶ **Boldfacing:** Click the Bold button or press Ctrl+B.

▶ **Italicizing:** Click the Italicize button or press Ctrl+I.

▶ **Underlining:** Click the Underline button or press Ctrl+U.

▶ **Resizing text:** Select the text and click an option on the Font Size drop-down list, or choose Format⇨Font and then choose a Size option.

▶ **Changing fonts:** Click the Font drop-down list word choose a font name, or choose Format⇨Font and select a font in the dialog box.

Dummies 101™ Word For Windows® 95

CHEAT SHEET

Editing Techniques

♦ **Entering text:** Start typing. Letters that you enter push aside the words that are already there. Press the Insert key or double-click OVR on the status bar to make the characters that you enter cover up the letters that are already there.

♦ **Deleting text:** Press Backspace or Delete to delete a character at a time. Select the text that you want to delete and press the key.

♦ **Starting a paragraph:** Press Enter to start a new paragraph.

♦ **Selecting text:** Double-click a word to select it. Drag across text to select it. Double-click in the left margin to select a paragraph.

♦ **Moving text:** Select the text that you want to move and then drag it to a new place. You can also click the Cut button and paste the selected text elsewhere with the Paste button; choose Edit⇨Cut and then Edit⇨Paste; or press Ctrl+X and then Ctrl+V.

♦ **Copying text:** Select the text and drag it elsewhere while holding down the Ctrl key. After you select text, you can also click the Copy button and then the Paste button; choose Edit⇨Copy and then Edit⇨Paste; or press Ctrl+C and then Ctrl+V.

Moving Around in Documents

Press This Key	To Move Here
Ctrl+↑	Up one paragraph
Ctrl+↓	Down one paragraph
Page Up	Up one screen
Page Down	Down one screen
Ctrl+Page Up	Top of screen
Ctrl+Page Down	Bottom of screen
Ctrl+Alt+Page Up	Up one page
Ctrl+Alt+Page Down	Down one page
Ctrl+Home	Start of document
Ctrl+End	Bottom of document
Ctrl+→	Right one word
Ctrl+←	Left one word
Home	Start of line
End	End of line

IDG BOOKS WORLDWIDE™

DUMMIES 101™: WORD FOR WINDOWS® 95

DUMMIES 101:™ WORD FOR WINDOWS® 95

by Peter Weverka

IDG Books Worldwide, Inc.
An International Data Group Company

Foster City, CA ✦ Chicago, IL ✦ Indianapolis, IN ✦ Braintree, MA ✦ Southlake, TX

Dummies 101™: Word For Windows® 95

Published by
IDG Books Worldwide, Inc.
An International Data Group Company
919 E. Hillsdale Blvd.
Suite 400
Foster City, CA 94404

Library of Congress Catalog Card No.: 96-75108

ISBN: 1-56884-632-0

Printed in the United States of America

10 9 8 7 6 5 4 3 2 1

1M/RU/QS/ZW/IN

Distributed in the United States by IDG Books Worldwide, Inc.

Distributed by Macmillan Canada for Canada; by Computer and Technical Books for the Caribbean Basin; by Contemporanea de Ediciones for Venezuela; by Distribuidora Cuspide for Argentina; by CITEC for Brazil; by Ediciones ZETA S.C.R. Ltda. for Peru; by Editorial Limusa SA for Mexico; by Transworld Publishers Limited in the United Kingdom and Europe; by Al-Maiman Publishers & Distributors for Saudi Arabia; by Simron Pty. Ltd. for South Africa; by IDG Communications (HK) Ltd. for Hong Kong; by Toppan Company Ltd. for Japan; by Addison Wesley Publishing Company for Korea; by Longman Singapore Publishers Ltd. for Singapore, Malaysia, Thailand, and Indonesia; by Unalis Corporation for Taiwan; by WS Computer Publishing Company, Inc., for the Philippines; by WoodsLane Pty. Ltd. for Australia; by WoodsLane Enterprises Ltd. for New Zealand.

For general information on IDG Books Worldwide's books in the U.S., please call our Consumer Customer Service department at 800-762-2974. For reseller information, including discounts and premium sales, please call our Reseller Customer Service department at 800-434-3422.

For information on where to purchase IDG Books Worldwide's books outside the U.S., contact IDG Books Worldwide at 415-655-3021 or fax 415-655-3295.

For information on translations, contact Marc Jeffrey Mikulich, Director, Foreign & Subsidiary Rights, at IDG Books Worldwide, 415-655-3018 or fax 415-655-3295.

For sales inquiries and special prices for bulk quantities, write to the address above or call IDG Books Worldwide at 415-655-3200.

For information on using IDG Books Worldwide's books in the classroom, or ordering examination copies, contact the Education Office at 800-434-2086 or fax 817-251-8174.

For authorization to photocopy items for corporate, personal, or educational use, please contact Copyright Clearance Center, 222 Rosewood Drive, Danvers, MA 01923, or fax 508-750-4470.

is a trademark under exclusive license to IDG Books Worldwide, Inc., from International Data Group, Inc.

About the Author

Peter Weverka

Peter Weverka is the author of *Word For Windows 95 For Dummies Quick Reference* (IDG Books Worldwide, Inc., 1995) and the editor of 75 computer books on topics ranging from the Internet to desktop publishing. His humorous articles and stories (none related to computers, thankfully) have appeared in *Harper's* and *Exquisite Corpse*.

Welcome to the world of IDG Books Worldwide.

IDG Books Worldwide, Inc., is a subsidiary of International Data Group, the world's largest publisher of computer-related information and the leading global provider of information services on information technology. IDG was founded more than 25 years ago and now employs more than 7,700 people worldwide. IDG publishes more than 250 computer publications in 67 countries (see listing below). More than 70 million people read one or more IDG publications each month.

Launched in 1990, IDG Books Worldwide is today the #1 publisher of best-selling computer books in the United States. We are proud to have received 8 awards from the Computer Press Association in recognition of editorial excellence and three from Computer Currents' First Annual Readers' Choice Awards, and our best-selling ...*For Dummies®* series has more than 19 million copies in print with translations in 28 languages. IDG Books Worldwide, through a joint venture with IDG's Hi-Tech Beijing, became the first U.S. publisher to publish a computer book in the People's Republic of China. In record time, IDG Books Worldwide has become the first choice for millions of readers around the world who want to learn how to better manage their businesses.

Our mission is simple: Every one of our books is designed to bring extra value and skill-building instructions to the reader. Our books are written by experts who understand and care about our readers. The knowledge base of our editorial staff comes from years of experience in publishing, education, and journalism — experience which we use to produce books for the '90s. In short, we care about books, so we attract the best people. We devote special attention to details such as audience, interior design, use of icons, and illustrations. And because we use an efficient process of authoring, editing, and desktop publishing our books electronically, we can spend more time ensuring superior content and spend less time on the technicalities of making books.

You can count on our commitment to deliver high-quality books at competitive prices on topics you want to read about. At IDG Books Worldwide, we continue in the IDG tradition of delivering quality for more than 25 years. You'll find no better book on a subject than one from IDG Books Worldwide.

John J. Kilcullen

John Kilcullen
President and CEO
IDG Books Worldwide, Inc.

IDG Books Worldwide, Inc., is a subsidiary of International Data Group, the world's largest publisher of computer-related information and the leading global provider of information services on information technology. International Data Group publishes over 250 computer publications in 67 countries. Seventy million people read one or more International Data Group publications each month. International Data Group's publications include: **ARGENTINA:** Computerworld Argentina, GamePro, Infoworld, PC World Argentina; **AUSTRALIA:** Australian Macworld, Client/Server Journal, Computer Living, Computerworld, Digital News, Network World, PC World, Publishing Essentials, Reseller; **AUSTRIA:** Computerwelt, PC TEST; **BELARUS:** PC World Belarus; **BELGIUM:** Data News; **BRAZIL:** Annuário de Informática, Computerworld Brazil, Connections, Super Game Power, Macworld, PC World Brazil, Publish Brazil, SUPERGAME; **BULGARIA:** Computerworld Bulgaria, Networkworld/Bulgaria, PC & MacWorld Bulgaria; **CANADA:** CIO Canada, ComputerWorld Canada, InfoCanada, Network World Canada, Reseller World; **CHILE:** Computerworld Chile, GamePro, PC World Chile; **COLUMBIA:** Computerworld Colombia, GamePro, PC World Colombia; **COSTA RICA:** PC World Costa Rica/Nicaragua; **THE CZECH AND SLOVAK REPUBLICS:** Computerworld Czechoslovakia, Elektronika Czechoslovakia, PC World Czechoslovakia; **DENMARK:** Communications World, Computerworld Danmark, Macworld Danmark, PC World Danmark, PC World Danmark Supplements, TECH World; **DOMINICAN REPUBLIC:** PC World Republica Dominicana; **ECUADOR:** PC World Ecuador, GamePro; **EGYPT:** Computerworld Middle East, PC World Middle East; **EL SALVADOR:** PC World Centro America; **FINLAND:** MikroPC, Tietoverkko, Tietoviikko; **FRANCE:** Distributique, Golden, Info PC, Le Guide du Monde Informatique, Le Monde Informatique, Reseaux & Telecoms; **GERMANY:** Computer Business, Computerwoche, Computerwoche Extra, Computerwoche Focus, Electronic Entertainment, GamePro, I/M Information Management, Macwelt, PC Welt; **GREECE:** GamePro, Macworld & Publish; **GUATEMALA:** PC World Centro America; **HONDURAS:** PC World Centro America; **HONG KONG:** Computerworld Hong Kong, PCWorld Hong Kong, Publish in Asia; **HUNGARY:** ABCD CD-ROM, Computerworld Szamitastechnika, PC & Mac World Hungary, PC-X Magazine; **INDIA:** Computerworld India, PC World India, Publish in Asia; **INDONESIA:** InfoKomputer PC World, Komputek Computerworld, Publish in Asia; **IRELAND:** ComputerScope, PC Live!; **ISRAEL:** PC World 32 BIT, People & Computers; **ITALY:** Computerworld Italia, Computerworld Italia Special Editions, Lotus Italia, Macworld Italia, Networking Italia, PC Shopping, PC World Italia, PC World/Walt Disney; **JAPAN:** Macworld Japan, Nikkei Personal Computing, SunWorld Japan, Windows World Japan; **KENYA:** East African Computer News; **KOREA:** Hi-Tech Information/Computerworld, Macworld Korea, PC World Korea; **MACEDONIA:** PC World Macedonia; **MALAYSIA:** Computerworld Malaysia, PC World Malaysia, Publish in Asia; **MEXICO:** Computerworld Mexico, GamePro, Macworld, PC World Mexico; **MYANMAR:** PC World Myanmar; **NETHERLANDS:** Computable, Computer! Totaal, LAN Magazine, Macworld, Net Magazine; **NEW ZEALAND:** Computer Buyer, Computerworld New Zealand, MTB, Network World, PC World New Zealand; **NICARAGUA:** PC World Costa Rica/Nicaragua; **NIGERIA:** PC World Africa; **NORWAY:** Computerworld Norge, Computerworld Privat, CW Rapport Klient/Tjener, CW Rapport Nettverk & Telecom, CW Rapport Offentlig Sektor, IDG's KURSGUIDE, Macworld Norge, Multimedia World, PC World Ekspress, PC World Nettverk, PC World Norge, PC World's Produktguide, Windows Spesial; **PAKISTAN:** Computerworld Pakistan, PC World Pakistan; **PANAMA:** GamePro, PC World Panama; **PARAGUAY:** PC World Paraguay; **P. R. OF CHINA:** China Computerworld, China Infoworld, Computer & Communication, Electronic Product World, Electronics Today, Game Camp, PC World China, Popular Computer Week, Software World, Telecom Product World; **PERU:** Computerworld Peru, GamePro, PC World Profesional Peru, PC World Peru; **POLAND:** Computerworld Poland, Computerworld Special Report, Macworld, Networld, PC World Komputer; **PHILIPPINES:** Computerworld Philippines, PC Digest, Publish in Asia; **PORTUGAL:** Cerebro/PC World, Correio Informático/Computerworld, Mac•In/PC•In Portugal; **PUERTO RICO:** PC World Puerto Rico; **ROMANIA:** Computerworld Romania, PC World Romania, Telecom Romania; **RUSSIA:** Computerworld Rossiya, Network World Russia, PC World Russia; **SINGAPORE:** Computerworld Singapore, PC World Singapore, Publish in Asia; **SLOVENIA:** MONITOR; **SOUTH AFRICA:** Computing S.A., Network World S.A., Software World; **SPAIN:** Computerworld España, COMUNICACIONES WORLD, Dealer World, Macworld España, PC World España; **SWEDEN:** CAP&Design, Computer Sweden, Corporate Computing, MacWorld, Maxi Data, MikroDatorn, Nätverk & Kommunikation, PC/Aktiv, PC World, Windows World; **SWITZERLAND:** Computerworld Schweiz, Macworld Schweiz, PCtip; **TAIWAN:** Computerworld Taiwan, Macworld Taiwan, PC World Taiwan, Windows World; **THAILAND:** Thai Computerworld, Publish in Asia; **TURKEY:** Computerworld Monitör, MACWORLD Türkiye, PC WORLD Türkiye; **UKRAINE:** Computerworld Kiev, Computers & Software Magazine, PC World Ukraine; **UNITED KINGDOM:** Acorn User, Amiga Action, Amiga Computing, Amiga, Appletalk, CD Powerplay, CD-ROM Now, Computing, Connexion, GamePro, Lotus Magazine, Macaction, Macworld, Open Computing, Parents and Computers, PC Home, PC Works, The WEB; **UNITED STATES:** Cable in the Classroom, CD Review, CIO Magazine, Computerworld, Computerworld Client/Server Journal, Digital Video Magazine, DOS World, Electronic, InfoWorld, I-Way, Macworld, Maximize, MULTIMEDIA WORLD, Network World, PC World, PUBLISH, SWATPro Magazine, Video Event, WebMaster; **URUGUAY:** PC World Uruguay; **VENEZUELA:** Computerworld Venezuela, GamePro, PC World Venezuela; and **VIETNAM:** PC World Vietnam   10/17/95

Dedication

for Sofia

Credits

Senior Vice President and Publisher
Milissa L. Koloski

Associate Publisher
Diane Graves Steele

Brand Manager
Judith A. Taylor

Editorial Managers
Kristin A. Cocks
Mary C. Corder

Product Development Manager
Mary Bednarek

Editorial Executive Assistant
Richard Graves

Editorial Assistants
Constance Carlisle
Chris Collins
Kevin Spencer

Marketing Assistant
Holly Blake

Assistant Acquisitions Editor
Gareth Hancock

Production Director
Beth Jenkins

Production Assistant
Jacalyn L. Pennywell

Supervisor of Project Coordination
Cindy L. Phipps

Supervisor of Page Layout
Kathie S. Schnorr

Supervisor of Graphics and Design
Shelley Lea

Production Systems Specialist
Steve Peake

Reprint/Blueline Coordination
Tony Augsburger
Patricia R. Reynolds
Todd Klemme
Theresa Sánchez-Baker

Media/Archive Coordination
Leslie Popplewell
Melissa Stauffer
Jason Marcuson

Project Editors
Pamela Mourouzis
Bill Helling

Editors
Kelly Ewing
Suzanne Packer

Technical Reviewer
Jim McCarter

Project Coordinator
Sherry Gomoll

Graphics Coordination
Gina Scott
Angela F. Hunckler
Carla Radzikinas

Production Page Layout
Shawn Aylsworth
Brett Black
Cameron Booker
Linda M. Boyer
Kerri Cornell
Jane Martin
Drew R. Moore
Anna Rohrer
Kate Snell

Proofreaders
Henry Lazarek
Gwenette Gaddis
Dwight Ramsey
Carl Saff

Indexer
Lori Lathrop

Cover Design
Kavish + Kavish

Disk Design
Access Technology

Acknowledgments

I owe a very big "thank you" to a lot of different people for helping me with my book. I would especially like to thank Diane Steele for giving me the opportunity to write it and IDG Books editor Pam Mourouzis for recommending me to Diane.

I am also grateful to copy editors Kelly Ewing, Suzanne Packer, and Debra Hart May. The public doesn't know it yet, but there is a worldwide shortage of good copy editors. Given the gravity of the editorial crisis under which we must toil, I was very pleased to have such good copy editors working on my book.

Thanks also go to Bill Helling, who has nerves of steel and a good sense of humor, two qualities that all good project editors should have, and to technical editor Jim McCarter, who made sure that all the instructions given in this book are indeed accurate. I would also like to thank Lori Lathrop for her index and Access Systems for designing the *Dummies 101* series disk.

These people worked very hard on my book, and for that I am very grateful: Sherry Gomoll, Linda Boyer, Lori Lathrop, Henry Lazarek, and the rest of the folks in Production.

Finally, thanks to my family, Sofia, Henry, and Addie, for indulging my strange working hours and scruffy appearance in the morning.

(The publisher would like to give special thanks to Patrick J. McGovern, without whom this book would not have been possible.)

Contents
at a Glance

Files
at a Glance

Part I	Description	Filename
2-1	Button practice	Buttons
2-2	Shortcut keys	Shortcut Keys
2-3	Menu practice	Menu Commands
3-1	Type over text	Typeover
3-2	Select text	Select
3-3	Move text	Move
3-4	Copy text	Copy
3-5	Delete text	Delete
Unit 3 Exercise		Unit 3 Exercise
4-1	Scroll practice	Jump
4-2	Jump around	Jump
Unit 4 Exercise		Jump
Part I Lab Assignment		Where Are They Now

Part II	Description	Filename
6-1	Bold text	Bold
6-2	Italicize text	Italics
6-3	Underline text	Underline
6-4	Special effects	Effects
Unit 6 Quiz		Character Styles
7-1	Change type size	Type Size
7-2	Change font size	Font
7-3	Change text color	Color
7-4	Highlight text	Highlight
Unit 7 Exercise		Unit 7 Exercise
8-1	Justify text	Justify

Table of Contents

Introduction

This book is designed to turn you into an experienced user of Microsoft Word for Windows 95, also known as Word 7, in the shortest possible time. Its 67 lessons cover the most important features of the program in a thorough, step-by-step fashion. When you are finished with this book, you will have explored and learned about everything you need to know to be a good word processor.

How you make use of this book is up to you. You can study it from beginning to end, or you can dive in where you need instructions for doing a particular task. You decide. The important thing to know is that the lessons are presented so that you can learn at your own pace. If you want to speed through this book, more power to you, and if you're one of those people who learns things slowly but thoroughly (I am), this book's method of presenting instructions will also serve you well.

Accompanying most of the lessons is a practice file. By using the practice files on the disk that comes with this book and following the instructions in the lessons, you will get hands-on learning experience in using Word 95. You will acquire skills that would take hours and hours to acquire on your own. And you will discover shortcuts and techniques for doing tasks that you would likely not discover if you didn't have this book.

On the disk are over 50 practice files, including letters, reports, memos, and simple one- and two-paragraph messages. Each file is a stand-in for a Word 95 file that you might work on at home or at the office. As you follow the lessons and work with the practice files, you will encounter the same problems and obstacles that you normally encounter when you use Word 95. The only difference is that I will show you how to solve the problems and get around the obstacles. You are about to become the beneficiary of my many years of blind groping and daring experimentation. You are about to become a very proficient, confident user of Word 95.

Whom This Book Is For

This book is for beginning to intermediate users of Microsoft Word for Windows 95 (or Microsoft Word 7), the latest version of Word. When you first start the program, you see a screen that welcomes you to Microsoft Word for Windows 95, Version 7. That's a mouthful, so to keep it simple, I'll just call the program Word 95 in this book. This book does not cover Microsoft Word 6 (although *Dummies 101: Word 6 For Windows,* also published by IDG Books Worldwide, Inc., and written by yours truly, covers that topic).

If you got this book as a birthday present and can't exchange it, or you are cabin-bound on the Aleutian Islands and the bookstores haven't thawed out yet, don't despair if you have the wrong book. Most of the instructions in this book will work if you have Word 6. Most of the command and option names are the same. The Help program (covered in Unit 5) did change significantly from Word 6 to Word 95, and the means of opening and closing document windows changed as well. Except in those areas, however, this book can serve in a pinch to help you with Word 6.

What's in This Book, Anyway?

This book is a tutorial. It explains, in step-by-step fashion, how to do word processing tasks with Word 95. Simple tasks such as opening and creating documents are covered at the start of the book. As the book progresses, the lessons become more difficult, the idea being that the skills you acquire in the early going will enable you to complete the complex tasks that come at the end of the book.

You will find 67 lessons in all. Lessons that cover similar tasks are grouped in units. At the end of each unit is a short quiz so that you can test yourself and find out how much you learned. At the end of each part is a longer test (the answers to the tests are in Appendix A). The book is divided into five parts, which the following sections describe in more detail.

Part I: Getting Acquainted with Word for Windows 95

Part I explains the basics of using Word 95. Here, you'll learn how to do the tasks that most users do whenever they run the program — such as opening, closing, and saving documents, giving commands, and moving around in documents. The end of Part I explains how to get help when you don't know how to do a task.

Part II: Deciding on the Look of Documents

Part II explains how to change the *look* of text and documents. It shows you how to change the size and typeface of text, boldface text and embellish it in other ways, align text on the page, and deal with margins, indentation, and line spacing, among other things.

Part III: Printing Documents, Envelopes, and Labels

Part III explores printing. It describes how to preview a file before you print it, tell Word 95 how your printer handles files, and print documents in various ways. For example, you'll learn how to print on both sides of the paper, print on envelopes, and print all or part of a document.

Part IV: Streamlining Your Work

Part IV shows you how to take command of Word 95. You'll learn, among other things, how to change the look of the screen itself, get different views of your documents, check for spelling errors, use the Thesaurus, number the pages of a document, create numbered and bulleted lists, and add headers and footers.

Part V: Appendixes

Appendix A gives you the answers to the questions in the tests at the end of Parts I through IV. It also tells you which lessons to review if you get an answer wrong.

For people like me who can't remember what all the buttons on the toolbars do, Appendix B shows each button and describes why you would click it.

About the Disk

To get the most out of this book, you absolutely must use the practice files. You will find the practice files on the disk that comes with this book. Most lessons bid you to use a practice file, so you will do yourself a favor by copying the practice files from the disk onto your computer.

Lucky for you, the disk that comes with this book includes a handy installation program that makes copying the practice files onto your computer very, very easy.

To install the practice files, follow these steps:

1 Insert the Dummies 101 disk into your computer's 3¹/₂-inch floppy disk drive.

The 3¹/₂-inch drive is the only drive that the disk will fit in. If you have two 3¹/₂-inch drives, use the one on top or on the left.

2 From the Start menu, click Settings and then choose Control Panel.

3 Double-click the Add/Remove Programs icon in the Control Panel.

The Add/Remove Properties dialog box appears.

4 Click the Install button in the dialog box.

5 Click the Next button to ask Windows 95 to search for the installation program.

6 Click the Finish button to tell the installation program to do its work and copy the practice files to your computer.

7 Follow along with the installation screens.

A series of installation screens appears and suggests what type of installation you need and where you should install the practice files. Unless you are quite sophisticated and want to do things your own way, keep clicking the Next button to accept the installation type and installation directory that the installation program suggests. If you need more information at any time, click the Help button.

After you complete the installation process, all the files you need for this book will be copied to the C:\MSOffice\Winword\Practice folder. They are ready and waiting for you to use them along with the lessons in this book.

Now that the practice files have been copied to your computer, store the floppy disk where it will be free from harm. That way, you can reinstall a practice file if you mess up the one that you copied to your computer.

Notes:

The Cast of Icons

To help you get more out of this book, I've placed icons here and there. Here's what those icons mean:

heads up

Where you see the Heads Up icon, pay close attention. This icon marks passages that give especially good advice — advice that you should remember. It also alerts you to places where I describe risky techniques or ask you to make decisions that could change the way Word 95 works or could alter a file, for example.

on the test

Information that you will need to know for the tests at the end of each part are marked with the On the Test icon (questions on the quizzes at the end of each unit are not marked with this icon). I want you to do well on the tests, so prick up your ears when you see this icon. If you stumble on a test question, look in Appendix A to find out which lesson provides the answer to the question and then turn to the lesson, find the On the Test icon, and get the right answer.

on the disk

Most of the lessons in this book require you to use a practice file. When I tell you to open a practice file, you will see the On the Disk icon. Also, a list at the beginning of each unit tells which files you need to complete the lessons in the unit.

Conventions of This Book

To help you learn quickly and get the most out of this book, I've adopted a few conventions.

Save button

Where I tell you to click a button, a picture of the button appears in the margin of the book. For example, the button you see here is the Save button. Where I tell you to click the Save button to save your document, you'll see the Save button in the margin.

Besides clicking buttons, you can do tasks in Word 95 by pressing combinations of keys. For example, you can also save a document by pressing Ctrl+S. In other words, you press the Ctrl key and the S key at the same time. Where you see Ctrl+, Alt+, or Shift+ followed by a key name (or maybe more than one key name), you press the keys simultaneously.

To show you how to issue commands, I use the ⇨ symbol. For example, you can choose File⇨Save to save a command. The ⇨ is just a shorthand method of saying, "Choose Save from the File menu."

Notice how the *F* in File and the *S* in Save are underlined in the preceding paragraph. Those same characters are underlined in the command names in Word 95. You can press underlined letters to give commands on menus and press the Alt key and underlined letters to make selections in dialog boxes. Where a letter is underlined in a command name or on a dialog box option in Word 95, it is also underlined on the pages of this book.

Where you see letters in boldface text in this book, I want you to type the letters. For example, if you read, "Type **annual report.doc** in the File name text box to name your document," you should do just that: You should type those very same letters.

At the start of each unit is a list of prerequisites. The prerequisites explain what you need to know to complete the unit successfully. For example, before you can open a file, you need to know how to create one, so creating a file is a prerequisite for opening a file. Next to each prerequisite on the list is the lesson or unit in this book that you can refer to if you don't know a prerequisite and need to brush up on it.

At the end of each lesson, you will find a progress check. Progress checks describe precisely what you need to have learned from each lesson before going on to the next lesson. After you complete a lesson, read the progress check to make sure that you are ready to move ahead.

Notes in the margin of this book tell you the names of buttons, provide shortcuts for doing tasks, and give word definitions, among other things. Don't forget to glance at the margin notes to pick up this valuable information.

Last, but not least, I've included recesses. This book is packed with information, and no mortal soul can take in all the information quickly. When I think it is time for a rest, I insert a brief recess in the text. Recesses are meant to help you take stock of what you have learned and point to places where you should take a breather.

Notes:

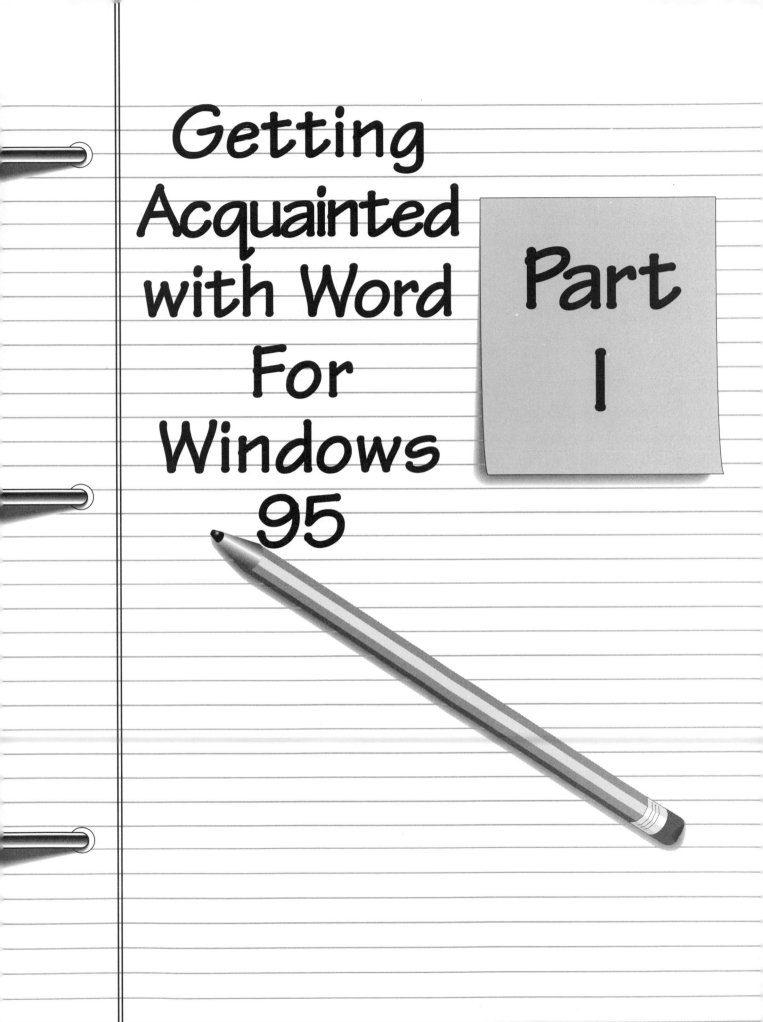

Getting Acquainted with Word For Windows 95

Part I

In this part . . .

art I teaches you the basics of Word 95. The tasks that are described here are tasks that everybody who uses Word 95 does whenever they use the program. In Part I, you learn how to open, close, and save documents; give commands; and move around in documents. The end of Part I explains how to get help when you don't know how to do a task.

My Word, you have a lot of important things to learn here!

The Fundamentals

Prerequisites
- Turning on your computer
- Installing the program
- Looking sharp and keeping your nose clean

Objectives for This Unit

✓ Starting the program

✓ Creating, saving, and naming a document

✓ Opening and closing a document

✓ Learning what the things on-screen are

✓ Exiting Word for Windows 95

This unit explains the basics of using Word for Windows 95. Some readers may know the program as Word 7, but for the purposes of this book, I'll call the program Word 95.

The tasks covered in this unit are tasks that you will do whenever you run the program. Learn these tasks now, and you can take a giant first step toward becoming one of those people whom others seek out when they have a word processing question.

In Unit 1, you learn how to start Word for Windows 95. Then you learn how to create, save, and name a document so that you can open it later. This unit also tells you how to open a document that you worked on previously and how to close a document, as well as how to exit Word for Windows 95.

If you've poked around in Word 95, you already know that the screen is cluttered with buttons, icons, and strange arrows that point east, west, north, and south. You learn what all that stuff is in Unit 1.

Starting Word 95   Lesson 1-1

Before you can start Word 95, of course, you have to turn on your computer. To turn on most computers, you either press a button on the front panel or flick a switch on the side.

A few colorful screens appear and inform you that your computer is starting Windows 95. Eventually, you see a mostly blank screen with a few icons on it.

Figure 1-1: Starting Word for Windows 95.

Figure 1-2: After Word 95 is up and running, you see this screen.

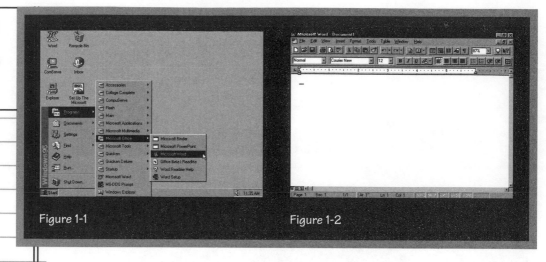

Figure 1-1   Figure 1-2

mouse pointer

☑ **Progress Check**

If you can do the following, you've mastered this lesson:

❑ Turn on your computer.

❑ Start Word for Windows 95.

Along the bottom of this screen is the *taskbar*. On the left side of the taskbar is the Start button; on the right is a digital clock. Now you're ready to start Word 95 by doing the following:

1 Click the Start button.

Click simply means to put the mouse pointer over something and tap the left mouse button once. When you roll the mouse cursor over the screen in Windows 95, it looks like a large egotistical *I*, but as soon as you roll it over a button or something else that can be selected, the cursor turns into a pointing arrow.

When you click the Start button, a menu appears on-screen.

2 Choose Programs, the first menu item.

To choose Programs, you point to the word *Programs*, press P on your keyboard, or press the up arrow on your keyboard until *Programs* is high-lighted and then press Enter. A second menu appears beside the first one. This new menu offers a number of choices in alphabetical order.

3 Choose Microsoft Office on the new menu.

To choose Microsoft Office, either point to this menu item with your mouse or press the ↓ key until Microsoft Office is highlighted and then press Enter.

Yet another menu appears to the right of the Microsoft Office menu. On this menu are the Microsoft Office programs that you or somebody else installed on your computer. Your screen looks something like Figure 1-1. Microsoft Word should be one of the options on the new menu.

4 Choose Microsoft Word to start the program.

To choose Microsoft Word, you can either click the name or press the arrow keys until the name is highlighted and then press Enter.

You see a colorful title screen, and then the program opens, as Figure 1-2 shows.

Lesson 1-2   Creating Your First Document

This lesson shows you how to create a simple document. You learn how to enter text on-screen, end a line of text, and begin a new one. This lesson also describes a few simple techniques for editing text.

When you first start Word 95, you are presented with a new document. That's simple enough. You can start typing, formatting, and doing any number of things to the new document. If you want to create a new document on your own, however, you have to tell Word 95 to create a new document. This lesson explains how to do that.

To create a document, do the following:

on the test

1 Click the New button.

You can also choose File⇨New or press Ctrl+N. As you learn in Unit 2, you often can give a command in more than one way. Opening a new document is a common task, so Word 95 offers three different ways to give the File⇨New command.

If you click the New button or press Ctrl+N, you go straight to a blank screen. If you opt for File⇨New, you see the New dialog box with a bunch of stuff in it. For the moment, don't worry about letters, faxes, reports, memos, templates, or anything else in the New dialog box. Just double-click the Blank Document icon or click OK.

On the blank screen, notice the text cursor in the upper-left corner (the *text cursor* is the blinking vertical line that marks the place where text appears when you start typing). By typing text, pressing keys, and choosing formatting commands, you can create a document.

2 Type your first name and press Enter.

When you press Enter, the cursor drops down a line. Press Enter when you want to end one line and begin another.

3 Type the following sentence twice: The quick brown fox jumped over the lazy dog.

Notice how Word 95 moves the text to the next line automatically when the text reaches the right side of the screen. With Word 95, you don't have to worry about text falling off the right side of the screen, because Word 95 "wraps" the text to the next line automatically.

4 Hold down the Backspace key until all the words in the second sentence you typed have been erased.

Word 95 offers many ways to *delete*, or erase, text, and using the Backspace key is the simplest method. By pressing the Backspace key, you can erase characters to the left of the text cursor. The Backspace key, located just above the Enter key, has a left-pointing arrow on it.

5 Move the mouse cursor to the start of the sentence and then click the left mouse button once.

By doing so, you move the text cursor to a new position — in this case, the start of the sentence.

The mouse cursor is the large egotistical *I*. As you roll the mouse with your hand, the mouse cursor moves across the screen. When the mouse cursor is in the spot where you want to start entering text, click the mouse button to move the text cursor to that spot. Your text cursor should now be blinking on and off at the start of the first sentence you entered in step 3.

6 Type a capital A.

To do so, hold down the Shift key and press A. Notice how the other letters move to the right to make room for the new letter.

New button

Notes:

I
mouse cursor

7 **Press the Delete key three times to erase the word *The*.**

In addition to pressing the Backspace key, you can erase characters by pressing the Delete key. Notice, however, that pressing Delete erases characters to the right of the text cursor, whereas pressing Backspace erases characters to the left of the text cursor.

Two delete keys are on your keyboard. One, called Delete, is to the right of the Enter key. The other, called simply Del, is on the numeric keypad on the right side of your keyboard next to the 0 key. (If you press Del and get a period, the Num Lock feature is turned on. When you press the Num Lock key located at the top of the numeric keypad, the keys on the keypad work like number keys. Press Num Lock again to turn Num Lock off and make the Del key erase characters.)

8 **Press and hold down the → key to move the text cursor to the end of the sentence.**

Besides rolling the mouse and clicking to move the text cursor (as you did in step 5), you can move the text cursor by pressing an arrow key. Your keyboard has two sets of arrow keys, one to the left of the numeric keypad and one on the numeric keypad. Press the ← or → key to move the text cursor left or right across the screen.

9 **Press the ← key until the text cursor butts its head on the top of the screen.**

To move up or down from line to line, press the ↑ or ↓ key.

Congratulations! You've created a document. *Document*, by the way, is just another name for a computer file. In Word 95, files are called documents. In the next lesson, you learn how to save and name your document.

☑ Progress Check

If you can do the following, you've mastered this lesson:

❏ Create a new document.

❏ Enter text on-screen.

❏ Move the text cursor by pressing the arrow keys or by using the mouse.

❏ Delete text.

Lesson 1-3   Saving and Naming a Document

After you create a document, you have to save it if you intend to use it ever again. *Saving* means to move data to the computer's hard disk or to a floppy disk. Text that you enter is not stored on the hard disk — it is stored in the computer's memory. You have to save your document if you want the data to be stored permanently.

After you save a document the first time, you have to save it from time to time as you work on it. When you save a document, Word 95 takes the work you've done since the last time you saved your document and stores the work safely on the hard disk or on a floppy disk.

As yet, the document you created in Lesson 1-2 doesn't have a name. If you look at the *title bar* (the strip along the top of the screen), you see the generic name "Document2." (It says "Document2" and not "Document1" because, when you first start Word 95, the program opens up a new document automatically — Document1. You created the second document yourself.) In this lesson, you will save and name your document. When you are done, you will see your name followed by the letters *.doc* on the title bar. This lesson also explains how to save a file that you've already saved and named.

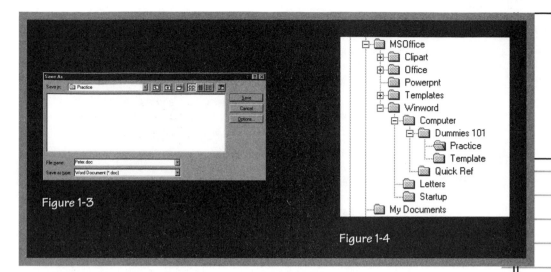

Figure 1-3

Figure 1-4

Figure 1-3: Saving and naming a file for the first time.

Figure 1-4: A folder hierarchy. Double-click folders in the Save As dialog box to move down the hierarchy.

Saving a document for the first time

on the test

As part of saving a document for the first time, Word 95 opens a dialog box and invites you to give the document a name. So the first time you save, you do two things at once — you save your work and name your document.

To save a document for the first time, do the following:

1 Choose File⇨Save.

on the test

You can also press Ctrl+S or click the Save button. No matter which method you choose to give the command, the Save As dialog box appears on-screen, as shown in Figure 1-3. Notice your name followed by the letters *.doc* in the File name box.

2 Find the folder that you want to save the document in and click to make it appear in the Save in box. For this exercise, save the file in the Practice folder.

In Windows 95, all files are saved in *folders.* To find the Practice folder, you may have to click the Up One Level button (the first button to the right of the Save in box) to go a step higher in the folder hierarchy. Then double-click folders in the main box until you arrive at the correct folder. When you're done, the folder in which you are saving your document should appear in the Save in box.

Figure 1-4 shows the folder hierarchy on my computer. I'm saving my file in the Practice folder, and to get to that folder I have to do a bit of clicking in the Save As dialog box. First, I click the Up One Level button to see all the major folders on my C drive. Then, to slide down the hierarchy, I double-click the MSOffice folder, double-click the Winword folder, and double-click the Practice folder.

3 Enter a new file name in the File name box or keep the one that Word 95 suggests.

Word 95 suggests a name in the File name box (the name comes from the first word or few words in the document), but if that name isn't suitable, you can enter another. To do so, click in the box and start typing. Press the Delete and Backspace keys to erase characters.

For this exercise, keep the document name that Word 95 suggests. That name should be the letters in your name followed by *.doc.*

Notes:

Save button

Save button

Ctrl+S is shortcut
for File→Save

☑ Progress Check

If you can do the following,
you've mastered this lesson:

❑ Save and name a
document.

❑ Save a previously named
document.

When you're choosing a name for a document, be sure to choose one that you will remember later. A document name should give a Texas-sized clue about what is in the file.

Document names can be 255 characters long and can include all characters and numbers except the following: / ? : * " < > |. Document names can even include spaces.

on the test

Whatever you do, keep the *.doc* ending on all Word 95 documents. This ending, called a *file extension,* is how your computer knows that the document is a Word document and not a file from another computer program. If you have trouble remembering what the *.doc* file extension is, just remember what Bugs Bunny said when he opened his first Word 95 document: *"What's up, .doc?"*

heads up

Instead of long document names, you might consider sticking with the old 8-character file names that DOS uses. The problem with long names is that many of your friends and coworkers have applications that accept only 8-character file names (11 characters if you count the 3-letter file extension). If you trade files with friends and your file names are longer than 8 letters, your friends will have a hard time reading the long file names.

4 Click the Save button.

Now that you've saved your document, your name followed by the letters *.doc* appears in the title bar at the top of the screen.

Saving a document you've already saved and named

Because saving a document is such a common and necessary chore, Word 95 offers three different ways to do so:

- ◗ Click the Save button.
- ◗ Choose File⇨Save.
- ◗ Press Ctrl+S.

After you give the Save command, your hard disk makes a sound similar to the noise made by cockroaches scuttling across linoleum. That's the sound of your data being transferred from the computer's memory banks to the hard disk. Now that your data is safe, you can get back to work.

Save documents early and often. Make it a habit to click the Save button or press Ctrl+S whenever you leave your desk, let the cat out, or sprint to see which neighborhood prankster has rung your doorbell and run away. If you don't save your work and a power outage occurs or somebody trips over the computer's power cord and unplugs your computer, you lose all the work you did since the last time you saved your document. When you save a document, you transfer all its data safely to the hard disk.

Closing a Document   Lesson 1-4

In the preceding lesson, you saved a document for the first time. In so doing, you named the document. In this lesson, you will close the document you just saved and named. This lesson also explains what happens when you try to close a document without saving it first.

Before you close a document and remove it from the screen, Word 95 wants to be sure that all the text you put in the document is saved. The program doesn't want you to lose data when you close a document, and if you try to close a document without having saved the data inside it, Word 95 gives you one last chance to save your file before you close it. To see how it works, do the following:

1 **Type this sentence anywhere in your document:** I'm going to close without saving.

The sentence you just entered is on-screen but hasn't been saved to the hard disk.

2 **Choose File⇨Close.**

File⇨Close is the command for closing a document. However, you didn't save your file since entering the sentence in step 1, so Word 95 displays a dialog box that asks, Do you want to save changes to (the name of your file)?

3 **Click the Cancel button or press Esc to close the dialog box.**

Normally you click Yes or press Y to have Word 95 save the file and then close it. I had you choose Cancel in step 3 because I want you to keep the file open for the next exercise.

heads up

By the way, is there a good reason for choosing No in this dialog box? There is, as a matter of fact. If you start working on a file and make a total mess of it, you can choose File⇨Close and click No when Word 95 asks whether you want to save your changes to the file. That way, you abandon the changes you made to the file and get your original file back, sans the horrible mess you made.

In the next step, you will close a file and remove it from the screen.

4 **Click the Save button, choose File⇨Save, or press Ctrl+S to save the file one last time.**

Now Word 95 doesn't ask whether you want to save your changes, because you just did it.

5 **Choose File⇨Close.**

The file disappears from the screen. That's all she wrote.

Recess

The last couple of lessons about saving, naming, and closing documents were grueling, were they not? But you learned something very important: how to save a document and close it so that you can retrieve it later. You will save many important documents in your long and storied career, so the lessons you just learned are valuable indeed. You deserve a break. Make yourself an egg salad sandwich and be sure to include Tabasco sauce and capers in the mix.

☑ **Progress Check**

If you can do the following, you've mastered this lesson:

❑ Close an unsaved document.

❑ Close a saved document.

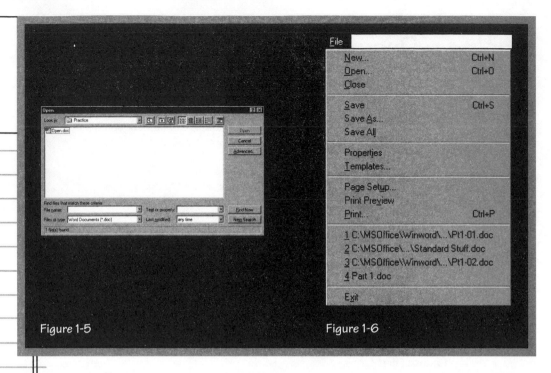

Figure 1-5: The Open dialog box.

Figure 1-6: Click a file name at the bottom of the File menu to open a file.

Figure 1-5   Figure 1-6

Lesson 1-5

Opening an Existing Document

In this lesson, you will open a document and display it on-screen so that you can work with it. The document you will open is the one you created in Lesson 1-2, saved and named in Lesson 1-3, and closed in Lesson 1-4. This document is named after someone you know and love very much — yourself. It is located in the Practice folder.

To open a document that is stored on your hard disk, do the following:

on the test

1 Choose File⇨Open.

You can also press Ctrl+O or click the Open button. No matter how you give the Open command, the Open dialog box appears on-screen, as shown in Figure 1-5.

2 Find the folder where the file is — in this case, the Practice folder.

How you get to the Practice folder depends on where you start. If you haven't exited Word 95 or saved any files since you saved your first file in the Practice folder in Lesson 1-3, the Open dialog box opens to the Practice folder, and you see the contents of this folder in the dialog box.

However, if the Open dialog box doesn't open to the Practice folder, you have to root around to find it. Click the Up One Level button, the button to the right of the Look in text box, to see the major files on the C drive. Then double-click the MSOffice folder, double-click the Winword folder, and double-click the Practice folder to see your practice files.

3 Click on the document named after you.

By clicking, you select the document. You can tell that the document has been selected because it is highlighted. That is, its letters appear before a dark background.

Open button

double-clicking means to press the left mouse button twice very quickly

4 **Click the Open button or press Enter.**

Your file appears on-screen.

By the way, you can bypass step 4 in the preceding exercise by double-clicking the file you want to open in step 3 instead of merely clicking it. Double-clicking a file in the Open dialog box opens the file straightaway.

on the test

Here's another shortcut for opening documents: Click File on the menu bar (or press Alt+F) to pull down the File menu, as shown in Figure 1-6. On the bottom of the File menu are the names of the last four files you worked with in the order in which you opened them. The files are numbered 1 through 4. If one of these files is the one you want to work with, either click it or press its number on the keyboard.

☑ **Progress Check**

If you can do the following, you've mastered this lesson:

❑ Find a document in the Open dialog box.

❑ Open a document.

Finding Your Way around the Screen

Lesson 1-6

The Word 95 screen is a bit overwhelming. What are all those buttons, arrows, words, and numbers about? This lesson briefly explains everything. No, you aren't tested on anything here. This lesson is meant to help you get acquainted with the screen, not to baffle or befuddle you.

As you read the following table, look at Figure 1-7, which shows everything's location on-screen.

Notes:

Table 1-1	**What Everything Is On-Screen**
Part of Screen	*What It Is*
title bar	Tells you the name of the document you're working on.
Control menu	Click here to pull down a menu with options for minimizing, maximizing, moving, and closing the window.
Minimize, Restore, Close buttons	Click these buttons to shrink, enlarge, or close the window.
menu bar	The main menu options you can choose to give Word 95 commands. When you click on these menu names, a menu appears.
document window buttons	Click these buttons to shrink, enlarge, or close the document window.
Standard toolbar	Offers buttons that you can click to execute Word 95 commands.
Formatting bar	Offers formatting buttons and pull-down lists for changing the appearance and alignment of text.
document window	Where you do the real work of writing words and laying out text.

(continued)

Figure 1-7: What all that stuff on-screen is.

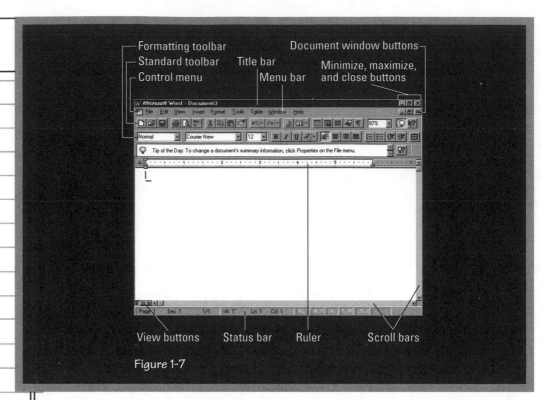

Figure 1-7

✓ Progress Check

If you can do the following, you've mastered this lesson:

❑ Find your way around on-screen.

❑ Use some of the screen's shortcuts.

Table 1-1 *(continued)*

Part of Screen	What It Is
ruler	Shows the width of margins and tab stop locations.
scroll bars	Help you move around in a document.
View buttons	Click to change your document view to Normal, Page Layout, or Outline view.
status bar	Offers basic information about where you are and what you're doing in a document.

Lesson 1-7   Exiting Word 95

Sooner or later, you will decide to stop word processing and get on with your real life. When that happens, you have to exit Word 95. This lesson explains how to do that.

Before you leave the program, close and save all the documents you've been working on (Lesson 1-4 explains how to do so). Then do one of the following:

on the test

● Choose File⇨Exit.

● Click the Close button in the upper-right corner of the application window.

If perchance you forgot to save and close a document, you see the `Do you want to save changes?` dialog box. Click Yes.

heads up

Never close Word 95 by turning off your computer. Doing so can damage your hard disk and the documents you worked so hard to create.

☑ **Progress Check**

If you can do the following, you're ready to move on to the Unit 1 quiz:

❑ Close a document before you exit Word.

❑ Exit Word 95.

Unit 1 Quiz

This short quiz is designed to help you remember what you learned in Unit 1. For the following questions, circle the letter of the correct answer or answers. Each question may have more than one right answer.

1. **To start Word 95, you do the following:**

   A. Turn on your computer.

   B. Click the Start button, choose Programs, choose Microsoft Office, and choose Microsoft Word.

   C. Press Ctrl+S.

   D. Tap three times on your computer and whistle "Dixie."

   E. Choose File⇨Open.

2. **To open a brand-new document, you do the following:**

   A. Give the computer a vigorous shake.

   B. Choose File⇨New or press Ctrl+N.

   C. Choose File⇨Open.

   D. Click the New button.

   E. Place a floppy disk in the floppy drive.

3. **To end one line of text and begin another, you do the following:**

   A. Keep pressing the spacebar until you get to the end of the line and move to the next one.

   B. Press Enter.

   C. Move the mouse cursor to the next line and click once.

   D. Press Tab.

   E. Press any key until you reach the end of the line and go to the next one.

Notes:

4. **Which button is this?**

   A. Open

   B. Save

   C. New

   D. Floppy Disk

   E. Print

5. **Saving documents is very important because:**

   A. It just is, that's all.

   B. By saving a document, you move its data to the hard disk, where the data is stored permanently and safely.

   C. You should save data for a rainy day.

   D. Americans don't save nearly enough, and that means less money is available to borrow, which increases competition for loans and drives up interest rates.

   E. Listening to the sound the computer makes when you save a document is fun.

6. **To close a document, you do the following:**

   A. Choose File⇨Close.

   B. Save your document and choose File⇨Close.

   C. Take off your clothes.

   D. Turn off your computer.

   E. Choose File⇨Open.

7. **To exit Word 95, you do the following:**

   A. Look for the Exit sign and go out that door.

   B. Choose File⇨Exit.

   C. Save your documents and choose File⇨Exit.

   D. Click the Close button in the upper-right corner of the application window.

   E. Open the window, slide out, dangle from the window ledge, and jump to the back garden.

Unit 1 Exercise

1. Open the file you created in Lesson 1-3, the one with your name in it.

2. Enter your name and address at the top and drop down a line.

3. Enter the date.

4. Press Enter twice and type **I'm getting pretty good at this word processing business.**

5. Delete the sentence that begins "A quick brown fox. . . ."

6. Save the changes that you just made to the file.

7. Close the document.

Telling Word What You Want It to Do

Prerequisites
- Starting Word 95 (Lesson 1-1)
- Opening a document (Lesson 1-5)
- Finding your way around the screen (Lesson 1-6)

Objectives for This Unit

✓ Clicking buttons to give commands

✓ Giving commands by pressing shortcut keys

✓ Choosing commands from the menus

✓ Using shortcut menus

✓ Filling in a dialog box

on the disk
- Buttons
- Shortcut Keys
- Menu Commands

Until now, Word 95 has no doubt been bossing you around. The program has been twisting you out of shape and confusing you with its strange dialog boxes and weird command names. In Unit 2, however, you will turn the tables on Word 95. Unit 2 shows you how to give Word 95 commands and make the program do your bidding. Here, you'll take charge and become the master of your word processing destiny.

You can give commands in many ways, and as you become more comfortable with the program, you can decide which way is best for you. You can click buttons, press shortcut keys, or choose menu commands from the main menu or from shortcut menus. I explain all four techniques in this unit.

This short unit also tells you how to fill in *dialog boxes*. When Word needs a lot of information to complete a command, a dialog box appears on-screen. You have to fill out the dialog box before Word will do what you ask.

Giving Commands by Clicking Buttons   Lesson 2-1

The fastest way to give a command in Word 95 is to click a button on the Standard toolbar or the Formatting toolbar. The *Standard toolbar* is the row of buttons below the main menu bar. The *Formatting toolbar* is located right below the Standard toolbar.

Print button

Center button

☑ **Progress Check**

If you can do the following, you've mastered this lesson:

❑ Click buttons on the tool-bars to give commands.

❑ Click the Undo button to reverse your latest action on-screen.

Undo button

Save button

For Lesson 2-1, you will use a file in the Practice folder called Buttons. This file is on the disk that came with this book. Open Buttons now. If you haven't installed the files on the disk, see the instructions opposite the disk in this book or read "About the Disk" in the Introduction. Review Lesson 1-5 if you need help opening a document.

To experiment with buttons, do the following:

1 Move the mouse pointer over a button to find out what it does. For this exercise, move the mouse over the Print button on the Standard toolbar.

The mouse cursor changes into a pointer when it is on top of a button. The Print button is the fourth from the left. It has a little printer on it.

What appears below the button — in this case, the word *Print*— is the button's name. Meanwhile, the status bar along the bottom of the screen says, Prints the active document using the current defaults, which is what happens when you click the Print button.

2 In the Buttons file, move the text cursor anywhere on the line that says, "The Deluxe Motel."

To get to that line, you can either press the ↓ key several times or click anywhere on the line with the mouse.

3 Click the Center button on the Formatting toolbar.

The Center button is the eighth button from the right. When you click the Center button, Word 95 centers the words *The Deluxe Motel* between the margins of the page.

4 Press the ↓ key once to move to the following line.

5 Click the Center button again to center the address, "314 Happy Blvd."

Now the address of the party is centered in the document, which makes it stand out and makes it easier to read as well.

6 To get to the end of the document, press PgDn once or hold down the ↓ key until you get to the end.

7 Press Enter twice so that you can add a postscript.

8 Type P.S.

On the other hand, maybe you shouldn't write a postscript after all. Word 95 has a special button for reversing your most recent action: the Undo button.

9 Click the Undo button to erase the letters *P.S.*

The Undo button, located in the middle of the Standard toolbar, "undoes" your last action. When you click the Undo button, the letters *P.S.* disappear. You can also press Ctrl+Z to undo your latest action.

10 Click the Save button to save your changes to the document.

11 Close the Buttons file.

Word 95 offers 11 toolbars in all. All the buttons on the toolbars can help you perform tasks quickly. You'll use different toolbars throughout this book.

Giving Commands with Shortcut Keys   Lesson 2-2

Another way to give commands is to press shortcut keys. A *shortcut key* is actually two keys that you press simultaneously to give a command right away and bypass menus and buttons.

You've already seen three shortcut keys in this book: Ctrl+N to open a new document (Lesson 1-2), Ctrl+S to save a document (Lesson 1-3), and Ctrl+O to open a document (Lesson 1-5). Many shortcut keys are listed on the menus. For example, pull down the <u>F</u>ile menu, and you see the shortcut keys I just mentioned to the right of <u>N</u>ew, <u>O</u>pen, and <u>S</u>ave.

heads up

See whether the commands you use often have shortcut keys. You can save time by pressing shortcut key combinations instead of clicking in dialog boxes or making menu choices.

on the disk

For this lesson, open the Shortcut Keys file in the Practice folder. If this file looks familiar, that's because it is identical to the Buttons file you played with in Lesson 2-1. For this exercise, you do everything you did in the last lesson, only this time you use shortcut keys instead of buttons. Follow these steps:

1 **Press Ctrl+P to open the Print dialog box.**

If you want to print this document, you can do so by filling in this dialog box. Sometimes the fastest way to display a dialog box is to press a shortcut key like Ctrl+P.

2 **Press Esc to close the Print dialog box.**

3 **In the Shortcut Keys file, move the text cursor anywhere on the line that says, "The Deluxe Motel."**

Press the ↓ key several times or click the line.

4 **Press Ctrl+E to center the paragraph.**

In Lesson 2-1, you clicked the Center button to center a paragraph. Which is faster, clicking the Center button or pressing Ctrl+E? It depends on how well you type.

5 **Press the ↓ key once to move to the following line.**

6 **Press Ctrl+E again to center the address, "314 Happy Blvd."**

7 **To get to the end of the document, press Ctrl+End.**

The End key is on the numeric keypad (with the 1) and also on the group of keys to the right of the Enter key. Ctrl+End is a shortcut key for moving quickly to the end of a document. You will learn about many such shortcut keys in Unit 4.

8 **Press Enter twice so that you can add a postscript.**

9 **Type P.S.**

In Lesson 2-1, you clicked the Undo button to delete the *P.S.*, but you also can delete the *P.S.* in another way.

10 **Press Ctrl+Z to delete the *P.S.***

Ctrl+Z is the shortcut key for the Undo command. When you press Ctrl+Z, the *P.S.* is removed from the document.

Notes:

Ctrl+P displays Print dialog box

Ctrl+E is shortcut for centering text

☑ **Progress Check**

If you can do the following, you've mastered this lesson:

❑ Center text.

❑ Give commands with shortcut keys.

press Ctrl+Z to "undo" your latest action

press Ctrl+S to save a document

11 Click Ctrl+S to save your changes to the document.

12 Close the Shortcut Keys file.

Whether you click buttons or press shortcut keys to give commands is up to you. Sometimes clicking a button is easier, and sometimes pressing keys is easier. Which method you use depends on what you want to do, how good you are with the mouse, and how adept you are at typing. Besides shortcut keys and buttons, Word offers a third way to give commands — with the menus. Choosing commands from menus is the subject of the next lesson.

Lesson 2-3

Choosing Menu Commands

Yet another way to give commands is to choose them from the menus. With this technique, you *pull down* a menu from the menu bar along the top of the screen and then choose a menu option.

To pull down a menu, you can either click the menu name with the mouse or press the Alt key and the letter that is underlined in the menu name. For example, to pull down the <u>F</u>ile menu, either click the word <u>F</u>ile or press Alt+F. When you do, the <u>F</u>ile menu appears on-screen.

After you pull down a menu, you have several *menu commands* to choose from. To choose a command from a pull-down menu, either click the command name or press the letter that is underlined in the command name. Suppose you want to choose the <u>O</u>pen command on the <u>F</u>ile menu. After the <u>F</u>ile menu drops down, you can either click the word <u>O</u>pen or press O to open a new document.

on the disk

For this exercise, open the Menu Commands file in the Practice folder. I hope this file looks familiar to you, because it holds the same text you worked on in Lesson 2-1 and 2-2. This time, you do everything you did in those two lessons, except you use menu commands instead of buttons or shortcut keys. Follow these steps:

1 Pull down the <u>F</u>ile menu.

Of course, you can always press Alt+F to do so.

2 With the <u>F</u>ile menu open, press the P key.

By doing so, you choose the <u>P</u>rint command and open the Print dialog box. You can also click the word <u>P</u>rint on the <u>F</u>ile menu to open the Print dialog box.

3 Click the Cancel button or press Esc to leave the Print dialog box without printing anything.

4 In the Menu Commands file, move the text cursor anywhere on the line that says, "The Deluxe Motel."

In Lesson 2-1, you clicked the Center button to center these words between the margins. In Lesson 2-2, you pressed a shortcut key combination, Ctrl+E. Now you will center text with menu commands.

5 Click F<u>o</u>rmat on the main menu bar or press Alt+O to pull down the F<u>o</u>rmat menu.

6 Click <u>P</u>aragraph or press P to choose the Paragraph command. The Paragraph dialog box appears.

7 **Click the down-pointing arrow in the Alignment box on the lower-right side of the Paragraph dialog box, and choose Centered from the menu that drops down.**

To choose Centered, just click it. The word *Centered* appears in the Alignment box.

8 **Click OK or press Enter to close the dialog box and give the Centered command.**

Now the hotel name is centered. Going to all this work seems like an awful lot of trouble when you can just click the Center button or press Ctrl+E, but sometimes taking the long route with menu commands and dialog boxes has advantages. The Paragraph dialog box, for example, offers many settings in addition to Alignment settings. By choosing a command from a menu and opening a dialog box, you can often give several commands at once, as I'll show you in Lesson 2-5. With buttons and shortcut keys, you can give only one command at a time.

9 **Press the ↓ key once to move to the following line.**

10 **Repeat steps 5 through 8 to center the address, "314 Happy Blvd."**

Or if you don't feel like going to all that work, choose the Edit⇨Repeat Paragraph Formatting command.

11 **Press Ctrl+End to get to the end of the document.**

12 **Press Enter twice so that you can add a postscript.**

13 **Type** P.S.

In Lesson 2-1, you clicked the Undo button to "undo" the *P.S.* In Lesson 2-2, you pressed Ctrl+Z. Can you guess how to undo an action from the menu bar?

14 **Choose Edit⇨Undo Typing.**

Doing so removes the *P.S.* from the screen.

15 **Choose File⇨Save to save the changes to Menu Commands.**

16 **Choose File⇨Close to close the document.**

How you choose menu commands is up to you. You can either click the menu names or press the letters in the menu names that are underlined. In this book, I always underline the letters that are underlined in the command names. That way, you know which keys to press if you are the type who likes to give commands with the keyboard.

Notes:

☑ Progress Check

If you can do the following, you've mastered this lesson:

❑ Pull down a menu from the menu bar by pressing Alt and an underlined letter.

❑ Choose commands by typing the letters that are underlined in menu names and menu commands.

Taking Advantage of Shortcut Menus   Lesson 2-4

The words *taking advantage* are in the title of this lesson because most people neglect to use the shortcut menus. The shortcut menus can be very handy indeed, but you have to get in the habit of using them, and you have to know where they are.

To display a shortcut menu, you click with the right mouse button on a part of the screen or the text. Clicking with the right mouse button is called *right-clicking.* Usually, you click the left mouse button, but don't do that if you want to see a shortcut menu.

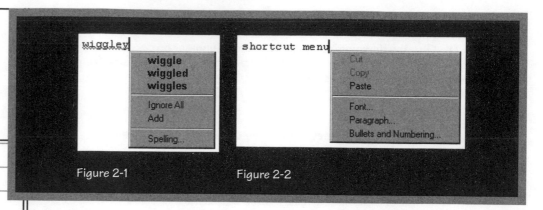

Figure 2-1: Right-click a misspelled word to display the spelling shortcut menu.

Figure 2-2: This shortcut menu is for editing and formatting text.

Figure 2-1   Figure 2-2

✓ **Progress Check**

If you can do the following, you've mastered this lesson:

❑ Right-click with the mouse.

❑ Display shortcut menus.

❑ Choose an option from a shortcut menu.

Do the following exercise to experiment with shortcut menus:

1 Type a few words on-screen and make sure that at least one of the words is misspelled.

You can tell when you've misspelled a word because the program puts a red wiggly line under misspelled words.

2 Right-click the misspelled word to display a spelling shortcut menu.

Figure 2-1 shows the shortcut menu you get by right-clicking the word *wiggley*. Because *wiggley* isn't a bona fide word, the shortcut menu offers three substitutes: *wiggle, wiggled,* and *wiggles.* To replace *wiggley* with *wiggles,* for example, you simply click the word *wiggles* on the shortcut menu.

You can also choose one of the other options: Ignore All ignores the misspelling, Add puts the word in your computer dictionary, and Spelling opens the Spelling dialog box. You will learn how to correct misspellings in Unit 14-1. For now, all you need to know is that a very handy shortcut menu for correcting misspellings is available.

3 Move the cursor to a word that is correctly spelled, and then click the right mouse button.

Now you see another kind of shortcut menu. As shown in Figure 2-2, this menu offers basic editing commands. The first three options are for cutting, copying, and pasting text. The last three are for changing fonts, changing paragraph alignments, and creating numbered or bulleted lists.

All you have to do is click an option to choose it from this shortcut menu. You'll learn about these options in Lesson 3-3 and 3-4.

4 Right-click the Standard or Formatting toolbar.

A shortcut menu appears. Besides right-clicking text, you can display shortcut menus by right-clicking parts of the screen, as this step demonstrates. This shortcut menu is for adding toolbars, removing toolbars, and telling Word 95 how to display toolbars.

Notice the check marks next to the Standard and Formatting options. Those check marks tell you that the Standard and Formatting toolbars currently appear on-screen. If you click Standard or Formatting on this menu, the Standard or Formatting toolbar disappears from the screen.

5 Click Formatting on the toolbar shortcut menu.

Now the shortcut menu disappears, and the Formatting toolbar is removed from the screen. Do you want the Formatting toolbar back? Go to the next step.

6 Right-click the Standard toolbar to see the shortcut menu again.

This time, a check mark does not appear next to the Formatting option because the Formatting toolbar isn't on-screen.

7 **Click Formatting on the shortcut menu.**

The Formatting toolbar reappears on-screen.

Word has many shortcut menus. I'll introduce you to the most important ones throughout this book.

Filling In Dialog Boxes   Lesson 2-5

Sometimes a dialog box appears on-screen after you choose a menu command. Word 95 displays a dialog box when it needs a lot of information to complete a task. Menu commands that produce dialog boxes have three dots after their names. For example, the File menu has several commands that produce dialog boxes, including New…, Open…, and Print….

The fast way to give commands is to click buttons or press shortcut keys, but if you want to be thorough or do something complicated, you often have to choose a menu command and fill in a dialog box. For example, you can print a document by clicking the Print button, but what if you want to print several copies of the document or print only the first few pages? In that case, you have to choose File⇨Print and fill in the Print dialog box.

Follow these steps to learn about dialog boxes:

1 **Choose File⇨Print to see the Print dialog box shown in Figure 2-3.**

The labels in Figure 2-3 describe the many ways that you tell Word 95 how to complete a command.

You can choose options in dialog boxes in two ways. You can either press Alt and the letter that is underlined in the option name or click the option with the mouse.

To move to an option in a dialog box, either click the option with the mouse, press Tab to move forward through the dialog box, or press Shift+Tab to move backward.

2 **In the Page range area of the dialog box, choose the Pages radio button by clicking it or by pressing Alt+G on the keyboard.**

Radio buttons are round and come in sets. In this dialog box, the Page range radio buttons tell Word which part of the document to print: all of it (All), the page where the cursor is (Current page), the text you've selected (Selection), or a range of pages (Pages).

You can choose only one radio button at a time, just as you can listen to only one radio station at a time. You can tell when a radio button has been selected because a round dot appears inside the circle.

3 **In the Pages text box, type** 1-2.

By typing **1-2**, you tell Word 95 to print pages 1 and 2. You'll learn about printing in Part III of this book. For now, you need to know that filling in a text box is one way to complete a command in a dialog box.

4 **Click the down-pointing arrow in the Print what drop-down list.**

A *drop-down list* is a list of options that appears when you click the arrow that points down. The down-pointing arrow is located on the right side of the drop-down list. When you click this arrow, a list appears.

Don't worry about the options in the Print what drop-down list for now. Just click Document to print the text in your document and not that other stuff on the Print what list.

Notes:

Figure 2-3: The Print dialog box.

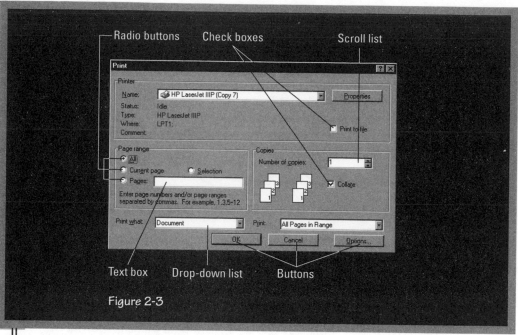

Figure 2-3

Besides the Print what drop-down list, the Print dialog box includes two other such lists, Name (at the top of the dialog box) and Print (in the lower-right corner).

5 **Go to the Number of copies scroll list and click the arrow that points up.**

When you click the up arrow, the number in the box changes to 2. Click again if you want three, four, or more copies. Click the little down-pointing arrow to get back to four, three, two, or one copy.

Scroll lists allow you to enter numbers by clicking arrows, but you can also type numbers directly into scroll lists. For example, you can type **2** in the Number of copies scroll list as well as click the arrow that points up.

6 **Click the Collate check box or press Alt+T.**

Check boxes work like radio buttons, except that you can select more than one check box at a time or none at all. Whereas radio buttons are round, check boxes are square.

When a check box option has been selected, a check mark appears inside it. When an option is not selected, no check mark appears.

7 **Click the Cancel button to close the Print dialog box without printing anything.**

Almost all dialog boxes have an OK and a Cancel button. Click OK (or press Enter) when you've filled out the dialog box and are ready for Word to execute the command. Click Cancel (or press Esc) to close the dialog box without giving the command.

Buttons in dialog boxes are rectangular and have their names listed on them. Four buttons are in the Print dialog box. Besides OK and Cancel, you see the Properties and Options buttons.

Tabs in dialog boxes

Some dialog boxes also include *tabs*. Click a tab to get another page of settings. For example, choose Format⇨Paragraph to see the two tabs in the Paragraph dialog box. By clicking the Text Flow tab (or pressing Alt+F), you can get to a second set of paragraph options. Click the Cancel button or press Esc to close this dialog box after you're done examining the tabs.

☑ **Progress Check**

If you can do the following, you've mastered this lesson:

❏ Move from option to option in a dialog box.

❏ Choose options in dialog boxes.

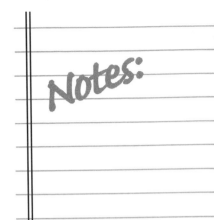

Recess

Unit 2 taught you how to give commands by clicking buttons, pressing shortcut keys, choosing menu commands and shortcut menu commands, and filling in dialog boxes. You learned a lot in Unit 2, and you deserve a reward. You deserve a trip to Puerto Escondido on Mexico's beautiful Pacific Coast. However, going to Puerto Escondido would mean flying to Oaxaca City and taking a long bus trip over the Sierra mountain range (and stopping in San Juan Del Pacifico to sample that town's famous agricultural products), and that would take a lot of time. So instead of going to Puerto Escondido, go to the backyard and water the plants. Nothing is more relaxing than gardening.

Unit 2 Quiz

For the following questions, circle the letter of the correct answer or answers. Each question may have more than one right answer.

1. **The fastest way to give a command is to do which of the following?**

    A. Threaten people with heavy, blunt objects.

    B. Click a button on a toolbar.

    C. Press a shortcut key combination.

    D. Choose a menu command and fill in a dialog box.

    E. Give the command in German.

2. **To find out what a button does, you do this:**

    A. Call the Microsoft Corporation help line at 800-936-5700.

    B. Place the mouse pointer on top of the button, read the button's name, and read its description on the status bar.

    C. Click the button and watch what happens.

    D. Stare hard at the image on the button until you can figure out what it represents.

    E. Go ask Mom.

3. **Which of the following statements about shortcut keys is incorrect?**

    A. Press Ctrl+N to open a new document.

    B. Press Ctrl+H to hatch an egg.

    C. Press Ctrl+S to save a document.

    D. Press Ctrl+O to open a document.

    E. Press Ctrl+P to display the Print dialog box.

4. **By pressing Alt+F, you open which of the following menus on the main menu?**

   A. View

   B. File

   C. Window

   D. Tools

   E. Format

5. **To open a shortcut menu, you do this:**

   A. Drop the mouse from a high place.

   B. Right-click on text or on a part of the screen.

   C. Right-click on a word with a red wiggly line underneath it.

   D. Yell "Right on!" and thrust your right fist in the air.

   E. Right-click on the Standard or Formatting toolbar.

6. **When you are finished filling in a dialog box, you do this:**

   A. Close the lid.

   B. Press OK to give a command or press Cancel to start all over.

   C. Give yourself a pat on the back.

   D. Choose a radio button and listen to a song.

   E. Click a tab to see what other options are available.

Unit 2 Exercise

1. In a new document, type your name in bold.

2. On the next line, type your address in normal text.

3. Skip a line and type today's date in bold.

4. Skip a line and type **Looking good.** in normal text.

5. Skip a line and type **Looking very good** followed by a comma, your name, and a period, all in bold.

6. Skip a line and type **Watch this:** in normal text, and then type **Looking very, very good indeed!** in bold.

Entering and Editing Text

Objectives for This Unit

✓ Entering text in insert mode and typeover mode

✓ Selecting text

✓ Cutting and pasting text

✓ Copying and pasting text

✓ Deleting text

✓ Changing the case of characters

✓ Putting symbols and special characters in documents

Prerequisites
▶ Starting Word 95 (Lesson 1-1)
▶ Opening a document (Lesson 1-5)
▶ Giving commands in Word 95 (Unit 2)
▶ Filling in dialog boxes (Lesson 2-5)

on the disk
▶ Typeover
▶ Select
▶ Move
▶ Copy
▶ Delete

In Units 1 and 2, you learned a few simple techniques for entering and editing text. You learned how to type letters on-screen and start a new line (by pressing Enter). You also learned how to delete text with the Backspace and Delete keys.

In Unit 3, you are going to become a sophisticated word processor.

This unit explains how to copy and move text from one place to another in a document. You have to "select" text to copy or move it, and this unit describes some very handy shortcuts for selecting words, sentences, paragraphs, and even entire documents. Unit 3 also offers shortcuts for changing the case of text — from uppercase to lowercase and vice versa. You also learn how to enter symbols and letters not found on the keyboard.

Insert Mode and Typeover Mode   Lesson 3-1

When you enter text in a document, the letters you enter push aside the letters that are already there. In other words, if you start typing in the middle of a document, new text is "inserted" between the letters that you already typed.

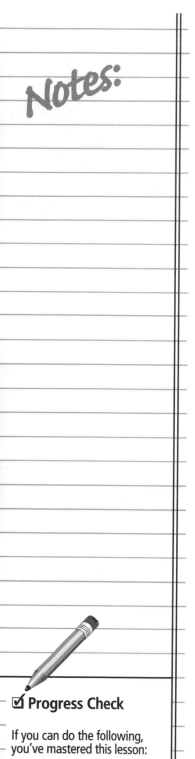

Notes:

However, inserting text isn't the only way to enter new letters and words. You can also enter text in *typeover mode* so that the letters you type delete the letters that are already in the document. Sometimes entering text in typeover mode is faster than entering it the usual way, in insert mode. Instead of erasing a word and typing a new one, you can switch to typeover mode and simply type the new word. The new word you enter covers up the word that you need to delete.

To switch from insert mode to typeover mode, either press the Insert (or Ins) key on your keyboard or double-click OVR on the status bar along the bottom of the screen. The Insert key is located to the right of the Backspace key. The Ins key is located on the numeric keypad, where it shares space with the 0.

on the disk

In this lesson, you will use the Typeover file to practice entering text in typeover mode. This file is on the disk that came with this book. (Read "About the Disk" in the Introduction if you haven't yet copied the files on the disk to your computer.)

To enter text in insert mode and typeover mode, open the Typeover file in the Practice folder and do the following:

1 Press Insert or double-click OVR on the status bar to switch from insert mode to typeover mode.

When you are in typeover mode, the letters OVR appear in dark text on the status bar.

2 Type Man.

If you read the Typeover file, you will see that this is a "Man Bites Dog" story. The headline is incorrect.

3 Move the text cursor to the start of the word *Man* at the end of the heading.

Remember, you can move the cursor by pressing the arrow keys or by clicking the mouse on a new location.

4 Type Dog.

Now the heading reads, "Man Bites Dog."

5 Switch back to insert mode by pressing the Insert key or double-clicking OVR on the status bar.

6 Move the cursor to the start of the word *onlookers* and type frightened, **followed by a space.**

As you type **frightened**, notice how the following words are pushed aside. You are in insert mode now.

When you are editing a document, you can save time by switching between insert and typeover mode.

☑ Progress Check

If you can do the following, you've mastered this lesson:

❑ Press the Insert (or Ins) key to switch to typeover mode.

❑ Double-click OVR on the status bar to switch to typeover mode.

❑ Press the Show/Hide¶ button to see how your document is formatted.

extra credit

Formatting characters

Telling where paragraphs begin and end and how many spaces are between words is sometimes hard when you are editing a document. To help you, Word 95 has the Show/Hide¶ button. Click this button, and formatting symbols appear on-screen to show you where paragraphs end, where you pressed the Tab key, and how many spaces are between words.

Figure 3-1 shows two pictures of the same screen. You can see the formatting symbols in the screen on the right. The ¶ symbol marks the end of a paragraph, and the → shows where you pressed the Tab key. Dots appear where blank spaces are.

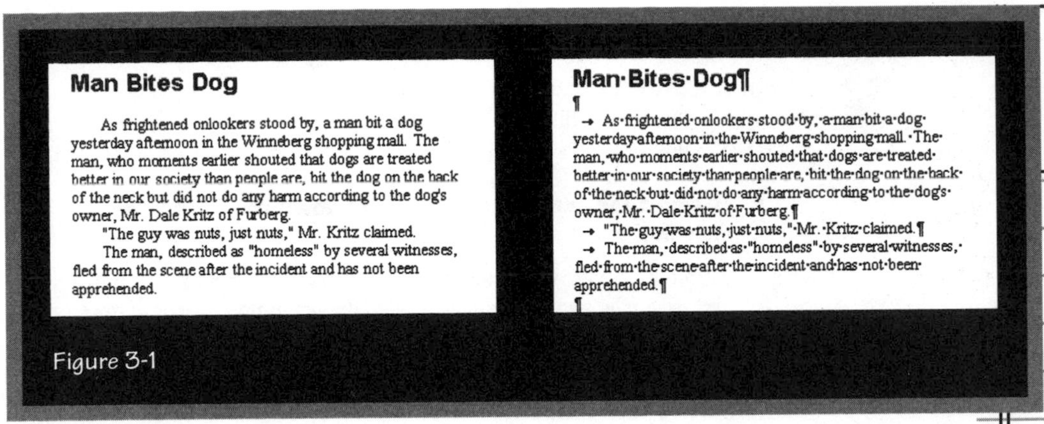

Figure 3-1

Figure 3-1: Press the Show/Hide¶ button to see the formatting characters in a document.

Selecting Text

Lesson 3-2

To move text from one place to another, you have to select it first. To copy text, you select it. To change characters from one font to another, you select the characters first. To delete large amounts of text, you select the text and then press Delete. I can give you about 101 reasons to select text, so it pays to know the many different shortcuts for selecting text in Word 95.

Selected text is highlighted on-screen. After you highlight the text, you can apply a command to all the text at once.

This lesson explains how to select text. Table 3-1 describes text selection techniques. You will get a chance to try out these techniques in the exercise that follows. Don't worry about remembering these techniques for now. This table is for reference purposes, and if I were you, I would fold back the corner of this page or put a yellow sticky note here. You will likely come back to this page later on.

Show/Hide¶ button

Table 3-1	Ways to Select Text
To Select This	**Do This**
A word	Double-click the word.
A line	Click in the left margin next to the line.
Several lines	Drag the mouse over the lines or drag the mouse down the left margin.
A paragraph	Double-click in the left margin next to the paragraph.
A mess of text	Click at the start of the text, hold down the Shift key, click at the end of the text, and let up on the Shift key.
A gob of text	Put the cursor where you want to start selecting text, press F8, and press the arrow keys or drag the mouse.
Yet more text	If you select text and realize that you want to select yet more text, double-click EXT (it stands for Extend) on the status bar and start dragging the mouse or pressing the arrow keys.
A document	Hold down the Ctrl key and click in the left margin, triple-click in the left margin, press Ctrl+A, or choose Edit⇔Select All.

drag means to hold
down the mouse
button and roll the
mouse cursor across
the screen

For this exercise, use the file called Select in the Practice folder. Each numbered step describes a different way to select text. When you are finished with each step, click once on-screen to unselect the text and go on to the next step.

on the disk

1 **To select the entire document, hold down the Ctrl key and click once in the left margin.**

The mouse pointer turns into an arrow when you move it to the left margin. Click when the arrow is pointing toward the upper-right corner of the screen, not the upper-left corner.

You can also select an entire document by triple-clicking in the left margin, pressing Ctrl+A, or choosing Edit⇨Select All.

2 **Drag the cursor across a few words to select them.**

You can select a handful of words by dragging the mouse over them. You can also click where you want to begin selecting, hold down the Shift key, and click at the end of the selection.

3 **Click once in the left margin to select a line of text.**

4 **Double-click in the left margin to select an entire paragraph.**

5 **Drag the cursor down the left margin to select several lines.**

As you drag, the lines to the right of the mouse cursor are selected.

6 **Move the cursor where you want the selection to begin, start dragging, and then press F8 or double-click EXT on the status bar. Now try clicking farther down the document or pressing the ↓ or → key.**

When you click farther down in the document or press an arrow key, you extend the selection. You can use this technique when you've made a selection but realize that you have fallen short. Double-click EXT (for "extend") or press F8 to extend a selection and then click elsewhere or start pressing arrow keys. To "unselect" the text that you've highlighted, double-click EXT on the status bar.

You can also press F8 or double-click EXT when you've overshot the mark and need to make the selection shorter. In that case, click farther up in the document or press the ↑ or ← key.

7 **To select everything from the cursor position to the start of the document, press F8 or double-click EXT and then press Ctrl+Home.**

8 **To select everything from the cursor position to the end of the document, press F8 or double-click EXT and then press Ctrl+End.**

After you press F8 or double-click EXT, all the keyboard shortcuts for moving the cursor in a document also work for selecting text. (You'll learn keyboard shortcuts for moving the cursor in Unit 4.) For example, press F8 or double-click EXT and then press End to select text to the end of the line. Press F8 or double-click EXT and press Home to select text to the start of the line.

9 **Double-click on a word to select it.**

☑ Progress Check

If you can do the following, you've mastered this lesson:

❑ Select text by dragging the mouse.

❑ Select text by clicking, double-clicking, or triple-clicking in the left margin.

❑ Select text by pressing F8 or double-clicking EXT and then pressing key combinations.

extra credit

Selecting text one character at a time

Word selects text one word at a time. Some people find that annoying. If you're one of those people, choose Tools⇨Options. On the Edit tab, click Automatic Word Selection to remove the check mark. Now Word 95 will select text one character at a time.

Moving Text to New Places On-Screen   Lesson 3-3

In the last lesson, you learned how to select text. Once you've selected text, you can cut it out of the document and paste it elsewhere. In other words, you can move text, which is the subject of this lesson.

Moving text is one of the most common word processing chores. Instead of retyping text that you've entered in the wrong place, all you have to do is select the text and move it. Word 95 offers five different ways to move text. After you select the text, you can

on the test

- Drag it to a new location.
- Choose Edit⇨Cut and then Edit⇨Paste.
- Press Ctrl+X and then Ctrl+V.
- Click the Cut button and then the Paste button.
- Right-click and choose Cut from the shortcut menu and then right-click and choose Paste from the shortcut menu.

In all but the first method in the preceding list, the text is cut from the document and copied to the *Clipboard*. The Clipboard is a kind of electronic holding tank. Text stays on the Clipboard, and after you give the Paste command, the text is moved from the Clipboard to your document. The Clipboard can only hold one item at a time. In other words, you can't cut four or five different things to the Clipboard at once. Cutting a new item replaces whatever was previously on the Clipboard.

on the disk

For this exercise, you will use a file called Move in the Practice folder. Open the Move file now. I don't mean to sound like Flaubert's parrot and repeat myself over and over again, but if you haven't loaded the files from the disk that came with this book, load them now. You will find instructions for loading them in the Introduction.

1 Double-click in the left margin beside the last paragraph.

Doing so selects the last paragraph. You will move the last paragraph to the top of the document.

2 Click the Cut button.

The last paragraph disappears. To cut text, you can also press Ctrl+X, choose Edit⇨Cut, or right-click the text you selected and choose Cut from the shortcut menu.

3 Move the text cursor to the start of the first paragraph in the document, right before the word *The*.

4 Click the Paste button.

To paste text, you can also choose Edit⇨Paste, press Ctrl+V, or right-click and choose Paste from the shortcut menu. The paragraph that you cut in step 3 appears at the top of the document.

5 Press Enter to put a blank line between paragraphs.

6 Select the new first sentence in the document, the one that begins "Please bring . . ."

7 Press Ctrl+X to cut this sentence.

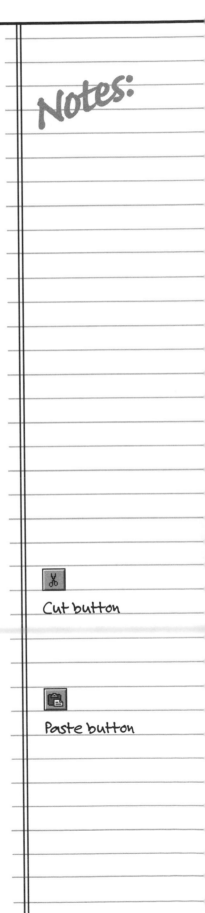

Cut button

Paste button

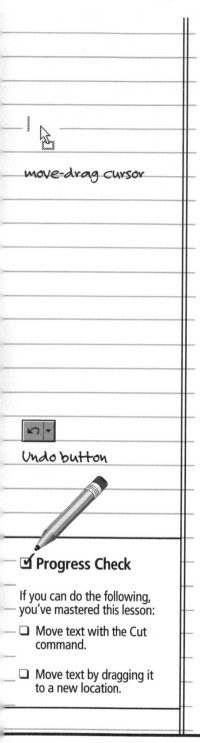

move-drag cursor

Undo button

☑ **Progress Check**

If you can do the following, you've mastered this lesson:

❑ Move text with the Cut command.

❑ Move text by dragging it to a new location.

8 **Move the mouse cursor to the end of the new first paragraph, right-click, and choose Paste from the shortcut menu.**

Now the sentence is the last one in the paragraph.

9 **Go to the bottom of the document and click once in the left margin next to Brian Cuong-Le's name.**

Doing so selects the entire line with Brian's name on it. Now you will move the name to a new location by dragging it.

10 **Hold down the mouse button and drag the mouse until the vertical line above the pointer is just to the left of Desiree Weaver's name, and then let go of the mouse button.**

Now Brian Cuong-Le appears before Desiree Weaver in the list.

When you move text by dragging it, the text is not copied to the Clipboard. Even though you just cut and pasted Brian Cuong-Le's name, "Brian Cuong-Le" is not on the Clipboard, as you will see shortly.

11 **Click in the left margin next to Salvador Perez's name to select that line and then drag the line with his name on it to the left of Desiree Weaver's name.**

Now the list is in alphabetical order.

12 **Move the mouse cursor to the very bottom of the document and click the Paste button, press Ctrl+V, or right-click and choose Paste from the shortcut menu to move what is on the Clipboard into the document.**

Instead of the name Salvador Perez, the sentence you copied in step 7 — "Please bring food and drink" — appears. That is because text is not copied to the Clipboard when you drag it.

13 **Click the Undo button to reverse what you did in step 13.**

14 **Type** Once again,.

15 **Press Ctrl+V to paste "Please bring food and drink."**

16 **Replace the uppercase *P* in *Please* with a lowercase *p* and then type** to the end-of-the-season party.

Now the sentence reads, "Once again, please bring food and drink to the end-of-the-season party."

Besides moving text from place to place in a document, you can move text from one document to another and even from one Windows 95 application to another. All you have to do is copy the text to the Clipboard with the Cut command and then paste the text in the other document.

Lesson 3-4

Copying and Pasting Text

In Word 95, copying text from one part of a document to another part is easy. There are lots of reasons for copying text. For example, if you want to enter a name many times in a document, you can enter the name once and then copy it into your document whenever you want to enter it again. Suppose that you are writing a paragraph that is nearly identical to one you wrote earlier. Instead of typing a new paragraph, you can copy the old one and then make the small changes you need to make to the new one.

Ways to copy and paste

You can copy text by selecting it and dragging it from one place to another or by selecting it and then choosing one of the following four commands:

on the test

- ▶ Choose Edit➪Copy and then Edit➪Paste.
- ▶ Press Ctrl+C and then Ctrl+V.
- ▶ Click the Copy button and then the Paste button.
- ▶ Right-click and choose Copy from the shortcut menu and then right-click and choose Paste from the shortcut menu.

When you copy text by choosing the Copy command or pressing Ctrl+C, the text is copied to the Clipboard. As you learned in the last lesson, the Clipboard is a temporary storage area where cut or copied text is kept. You can paste text from the Clipboard into your document as many times as you want.

on the disk

For this exercise, you will use a file called Copy in the Practice folder. Open the document now and follow these steps to practice copying text:

1 Select "the Poker World Championship in Reno, Nevada" in the first sentence in the first paragraph.

You will copy this text to the last paragraph.

2 Click the Copy button.

You can also choose the Copy command by pressing Ctrl+C, right-clicking the selection and choosing Copy from the shortcut menu, or choosing Edit➪Copy.

Now "the Poker World Championship in Reno, Nevada" has been copied to the Clipboard.

3 Select the word *it,* the third word in the first sentence of the last paragraph.

After you give the Paste command in step 4, "the Poker World Championship in Reno, Nevada" replaces the word *it.*

4 Right-click the word *it* and choose Paste from the shortcut menu.

You can also choose Edit➪Paste, press Ctrl+V, or click the Paste button to paste text you've copied to the Clipboard.

When you select something and then choose the Paste command, the text that you paste in replaces the text you selected.

5 Go to the top of the document and click in the left margin to select the first line, the row of clubs, hearts, diamonds, and spades.

6 Hold down the Ctrl key and, as you do so, drag the line with the card suits on it to the very bottom of the screen.

Now the line of card suits appears along both the bottom and top of the document.

on the test

The last lesson explained that you can move text by dragging it from one place to another. You can copy text by dragging it while holding down the Ctrl key. As you drag, two boxes appear below the mouse pointer, and the second box has a cross in it.

Even though you copied the first line in the document to a new place, "the Poker World Championship in Reno, Nevada" is still on the Clipboard (you copied it there in step 2). When you copy text by dragging it, the text isn't placed on the Clipboard. You can copy the text from the Clipboard into your document again, as you will do in step 7.

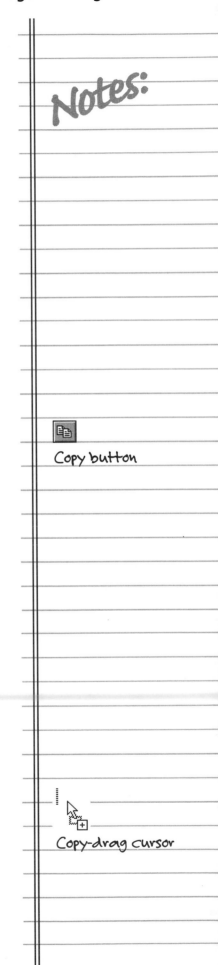

Notes:

Copy button

Copy-drag cursor

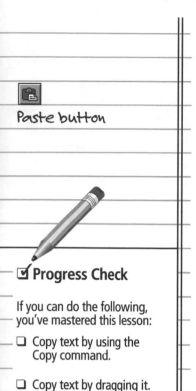

Paste button

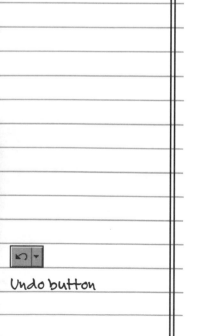

☑ **Progress Check**

If you can do the following, you've mastered this lesson:

❑ Copy text by using the Copy command.

❑ Copy text by dragging it.

❑ Copy text by using the shortcut menu.

7 **Place the cursor just to the left of the period at the end of the document.**

8 **Click the Paste button.**

Now the last sentence reads, "That's how I won the Poker World Championship in Reno, Nevada."

9 **Go the first paragraph and select "Texas Red and Willie the Cinch."**

10 **Choose Edit⇨Copy.**

Now "Texas Red and Willie the Cinch" has been copied to the Clipboard. The Clipboard can hold only one item at a time.

11 **Select "those other fellows" in the first line of the last paragraph.**

12 **Press Ctrl+V.**

Now the names of the other poker players appear in the sentence instead of the somewhat vague "those other fellows." You can use the Copy command when you edit your work to make your writing clearer.

13 **Close the document without saving it.**

Recess

You're not done with Unit 3 yet, but you have my permission to take a break. So far, you've learned about insert and typeover mode, selecting text, and moving and copying text. That's a lot to learn. Rest your brain a bit by staring off into space and remembering your elementary school years, when the world was fresh and new and all adults seemed strange and had wrinkles in weird places.

Lesson 3-5

Deleting Text

You've already learned how to delete text by pressing Delete or Backspace. Because deleting a paragraph or page by pressing those keys takes a long time, Word 95 offers another way to delete text: select all the text at once and press the Delete key. After you press Delete, all the text that you selected is erased from the document.

heads up

Deleted text is not placed on the Clipboard. The only way to get text back if you delete it accidentally is to use the Undo command (click the Undo button, choose Edit⇨Undo Clear, or press Ctrl+Z or Alt+Backspace). In this lesson's exercise, you will get a chance to recover deleted text with the Undo command.

on the disk

For this lesson, you will use the Delete file in the Practice folder. Open this file now and follow these steps to practice deleting text:

1 **Double-click any word in the first paragraph to select it and then press Delete.**

The word is deleted.

2 **Click the Undo button to bring back the word that you erased in step 1.**

Undo button

on the test

When you're working fast, deleting text accidentally is easy to do. Fortunately, you can always use the Undo command to get the text back. Besides pressing the button, you can also choose Edit⇨Undo.

3 **Double-click in the left margin beside the first paragraph to select the first paragraph and then press Delete.**

4 **Press Delete again to erase the blank line at the top of the remaining paragraph.**

5 **Choose Edit⇨Select All to select the entire document.**

You can also press Ctrl+A, hold down the Ctrl key and click in the left margin, or triple-click in the left margin to select an entire document.

6 **Press Delete.**

Now you have removed all the text in the document.

7 **Press Ctrl+Z to undo what you did in steps 5 and 6.**

8 **Click in the left margin beside the title "Pop Art" to select the line with the title on it.**

In the next step, you will enter a new title for this document.

9 **Type** Origins of Pop Art.

As soon as you type the first letter of the new title, the old title is erased. Deleting text by selecting it and then typing characters is a good editing technique and can speed up your work immeasurably.

10 **Close the document without saving it.**

If you regret deleting a bunch of text, you can always choose File⇨Close and answer No when Word 95 asks whether you want to save changes to your document. By not saving the changes you made to your document, you get your original document back the next time you open it.

As long as you know the techniques for selecting text, you can delete text quickly. Lesson 3-2 describes all the different ways to select text.

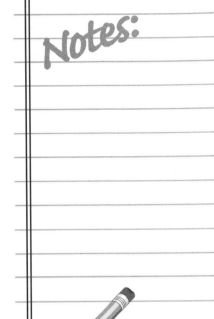

Notes:

☑ **Progress Check**

If you can do the following, you've mastered this lesson:

❏ Select and delete text.

❏ Choose the Undo command.

Changing the Case of Characters   Lesson 3-6

Case refers to whether the letters you type are capital letters. Capital letters, such as L and Z, are uppercase and other letters are lowercase (the terms come from the days when type was set by hand, and typesetters kept capital letters in the upper case, or tray, and other letters in the lower case).

Word 95 offers a couple of nifty shortcuts for changing the case of characters. If you accidentally press the Caps Lock key AND ENTER A BUNCH OF CHARACTERS IN UPPERCASE, for example, you can change them to lowercase very quickly and easily. You can change the case of characters in other ways as well.

Figure 3-2: You can change the case of text by pressing Shift+F3 or using the Change Case dialog box.

Figure 3-3: To start sentences with lowercase letters, click to remove the check mark from the Capitalize First Letter of Sentences option.

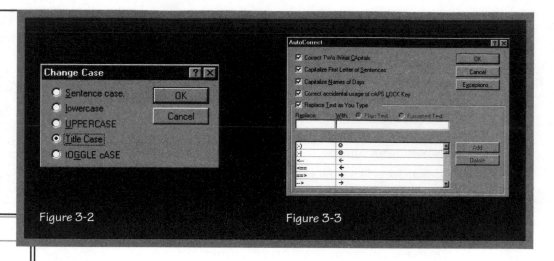

Figure 3-2   Figure 3-3

Notes:

Follow these steps to practice changing the case of characters:

1 **Open a new document, enter a few spaces, and type** Now I practice how I change case.

2 **Select the sentence you just typed and press Shift+F3.**

Now the sentence is in what is called Sentence case, with the first letter capitalized.

3 **Press Shift+F3 again.**

Now the sentence is all uppercase.

4 **Press Shift+F3 yet again.**

Now the sentence is all lowercase.

5 **Press Shift+F3 one last time.**

Now the sentence is in Sentence case again. As you press Shift+F3, the letters change to Sentence case, to all uppercase, and back to all lowercase again. You can keep pressing Shift+F3 until the letters are the right case, or you can select the text and choose Format⇨Change Case to get at a couple of other case options.

6 **Choose Format⇨Change Case.**

The Change Case dialog box appears, as in Figure 3-2. You are already familiar with the lowercase, UPPERCASE, and Sentence Case options, because you can get those by pressing Shift+F3. But what about the other two options in this dialog box, tOGGLE cASE and Title Case?

7 **Click the Title Case radio button (or press T) and then click OK (or press Enter) in the Change Case dialog box.**

Now your sample sentence reads, "Now I Practice How I Change Case." In title case, the first letter of each word is capitalized.

8 **Select the sentence, choose Format⇨Change Case, and this time choose the tOGGLE cASE option and click OK.**

Now the sentence reads, "nOW i PRACTICE HOW i CHANGE CASE." If you accidentally press the Caps Lock key and enter a whole bunch of characters in the wrong case, you can always correct your error with the tOGGLE cASE option.

9 **Repeat step 8.**

This time, when you choose the tOGGLE cASE option, the sentence is corrected and reads, "Now I practice how I change case."

extra credit

Starting a sentence with a lowercase letter

By now, you may have noticed that Word 95 does not allow you to start a sentence with a lowercase letter. Try to do so if you haven't noticed this feature yet. When you start a new paragraph with a lowercase letter or type a lowercase letter after you've typed a period and a space, Word 95 changes your lowercase letter to an uppercase letter as soon as you finish typing the word.

Word 95 capitalizes the first letter in sentences automatically, but if you have to enter computer code or something similar that begins with lowercase letters, you can tell the program to cut it out and stop capitalizing letters. Here's how:

1. With the cursor at the place in your document where you want to start sentences with lowercase letters, choose Tools⇨AutoCorrect.

   The AutoCorrect dialog box, shown in Figure 3-3, appears.

2. Press Alt+S or click to remove the check mark from the Capitalize First Letter of Sentences option.

3. Click OK or press Enter to close the dialog box.

4. Type the text that you want to begin with lowercase letters.

5. Repeat steps 1 and 2 to turn on automatic capitalization again.

   This time, when you choose the Capitalize First Letter of Sentences option, you place a check mark in the box and turn on the feature. The text that you entered with the feature turned off is not affected when you turn on the feature again. The first letters you entered are still lowercase.

   Most of the time, you do well to leave on the automatic capitalization feature because it corrects you if you mistakenly begin a sentence with a lowercase letter.

☑ Progress Check

If you can do the following, you've mastered this lesson:

❑ Change the case of letters by pressing Shift+F3.

❑ Change the case of letters by choosing Format⇨Change Case.

Entering Symbols and Special Characters

Lesson 3-7

on the test

You can enter many more characters in a document than are found on the keyboard. Word 95 offers the copyright symbol, foreign characters such as umlauts, accented letters, Greek letters, the smiley face, and the trademark symbol, to name only a few.

Which symbols you can use in your documents depends on which fonts are installed on your computer and printer. In any case, you can easily find out which characters are available, because Word 95 makes it simple to look over all the special characters and symbols that are available on your system.

Figure 3-4: Click a symbol and click the Insert button to insert a symbol in a document.

Figure 3-5: You can also insert special characters.

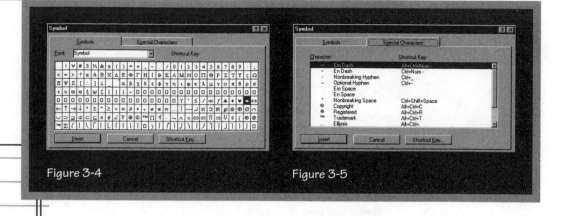

Figure 3-4   Figure 3-5

Notes:

☑ **Progress Check**

If you can do the following, you've mastered this lesson and can move on to the Unit 3 quiz:

❏ Insert a symbol in a document.

❏ Insert a special character.

In this exercise, you will review symbols and special characters and then enter one. You do not need to open a file to complete this exercise.

1 **Place the cursor where you want the symbol to go.**

2 **Choose Insert⇨Symbol.**

The Symbols tab of the Symbol dialog box, shown in Figure 3-4, appears. Take a look at the symbols that are available. If you see the one you are looking for, skip to step 5; otherwise, go to the next step.

3 **Click the down-pointing arrow beside the Font box to see a drop-down list of symbol sets on your computer.**

Different sets offer different varieties of symbols. For example, the Wingdings symbol set includes a skull and crossbones, a smiley face, and even a bomb symbol. The symbol set called Symbol offers Greek letters and mathematical symbols.

4 **Click a set name to see a new assortment of symbols in the dialog box.**

If necessary, keep choosing new symbol sets from the Font drop-down list until you see the symbol you are looking for in the dialog box. If you still can't find the symbol you need, you may want to check the Special Characters tab of the dialog box. To do so, skip to step 7.

5 **Click on the symbol you want.**

The symbol that you click is enlarged so that you can get a better look.

6 **Click Insert or press Alt+I to insert your symbol.**

Now your symbol is placed in the document. Meanwhile, the Symbol dialog box stays open so that you can insert another symbol if you want.

7 **Click the Special Characters tab (or press Alt+P) to see which special characters are available.**

The Special Characters tab, shown in Figure 3-5, appears.

8 **Click the special character that you want to insert.**

You may have to click the down-pointing arrow on the scroll bar to the right of the special character names to see the special characters at the bottom of the list.

9 **Click Insert (or press Alt+I) to insert the special characters.**

10 **Click Cancel or press Esc to close the dialog box when you're done entering symbols or special characters.**

Unit 3 Quiz

For the following questions, circle the letter of the correct answer or answers. Each question may have more than one right answer.

1. **You can tell when you are in typeover mode because:**

   A. You can feel it in the pit of your stomach.

   B. The letters OVR appear in dark text on the status bar.

   C. The letters you type cover the letters that are already present, rather than pushing them aside.

   D. Letters appear in boldface on-screen.

   E. You can enter letters more quickly.

2. **To select text, you do the following:**

   A. Double-click a word.

   B. Click in the left margin.

   C. Choose Edit⇨Select All.

   D. Drag the mouse down the left margin.

   E. All of the above.

3. **This button does the following:**

   A. Makes your lapels narrower.

   B. Places the text you selected on the Clipboard.

   C. Pastes what is on the Clipboard into the document.

   D. Removes the text that is highlighted from the document.

   E. Clips and saves the coupon so that you can redeem it for cash.

4. **This button does the following:**

   A. Shows you what is on the Clipboard.

   B. Pastes a copy of what is on the Clipboard in the document.

   C. Copies the text that is highlighted in the document.

   D. Tells you when you're in a clip joint.

   E. Turns on your VCR.

5. **Which of the following actions does *not* copy selected text to the Clipboard?**

   A. Choose Edit⇨Copy.

   B. Press Ctrl+X.

   C. Press Ctrl+C.

   D. Click the Copy button.

   E. Right-click and choose Copy from the shortcut menu.

6. **To drag text, do the following:**

    A. Grab the text by the hair and pull.

    B. Select the text, hold down the mouse button, and move the mouse pointer on-screen.

    C. Select the text, hold down the mouse button, and move the mouse cursor on-screen while holding down the Ctrl key.

    D. Select the text and press an arrow key.

    E. Select the text, click the Cut button, move the cursor, and then click the Paste button.

7. **Do the following to delete text:**

    A. Press Backspace until all the text is deleted.

    B. Select the text and press Delete.

    C. Press Delete until all the text is deleted.

    D. Select the text and choose Edit⇨Clear.

    E. Select the text and start typing.

Unit 3 Exercise

1. Open the Unit 3 Exercise file.

2. Switch to typeover mode and type **An Early Modern Artist** to give the article a new title.

3. Switch back to insert mode.

4. Find the name Honoré in the second paragraph and copy it to the very start of the first paragraph so that the essay starts with the artist's name, "Honoré Daumier." Copy the name by dragging it.

5. Click the Undo button and copy the name again, only this time do so by copying and pasting.

6. Move the first paragraph to the end of the second paragraph.

7. Click the Undo button and move the first paragraph to the end of the second paragraph in a different way.

8. Delete the third paragraph, the one that begins by describing when Daumier was born.

9. Change the title of the essay to all uppercase letters.

10. Go to the bottom of the document, open the Symbol dialog box, and see if you can find the symbol I entered in the document. If you can find it, enter a few more such symbols. If you can't find it, enter a few symbols of your own.

Moving Around in Documents

Objectives for This Unit

✓ Getting from place to place quickly

✓ Using the scroll bar to move around in documents

✓ Pressing keys to move around in documents

Prerequisites

▶ Opening a document (Lesson 1-5)

▶ Giving commands in Word 95 (Unit 2)

▶ Jump

on the disk

ocuments have a habit of getting longer and longer, and as they do, moving around in them gets harder and harder. If you are writing the conclusion of a 40-page report, for example, how can you get to the start of the report to make sure that the promises you made in the introduction are fulfilled in the conclusion? On that same 40-page report, how can you get quickly from page 32 to page 18?

This short unit explains the many ways to move around quickly in documents. Word 95 offers two means of doing so: with the scroll bar, located along the right side of the screen, and with keyboard shortcuts. I cover the scroll bar method in Lesson 4-1 and the keyboard shortcut method in Lesson 4-2.

Using the Scroll Bars to Move Around

Lesson 4-1

on the test

The Word 95 screen has two scroll bars. The one along the right side, called the *vertical scroll bar,* is for moving from page to page in documents and resembles an elevator shaft. The one along the bottom, called the *horizontal scroll bar,* is for moving from side to side to see a page when it doesn't fit entirely on-screen. Figure 4-1 shows the vertical scroll bar and describes how you use it to move throughout a document.

Figure 4-1: Use the vertical scroll bar to move around quickly in documents.

Notes:

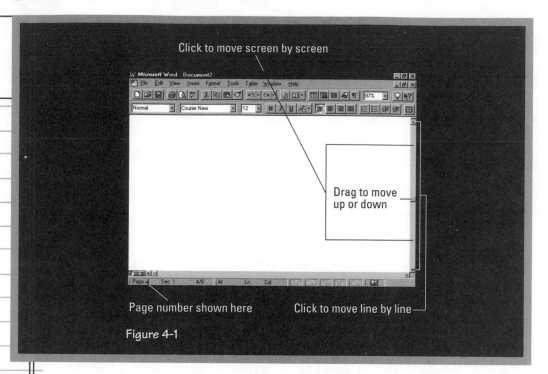

Click to move screen by screen

Drag to move up or down

Page number shown here   Click to move line by line

Figure 4-1

Here's how to move around with the vertical scroll bar:

- To move through a document quickly, grab the elevator (called the *scroll box*) and drag it up or down.

- To move line by line up or down, click the up or down arrow at the top or bottom of the scroll bar.

- To move screen by screen, click anywhere on the scroll bar except on the arrows or the elevator.

After you jump to a new place, you can tell where you are by looking at the status bar, the strip along the bottom of the screen. Table 4-1 explains the indicators on the status bar that tell you where you are in a document.

Table 4-1   Learning Where You Are from the Status Bar

Indicator	What It Tells You
Page	The page the cursor is in
Sec	The section the cursor is in
3/7	The page the cursor is in and the total number of pages in the document (in this example, the cursor is on page 3, and the document is 7 pages long)
At	How many inches down the page the cursor is
Ln	How many lines down the page the cursor is
Col	In a page with columns, which column the cursor is in

on the disk

For this exercise, you will use the Jump file in the Practice folder. Open that file now and follow these steps to practice using the scroll bars:

1 **Click the down-pointing arrow on the bottom of the vertical scroll bar a few times.**

As you click this arrow, text on-screen scrolls up one line at a time.

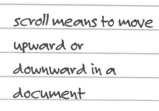

scroll means to move upward or downward in a document

2 **Click the up arrow at the top of the vertical scroll bar.**

Now text scrolls down a line at a time.

3 **Go back to the down arrow, but this time when you click the mouse button on the arrow, hold the mouse button down.**

Text moves very quickly upward one line at a time.

4 **Drag the scroll box down the elevator shaft.**

To do so, move the mouse cursor on top of the scroll box. When the mouse cursor changes into an arrow, hold down the mouse button and move the box downward.

By dragging the scroll box, you can move several pages at once.

5 **Click the scroll box and hold down the mouse button without moving the scroll box anywhere.**

A little yellow box with a page number inside it appears on-screen. This box quickly tells you the page you are on.

6 **Place the cursor above the scroll box — but not on the up arrow at the top of the elevator shaft — and click a few times.**

Each time you click, you move up one screen.

7 **Place the cursor below the scroll box and click a few times.**

Now you move downward one screen at a time.

8 **Place the cursor just above the down arrow at the bottom of the elevator shaft (but not on it) and keep holding down the mouse button as you click the mouse.**

Doing so moves you very quickly through the document, one screen at a time, to the bottom.

9 **Press the spacebar to enter a blank space.**

Now the document scrolls back to where you started. When you move with the scroll bar to a new place on-screen, the text cursor does not move. By using the scroll bar, you change only your view of the document; you don't change the location of the text cursor. To change the text cursor's location, you have to click on-screen after you move to a new place.

10 **Repeat step 8: Click near the bottom of the elevator shaft until you get to the bottom of the document.**

11 **Click on-screen and press the spacebar.**

This time, you enter a blank space at the bottom of the document in the place you moved to, not the place you started from.

12 **Click the right-pointing arrow on the right side of the horizontal scroll bar.**

The horizontal scroll bar, you remember, lies along the bottom of the screen. When you click this arrow, text moves to the left.

13 **Click the left-pointing arrow on the left side of the scroll bar at the bottom of the screen.**

Now text moves to the right. The horizontal scroll bar works just like its vertical cousin, only text moves from side to side instead of upward and downward. You can drag the scroll box on the horizontal scroll bar or click the horizontal scroll bar to move from side to side.

14 **Drag the scroll box on the vertical scroll bar to the top of the elevator shaft to get back to the beginning of the document.**

Using the scroll bars isn't the only way to move from place to place. You can also use keyboard shortcuts, but to learn about them, you have to go on to the next lesson. If you intend to do so, keep the Jump file open.

☑ Progress Check

If you can do the following, you've mastered this lesson:

❑ Use the vertical scroll bar to move up and down in documents.

❑ Use the horizontal scroll bar to move side to side on a page.

Lesson 4-2

Using the Keyboard to Move Around

Sometimes, using the keyboard to move around in documents is easier than using the scroll bars. For example, you can press Ctrl+Home to move straight to the beginning of a document and Ctrl+End to move straight to the end. This lesson explains which keys to press to move around in documents.

Table 4-2 lists all the keyboard shortcuts for moving around in documents. Don't worry about learning all the shortcuts. In the exercise that follows, I'll show you which shortcuts are definitely worth knowing.

Table 4-2	Keyboard Shortcuts for Moving Around in Documents
Press	*To Move Here*
Ctrl+↑	Up one paragraph
Ctrl+↓	Down one paragraph
PgUp	Up one screen
PgDn	Down one screen
Ctrl+PgUp	The top of the screen
Ctrl+PgDn	The bottom of the screen
Ctrl+Alt+PgUp	Up one page
Ctrl+Alt+PgDn	Down one page
Ctrl+Home	The start of the document
Ctrl+End	The end of the document
Ctrl+→	Right one word
Ctrl+←	Left one word
Home	The start of the line
End	The end of the line

You already know that you can press the → key to move the cursor to the right on a line and the ← key to move to the left.

on the disk

For this exercise, you need the Jump file that you opened in Lesson 4-1. Open that file now if it isn't already open. As you do this exercise, jot down the keyboard shortcuts that will be useful for you. These shortcuts can come in very, very handy.

1 **Press Ctrl+End to move to the end of the document.**

Notice how the text cursor moves to the end of the document. When you moved to the end of the document with the scroll bar in the last lesson, the text cursor stayed put. With the scroll bars, you change only which part of the document is shown on-screen. When you move through a document with keyboard shortcuts, you move the text cursor, too.

2 **Press Ctrl+Home to move to the document's first line.**

3 **Press End to move to the end of the first line.**

4 **Press PgDn.**

Pressing this key moves the cursor down one screen. Notice where the text cursor is now — in the middle of the line, not the beginning. Why is that?

The text cursor maintains its horizontal position on-screen when you move it up or down — that is, vertically — through a document. In step 3, you moved the text cursor to the end of the heading at the beginning of the document. That heading occupied about half a line. Therefore, when you pressed PgDn to move the text cursor one screen down in the text, the text cursor landed halfway through a line, roughly in the middle.

5 **Press Home to move the cursor to the start of the line.**

Now when you move the cursor down the screen in the next step, you will know where to find it. The cursor will be on the left side of the screen because the cursor maintains its horizontal position when you move it.

6 **Press Ctrl+PgDn to move to the bottom of the screen.**

7 **Press Ctrl+PgUp to move to the top of the screen.**

Strange, but when I do so, my cursor actually moves one line above the top of the screen, and I have to click the up arrow on the vertical scroll bar to move up one line and get to my cursor.

8 **Press Ctrl+↑ to move up one paragraph.**

In Word 95, a paragraph is simply what you put on-screen before you press Enter. A paragraph can be a heading, a blank line, or a single word on a line.

9 **Press Ctrl+Alt+PgDn to move down one page.**

Take notice: If you want to move down a page, press this shortcut key combination, not the PgDn key. Press PgDn to move the cursor down one screen, not one page.

10 **Press Ctrl+Home to move back to the start of the document.**

Moving around with the Go To command

Besides pressing shortcut keys and using the vertical scroll bar, you can also go from place to place with the Edit⇨Go To command. Here's how:

1. Choose Edit⇨Go To (or press Ctrl+G). The Go To dialog box appears.
2. Type the page number you want to go to in the Enter Page Number box.
3. Click the Go To button.

☑ Progress Check

If you can do the following, you've mastered this lesson and are ready to move on to the Unit 4 quiz:

❑ Press Ctrl+Home to move to the start of a document.

❑ Press Ctrl+End to move to the end of a document.

❑ Press Home to move to the start of a line.

Unit 4 Quiz

For the following questions, circle the letter of the correct answer or answers. Each question may have more than one right answer.

1. **Where is the scroll bar located?**

   A. Along the right side of the screen

   B. Along the bottom of the screen

   C. In the Outer Hebrides Islands

   D. Right above the status bar

2. **To move upward in a document with the vertical scroll bar, you do this:**

   A. Click the up arrow at the top.

   B. Drag the scroll box upward.

   C. Click on the scroll bar above the scroll box.

   D. All of the above.

3. **You can tell which page in a document you are on by doing this:**

   A. Dialing 911

   B. Checking out the page indicator on the status bar

   C. Clicking and holding down the mouse button on the scroll box

   D. Counting the number of lines on-screen and dividing by 50

4. **The fastest way to move to the top of a document is to do this:**

   A. Just keep pressing PgUp.

   B. Press Ctrl+Home.

   C. Press the ↑ key until your eyes start watering.

   D. Scream "Tallyho!" and slap your thigh.

5. **To move the cursor to the start of a line, you do this:**

   A. Press the End key.

   B. Press the Home key.

   C. Just keep right on pressing the ← key.

   D. Click the mouse cursor at the start of the line.

Unit 4 Exercise

on the disk

1. Open the Jump file.

2. Move to the end of the document by pressing a keyboard shortcut.

3. Move back to the start of the document with the vertical scroll bar.

4. Move to the bottom of the screen.

5. Move to the end of the line.

6. Move to the start of the line.

Getting Help When You Need It

Prerequisites

- Starting Word 95 (Lesson 1-1)
- Giving commands by clicking buttons (Lesson 2-1)
- Choosing menu commands (Lesson 2-3)
- Filling in dialog boxes (Lesson 2-5)
- Using the scroll bars to move around (Lesson 4-1)

Objectives for This Unit

✓ Getting help by looking up Help categories

✓ Finding help in the index

✓ Searching for information in the Help program

✓ Asking the Answer Wizard for help

✓ Using the Help buttons

✓ Learning from the TipWizard

✓ Getting Help from Microsoft

Dare I say it, but this book cannot teach you everything you need to know about Word 95. Quite soon, you will become a confident user of the program, and you will branch out on your own and try new things. You will become downright cocky, I imagine, and will want to create indexes, import clip art graphics, and create tables of contents. When that happens, how will you find out how to complete these tasks?

heads up

One way is to use the Word 95 Help program. The Help program offers instructions for doing all tasks (sometimes Help explains tasks well, and sometimes it doesn't). Besides the Help program, you can also click the Help button on the Standard toolbar or the Help button in a dialog box. And you can try your luck with the TipWizard and Answer Wizard. I explain all these techniques in Unit 5.

Getting Help by Category   Lesson 5-1

One way to get help is to obtain a general-purpose description of how to perform a task. With this technique, you start with a broad category in the Help program and try to zero in on the subject you need to know about. If you're new to a subject, starting with a broad category in the Help program is probably the best way to go.

Figure 5-1: Searching for help by category.

Figure 5-2: Double-click a question mark icon to see a list of instructions.

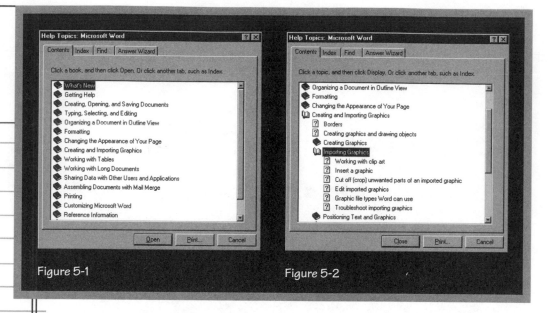

Figure 5-1

Figure 5-2

For this sample exercise, suppose that you want to import a clip art graphic into a document (doing so is a lot easier than you may think). You've never imported art, so you decide to search for help by category:

on the test

1 **Choose Help⇨Microsoft Word Help Topics to start the Help program.**

You can also press F1 to start the Help program. After a moment or two, the dialog box shown in Figure 5-1 appears. The dialog box should open to the Contents tab, but if it doesn't, click the Contents tab now.

Often you can't find the topic you're looking for when you search for help by category, but this time you're in luck. The eighth category is Creating and Importing Graphics.

2 **Double-click the book icon to the left of Creating and Importing Graphics.**

You can also open a topic by selecting it and clicking the Open button (or pressing O).

Now the book opens, and you see several subtopics. If you click a subtopic with a question mark, the program opens a list of instructions. However, you are interested in importing graphics, which is the fourth subtopic.

3 **Double-click the book icon next to Importing Graphics.**

As shown in Figure 5-2, the Importing Graphics book opens, and you see a bunch of subtopics with question marks next to their names. You are interested in the first two subtopics, Working with clip art and Insert a graphic.

4 **Double-click the question mark next to Working with clip art.**

An instruction screen, called Working with clip art, appears on-screen. Read the instructions. I hope they are helpful.

5 **When you're done reading the overview of clip art, click the Help Topics button in the upper-right corner of the screen.**

The Help Topics button sends you back to the Contents tab so that you can choose another Help topic.

6 **Double-click the question mark next to Insert a graphic.**

Another list of instructions appears on-screen. You can keep this instruction box on-screen as you follow its directions for inserting a graphic.

7 **Click the Minimize button on the Help instruction box.**

Now the box disappears from the screen. However, the Help program is still running. The Word 95 Help program can run at the same time as Word 95. Instead of closing the Help program altogether, you can minimize it until you need to read more instructions.

8 **Click the Help program icon on the taskbar to maximize the program.**

The Help program icon is the one with a question mark and the words *Microsoft Word*. The Help box reappears.

9 **Click the Back button.**

The Working with clip art screen you saw in step 4 reappears. Click the Back button when you want to see a Help screen that you saw previously. Click Help Topics to go back to the Help dialog box.

10 **Click the Help Topics button.**

At this point, you can either double-click another book or question mark to read another Help screen, or you can close the Help program. What happens if you double-click an open book?

11 **Double-click the open book icon next to Creating and Importing Graphics.**

The subtopic books are closed. Double-click an open book when you want to close its subtopics and get a better look at the categories in the dialog box.

12 **Click Cancel, press Esc, or click Close to close the Help program.**

Minimize button

☑ Progress Check

If you can do the following, you've mastered this lesson:

❑ Get help by category.

❑ Open an instruction list from the Contents tab of the Help Topics dialog box.

Using the Help Index

Lesson 5-2

Another way to seek help in Word 95 is to use the Help index, which works a bit like the index of a book. You type the name of the subject you need help with, and Word 95 throws up a list of topics that are related to that subject. After that, you choose a topic from the list and hope for the best.

To see how the Help index works, suppose that you need help creating a table of contents. Follow these steps:

1 **Choose Help⇨Microsoft Word Help Topics or press F1 to start the Help program.**

2 **Click the Index tab in the Help Topics dialog box.**

At the top of the Index tab is a text box in which you type the name of the topic you are looking for. Below the text box is an alphabetical list of a million or so Help topics.

3 **Type the first few letters of the topic you're interested in. For this exercise, type** table.

As you type, the alphabetical list scrolls to the T entries. Your screen should look like Figure 5-3. You can also get to the T entries by using the scroll bar on the right side of the dialog box, but that would take too long.

Notice the tables of contents entries on the bottom half of the topic list.

Figure 5-3: Looking for a topic in the Help index.

Figure 5-4: Click a square with arrows on it to see another instruction list.

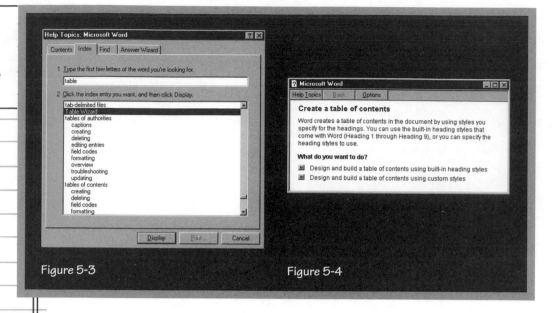

Figure 5-3   Figure 5-4

4 Under tables of contents, double-click creating.

You can also choose this subtopic by clicking it and then clicking the <u>D</u>isplay button.

Yet more subtopics are available under the creating option, so the Topics Found dialog box appears. The Topics Found dialog box offers two choices. You want the first choice, Create a table of contents.

5 Click the <u>D</u>isplay button.

Create a table of contents is already highlighted, so you don't have to click it before you choose <u>D</u>isplay. You can also open a subtopic by double-clicking it.

As shown in Figure 5-4, a Help screen called Create a table of contents appears. The overview at the top tells you about tables of contents. To get specific instructions, click one of the two squares with arrows in them under `What do you want to do?`

6 Click the first square with an arrow on it, the one called "Design and build a table of contents using built-in heading styles."

Do you see the little hand appear as you move the mouse pointer over the box? That hand means that you can click to select a Help topic.

Another Help screen appears. Notice that this screen also has squares with arrows on them that you can click. If the screen you see isn't the one you want, you can always go back to the preceding screen by pressing the <u>B</u>ack button.

7 Click the <u>B</u>ack button.

8 This time, click the second box with an arrow on it.

Another list of instructions appears.

9 If necessary, use the scroll bar to move down the instruction list.

Suppose this screen is just what you're looking for. In fact, you are so glad to have found this screen that you decide to print these instructions and post them on the wall beside your desk.

10 Click the <u>O</u>ptions button.

A drop-down menu appears with several options, including <u>P</u>rint Topic.

11 **Choose Print Topic.**

The Print dialog box appears. Make sure that your printer is on, and glance at the printer settings to make sure that they are all right.

12 **Click OK to print the list of instructions.**

The instructions are printed, and you see them again on-screen.

13 **Click Help Topics to get back to the Index tab of the Help Topics dialog box.**

At this point, you can find another help topic if you want.

14 **Click Cancel to close the Help Topics dialog box.**

All the instructions boxes in the Help program have Help Topics, Back, and Options buttons.

Searching in the Help Program   Lesson 5-3

Besides searching by category or looking up topics in the Help index, you can search for words in Help program files and see what comes up. With this technique, you type a word, and the Help program shows you a list of all its Help files in which it finds that word.

The first time you try to get help by searching for words in the Help program, Word 95 asks whether it should create an index file of words in the Help program. Click Yes. You cannot get help with the "word method" until Word creates this index file.

Searching for words in the Help files is the most cumbersome method of getting help, but sometimes it's the only way to go if you can't find what you're looking for in the Help index or in a Help category. For this exercise, suppose that you want to get swanky and spell *cooperate* with an umlaut, like so: coöperate. How do you get the two dots over the second *o*?

To find out, you can look for *umlaut* in the Help index. Umlaut is not there, however, so you have to search for *umlaut* in the Help program files. If you're indexing your files for the first time, do the following:

1 **Choose Help⇨Microsoft Word Help Topics or press F1 to start the Help program.**

2 **Click the Find tab in the Help Topics dialog box.**

A picture of a pencil and the words Loading Word List flash on-screen momentarily.

3 **In the text box at the top of the Find tab, type umlaut.**

Nothing happens! The second box, which normally shows phrases and option names with the word you typed in the first box, goes blank. The third box goes blank, too. Normally, the third box shows Help topics that you can choose to get the information you want.

You often have to thrash around on the Find tab to find what you're looking for.

Figure 5-5: Finding the elusive umlaut.

Figure 5-6: The umlaut found!

Notes:

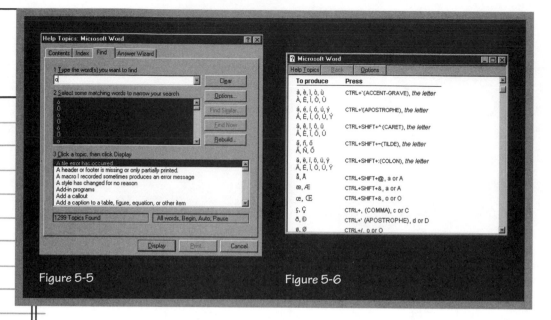

Figure 5-5   Figure 5-6

4. Delete the word *umlaut.*

5. Press O to see whether, on the off chance, you see an *o* with an umlaut.

Now you're on the right track. Some *o*'s with weird marks above them appear in the second box.

6. Click the down arrow on the scroll bar next to the second box until you see an *o* with an umlaut.

Your screen should look like Figure 5-5. The bottom of the dialog box tells you that 1,299 topics deal with the letter *o.* Better narrow the search down by choosing only one *o* in the second box.

7. Click the *o* with the umlaut.

That narrows down the list of topics considerably. Now only one topic, Type international characters, is in the third box.

8. Click the <u>D</u>isplay button.

You can also double-click a topic in the third box to display its list of instructions on-screen. The instruction list, shown in Figure 5-6, appears. If you look closely, you can find the instructions for entering an *o* with an umlaut on this list.

9. Click Help <u>T</u>opics to get back to the Find tab of the Help Topics dialog box.

10. Click the Close button to close the Help program.

heads up

Use the Find tab as a last resort when you can't get help with the Help index or Help category list. Finding a topic this way often leads to dead ends and can be frustrating.

Comparing the ways to get help

So far in Unit 5, you've learned three important ways to get help in Word 95. You've learned how to get help by category, use the Help index, and search the Help files for a particular word or subject. The Help program is a program unto itself. Remember that you can minimize the Help program by minimizing its window, do your work in Word 95, and get the Help program back when you need to by maximizing its window.

☑ **Progress Check**

If you can do the following, you've mastered this lesson:

❑ Conduct a word search in the Help program.

❑ Find and choose a topic on the Find tab of the Help Topics dialog box.

Recess

But you knew that already, so reward yourself by taking a break. Find a harmonica and blow on it, pretending all the while that you are Little Walter or James Cotton.

Asking the Answer Wizard for Help

Lesson 5-4

As if you haven't already learned enough ways to get help in Word 95, you have yet another option: you can ask the Answer Wizard. The Answer Wizard is sort of a craps shoot. You ask the Wizard a question and hope that it has an answer.

To practice using the Answer Wizard, suppose that you need help with passwords. You want to create a password so that only people in the know can open your document. To do so, follow these steps:

1 **Choose Help⇨Answer Wizard.**

The Answer Wizard tab of the Help Topics dialog box appears on-screen. You can also get to this tab by choosing Help⇨Microsoft Word Help Topics and clicking the Answer Wizard tab.

2 **Type a question in the first text box. For this exercise, type** How do I create a password?

3 **Click the Search button.**

A bunch of topic names appears in the second box. Will any of them explain how to create a password? I happen to know that *Protect a document* will, but most people don't know that because the word *password* isn't in the topic name. The Answer Wizard isn't always wise in its answers.

4 **Click Protect a document and then click the Display button.**

You can also double-click a topic to see its list of instructions. An exhaustive list of instructions and explanations appears on-screen.

5 **Scroll to the bottom of the instruction list and click the first box and two arrows icon.**

Click the box and two arrows next to *Require a password when a document is opened or accessed*. A new Help screen appears.

6 **Drag this Help screen to the side of the document window.**

To do so, move the mouse to the title bar of the Help screen. When the mouse cursor changes into a pointer, click, hold down the mouse button, and move the pointer to the side of the screen.

If you really want to create a password, you can read the instructions from the Help window as you give commands and complete all the necessary steps in Word 95. Remember that the Help program is a program unto itself. You can minimize the Help window or drag it around as you please.

7 **Click Help Topics to get back to the Answer Wizard.**

8 **Type** What goes well with a Caesar salad? **in the first box.**

☑ Progress Check

If you can do the following, you've mastered this lesson:

❑ Ask the Answer Wizard a question.

❑ Choose from the list of topics that the Answer Wizard offers.

9 **Click the Search button.**

Word 95 tells you, "Sorry, I don't know what you mean. Please rephrase your question."

No Wizard gets stumped as often as the Answer Wizard. The Answer Wizard is the least useful of all the Help commands.

10 **Click OK to tell Word 95 that you got the message.**

11 **Click Cancel to close the Help Topics dialog box.**

Lesson 5-5

Using the Help Buttons

Choosing the <u>H</u>elp command on the main menu bar isn't the only way to get help. You can also click the Help button on the Standard toolbar or click a Help button in a dialog box.

The Help button on the toolbar

Help button

The Help button is the right-most button on the Standard toolbar. When you click Help and move the mouse pointer on-screen, a question mark appears beside the pointer. As long as that question mark is beside the pointer, you can click on a part of the screen and maybe get an explanation of the part of the screen you clicked.

on the test

To see how the Help button works, type a few words and follow these steps:

1 **Click the Help button.**

A big, black question mark appears beside the mouse pointer.

2 **Move the mouse pointer on-screen and click the text you typed.**

A bunch of information appears on-screen. You see the font of the text and how the paragraph you clicked is formatted. The question mark still appears beside the pointer. You can click something else to get information about it.

3 **Click the status bar.**

As shown in Figure 5-7, a box appears to tell you what the status bar is good for. Now a question mark is not beside the mouse pointer. You're out of Help button mode.

4 **Click the Help button again.**

5 **Click either scroll bar.**

A box tells you what the scroll bars do.

6 **Click the Help button again to end this little adventure.**

When you need to shake the question mark pointer and get back to word processing as usual, click the Help button again.

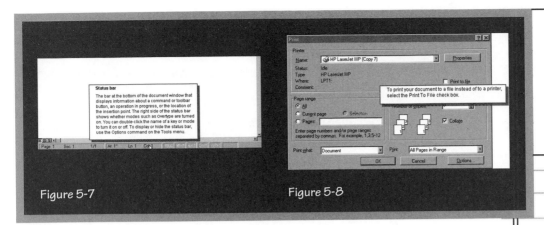

Figure 5-7

Figure 5-8

Figure 5-7: Click the Help button and then click a part of the screen to find out what that part of the screen does.

Figure 5-8: The Help button in dialog boxes is invaluable.

The Help button in dialog boxes

on the test

Every dialog box also has a Help button., You can find it in the upper-right corner next to the Close button (the X). To experiment with the Help button in a dialog box, do the following:

1 Press Ctrl+P to see the Print dialog box.

2 Click the Help button — it has a question mark on it — in the upper-right corner.

The familiar pointer and question mark appear.

3 Click the Print to file check box.

An explanation of why you might choose this option appears in a little box, shown in Figure 5-8.

4 Click the Help button again.

5 Click the Properties button.

An explanation of how to change printer properties appears in a little box.

6 Click Cancel to close the Print dialog box without printing anything.

The Help button in dialog boxes is invaluable. Click the Help button and click the part of the dialog box about which you have a question whenever you get stumped or when you merely want to learn more about an option.

☑ **Progress Check**

If you can do the following, you've mastered this lesson:

❑ Use the Help button on the Standard toolbar to get information about items on-screen.

❑ Use the Help button in a dialog box to find out more about the dialog box's options.

Getting Tips for Learning Word

Lesson 5-6

One final way to get advice for learning Word 95 is to read the tips from the TipWizard. You can read them along the tops of documents when you first start Word 95. After you finish reading a tip, click the TipWizard button, which is in the upper-right corner beside the Help button.

Try this experiment with the TipWizard:

1 Click the TipWizard button to turn on the feature if it is not already on.

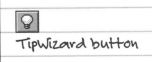

TipWizard button

Show Me button

2 **Type some gibberish and press Enter.**

The idea is to enter a misspelling. Because you entered misspelled words, the TipWizard says, `Click the right mouse button on the red wavy underlined words to correct them.`

3 **Click the Show Me button.**

An instruction box appears, telling you what the red wavy lines mean and how to make Word 95 take note of your misspellings if the program is not already doing so.

Click the Show Me button if you're from Missouri, or if you want to know more about the tip.

4 **Click the Close button (the X) to close the instruction box.**

5 **Click the up arrow on the right side of the TipWizard to see previous tips.**

You can always check out previous tips this way.

6 **Click the TipWizard button to remove the TipWizard from the screen.**

The TipWizard takes up valuable space on-screen. Most of the time, you do not want to see the TipWizard, but you can turn it on again merely by clicking the TipWizard button.

A word of advice about the Help program

Learning the many different ways to get help is not easy. So many techniques! So little time! Learning this stuff is important, however, because you spend a lot of time with the Help program and the Help buttons when you work with Word 95. If you get familiar with the many ways to get help early on, so much the better for you.

Recess

Before going on to the Unit 5 quiz, not to mention the Part I test, go to your nearest CD shop, find the Cuban jazz section, get a Barbito Diez recording, take it home, and play it. You will cool off in no time!

☑ Progress Check

If you can do the following, you've mastered this lesson and are ready to move on to the Unit 5 quiz:

❑ Click the TipWizard button to get a few words of wisdom.

❑ Click the Show Me button to investigate a tip.

Unit 5 Quiz

For the following questions, circle the letter of the correct answer or answers. Each question may have more than one right answer.

1. **To start the Word 95 Help program, you do this:**

   A. Ask Mom to help you.

   B. Press F1.

   C. Choose Help⇨Microsoft Word Help Topics.

   D. Type **help** and an exclamation point.

   E. Call a radio talk show, get angry, and complain because the poor get to use the Help program for free.

Notes:

2. **Following are techniques for getting help in Word 95:**

   A. Click the Help button and then click the part of the screen you need help with.

   B. Use the Find tab in the Help Topics dialog box to search for help.

   C. Use the Help index to find help about a topic.

   D. Click the Show Me button beside the tip at the top of the screen.

   E. Call the reference desk at your local library.

3. **When you click the <u>B</u>ack button in an instruction box, this happens:**

   A. You pass Go and collect $200.

   B. You go back to the last instruction box you saw.

   C. You go back to the Help Topics dialog box.

   D. You get a menu for printing the instruction box.

   E. You get relief from sore back pain.

4. **You can consult the following wizard to get answers to questions in Word 95:**

   A The Wizard of Oz

   B. Mr. Wizard

   C. The Wizard of Westwood

   D. The Answer Wizard

   E. The TipWizard

5. **To get information about an option in a dialog box, you do this:**

   A. Click the Help button, click the option, and read the instruction box.

   B. Read the manual.

   C. Choose the option and see what happens.

   D. Ask the youngster in the next cubicle.

   E. Call Microsoft Technical Support at 800-936-5700.

6. **In Help program instruction boxes, what happens when you click the little squares with arrows on them?**

   A. You hear "Moon Over Mandalay" played on a ukulele.

   B. You get more detailed information from another instruction box.

   C. You get a definition of a word.

   D. You make the box with arrows disappear.

   E. You get one trip to the cookie jar.

Unit 5 Exercise

Notes:

Get help for doing the following tasks. You can use whichever techniques you feel most comfortable using — the TipWizard, the Answer Wizard, the Help index, the Contents tab, the Find tab, or the Help buttons. You don't have to actually do these tasks. The purpose of completing this exercise is to learn how you would do these tasks if push came to shove and you really had to.

1. Create a table of contents.
2. Put borders around a text paragraph.
3. Create an index.
4. Create footnotes.
5. Number the pages of a document.

Unit 1 Summary

- **Starting:** Click the Start button, choose Programs, choose Microsoft Office, and then choose Microsoft Word.

- **Creating:** Choose File⇨New, press Ctrl+N, or click the New button.

- **Saving:** Choose File⇨Save, find the folder you want to save the file in, enter a new file name in the File name box, and click the Save button.

- **Closing:** Click the Save button, choose File⇨Save, or press Ctrl+S to save the file one last time, and then choose File⇨Close.

- **Opening:** Choose File⇨Open, press Ctrl+O, or click the Open button. Find the folder where the file is, select the document, and then click the Open button or press Enter.

- **Exiting:** Choose File⇨Exit.

Unit 2 Summary

- **Clicking buttons:** Move the mouse cursor over a button, and click when the mouse cursor changes into an arrow.

- **Shortcut keys:** Press Ctrl and a letter to give a shortcut key command.

- **Menu commands:** To pull down a menu, either click the menu name with the mouse or press the Alt key and the letter that is underlined in the menu name. To choose a command from a pull-down menu, either click the command name or press the letter that is underlined in the command name.

- **Shortcut menus:** Right-click on text or on a part of the screen, and a shortcut menu appears. You can choose a command from these menus.

- **Dialog boxes:** Often, you have to fill in a dialog box to complete a command. Dialog boxes may include radio buttons, scroll lists, check boxes, buttons, drop-down lists, and text boxes. Click the OK button when you're done filling the dialog box in.

Unit 3 Summary

- **Insert and typeover mode:** Press Insert or double-click OVR on the status bar to switch to typeover mode and have the letters you type cover up the ones that are already there. Press Insert or double-click OVR again to get back to insert mode and have the letters you enter push aside the other letters.

- **Selecting:** You can select text in many ways. Double-click a word to select it. Drag across text to select it. Double-click in the left margin to select a paragraph.

- **Moving:** Select the text you want to move and then drag it to a new place. You can also click the Cut button and paste the text elsewhere with the Paste button, choose Edit⇨Cut and then Edit⇨Paste, or press Ctrl+X and then Ctrl+V.

- **Copying:** Select the text and drag it elsewhere while holding down the Ctrl key. You can also click the Copy button and then the Paste button, choose Edit⇨Copy and then Edit⇨Paste, or press Ctrl+C and then Ctrl+V.

- **Deleting:** Select the text and press Delete.

- **Changing case:** To change the capitalization of letters, select them and press Shift+F3 or choose Format⇨Change Case and make a selection in the dialog box.

- **Entering symbols:** Choose Insert⇨Symbol, find the right font, choose the symbol by clicking it, and click Insert or press Alt+I.

Part I Review

Unit 4 Summary

▶ **Moving with the scroll bars:** Click the up or down arrow to move the screen one line at a time. Drag the scroll box to move large distances. Click on the scroll bar to move screen by screen.

▶ **Moving with keyboard shortcuts:** You can move the cursor in several different ways: Ctrl+Home moves it to the start of the document; Ctrl+End moves it to the end of the document; Home moves it to the start of a line; and End moves it to the end of a line.

Unit 5 Summary

▶ **Help by category:** Choose Help➪Microsoft Word Help Topics, double-click the book icon of the subject you're interested in on the Contents tab, and then double-click the question mark next to the subcategory you're interested in to see an instruction screen.

▶ **Help Index:** Choose Help➪Microsoft Word Help Topics, click the Index tab, type the first few letters of the topic you're interested in, and then double-click a subtopic in the index box to see an instruction screen.

▶ **Find tab:** Choose Help➪Microsoft Word Help Topics, click the Find tab, type the name of the topic you're looking for in the first box, select a topic in the second box to narrow your search, and then double-click a topic in the third box to see an instruction screen.

▶ **Answer Wizard:** Choose Help➪Answer Wizard, type a question in the first text box, click the Search button, and hope for the best.

▶ **Help buttons:** Click the Help button on the Standard toolbar and then click on text or a part of the screen to get information. Click the Help button in a dialog box and then click an option to learn about the option.

▶ **Tip Wizard:** Click the TipWizard button on the Standard toolbar and read the tip to learn more about Word 95.

Part I Test

This test will determine whether you spend the rest of your life in a mansion or a shotgun shack. It will determine what kind of car you drive: a roomy luxury model or a corroded fourthhand lemon. It will measure your worth as a human being. It will determine whether you sink or swim in today's hard-nosed global economy. It will show you once and for all how smart you really are and whether you deserve to be downsized. Are you intimidated by computers? Are you intimidated by this test? Well, you should be! Now hunker down and get to work.

Actually, I designed this test simply to help you find out how much you learned in Part I. The answers to the questions asked here can be found next to the "On the Test" icons scattered throughout Part I (the answers also appear in Appendix A). If you have trouble with a question, go back to the lesson in Part I that covers the topic you are having trouble with. This test is meant to help you use Word 95 better.

True   False

T F 1. Computers are smart and can think on their own.

T F 2. Click the New button to open a new document.

T F 3. The *.doc* at the end of file names is called a file extension, and it is how the computer identifies Word 95 files.

T F 4. Choose File⇨Close to exit Word 95.

T F 5. You can select text by dragging the cursor over it.

T F 6. You can enter only the characters that you see on your keyboard.

T F 7. There are two scroll bars, one along the side and one along the bottom of the screen.

T F 8. You can press F1 to start the Help program.

T F 9. In *The Wizard of Oz,* Dorthy was able to get back to Kansas by clicking the heels of her magic slippers and repeating, "There's no place like home."

T F 10. Click the Help button on the Standard toolbar to start the Help program.

Multiple choice

Circle the correct answer or answers to the following questions. Each question may have more than one right answer.

11. **Why should you save documents every so often as you work on them?**

    A. So that you can hear that disk-grinding sound on your computer

    B. To store the changes you've made to the hard disk, where they are stored permanently and won't be lost if there is a power failure or other untoward accident

    C. For the sheer fun of it

    D. So that your computer knows you are still awake

    E. To keep all the data on your computer intact

12. **Besides choosing File⇨Open, you can open a document in which of the following ways?**

    A. By clicking the Paste button

    B. By opening up the filing cabinet, taking out a manila folder, and pulling the document out

    C. By eavesdropping on the telephone conversations of the person in the next cubicle

    D. By pulling down the File menu and clicking one of the four file names at the bottom

    E. By choosing the File⇨New command

13. **You can tell what a button on a toolbar does by doing the following:**

    A. Placing the mouse pointer on it and reading its name

    B. Clicking it to see what happens

Part I Test

C. Staring hard at the little picture on the button until you realize what the little picture is supposed to mean

D. Placing the mouse pointer on it and reading the description on the status bar

E. Clicking the Help button and then clicking the toolbar button in question

14. **If you haven't studied adequately for a test and feel apprehensive or guilty about it, you will have which of the following dreams on the night before the test?**

A. You are dancing in the sunshine in a meadow of wildflowers.

B. You are strolling by the peaceful sea under a full moon.

C. You are walking naked through the hallways of your old high school and feel ashamed.

D. You have amazing leaping ability and are running joyously across a fantastic desert landscape.

15. **Which of the following is not a method of selecting text?**

A. Double-clicking a word

B. Dragging the mouse cursor down the left margin

C. Pressing F8 and then pressing arrow keys

D. Right-clicking in the left margin

E. Choosing Edit⇨Select All

16. **To copy text by dragging it, which key do you hold down as you drag the text?**

A. Ctrl

B. Alt

C. Shift

D. F2

E. None of the above

17. **If you accidentally delete text, you can still get it back with which of the following methods?**

A. By typing it back in the document

B. By clicking the Paste button

C. By begging Word 95 to forgive you

D. By clicking the Undo button

E. By pulling your hair out and swearing

18. **Why is there a question mark in the upper-right corner of all dialog boxes?**

A. To remind you of the universal question, "Why are we here?"

B. You can click it to close the dialog box.

C. It's the help button, and you can click it and then click an option to see what the option does.

D. It opens the Help program.

E. Don't worry about it. It's just a decoration.

Matching

19. **Match the following buttons with the corresponding commands:**

A.   1. File⇨Open

B.   2. Edit⇨Cut

C.   3. File⇨Save

D.   4. Edit⇨Copy

E.   5. File⇨New

20. **Match the following shortcut keys with the corresponding buttons:**

A. Ctrl+C   1.

B. Ctrl+Z   2.

C. Ctrl+V   3.

D. Ctrl+N   4.

E. Ctrl+O   5.

Part I Test

21. **Match the following actors and actresses with the movies in which they starred:**

    A. Vivien Leigh

    B. Humphrey Bogart

    C. Jean Seberg

    D. Rosenda Monteros

    E. Toshiro Mifune

    1. *The Magnificent Seven*

    2. *Casablanca*

    3. *A Streetcar Named Desire*

    4. *Seven Samurai*

    5. *Breathless*

22. **Match the following keyboard shortcuts with their related function:**

    A. Ctrl+X

    B. Ctrl+ S

    C. Ctrl+ C

    D. Ctrl+ V

    E. Ctrl+ Z

    1. Save

    2. Undo

    3. Cut

    4. Paste

    5. Copy

Part I Lab Assignment

This is the first of the lab assignments that you will find at the ends of Parts I through V of this book. The object of these assignments is to give you a chance to apply the things you learned in a realistic situation.

In the lab assignments, I won't tell you how to do things in step-by-step fashion as I did in the exercises in the lessons. Instead, these lab assignments give general instructions, the idea being for you to figure out how to do it yourself — or to already know how to do it yourself. By now, you are starting to feel like you have command of Word 95. I don't have to tell you to click this or press that anymore. You know how to do it.

For this lab assignment, imagine that you have just received a telephone call from the editor of *Silver Screen* magazine. The editor contacted you, a famous journalist and movie star biographer, because she was curious to know whatever happened to Rosenda Monteros, who starred in *The Magnificent Seven* beside Steve McQueen and Yul Brynner. In her ten-year career lasting from the mid-1950s to the mid-1960s, the talented and beautiful actress lit up the screen in movies such as *White Orchid* (1954) and *Tiara Tahiti* (1962). Rosenda Monteros was a great talent and one of the first Hispanic Americans to achieve national stardom. But where is she now?

Hundreds of magazine readers would give anything to find out, according to your editor.

Step 1: Opening the letter document

Well, it so happens that you've written this kind of "where are they now?" story before. On your computer is a letter that you wrote some time ago when you were trying to find out whatever happened to another actor. You just have to open that letter and change the date and some names around.

on the disk

Open the file called Where Are They Now in the Practice folder.

Part I Lab Assignment

Step 2: Copying text and moving around

Erase what's at the top of the letter and type in your name and address. Then copy your name and move to the bottom of the document by pressing keys. Erase the line at the bottom of the letter and paste in your own name. Then move back to the top of the document by using the scroll bar.

Step 3: Saving, typeover mode

Save the document (but don't close it). Then switch to typeover mode and type today's date where "June 1, 1993" is now. Switch back to insert mode when you're done.

Step 4: Selecting, copying, moving text

Erase "Ralph Meeker" in the first paragraph and type the name **Rosenda Monteros**. Then select her name and copy it to the Clipboard. Go to the third paragraph and select the name Ralph Meeker there, and then paste in Rosenda Monteros's name. Find "him" and "his" in the letter and replace these words with "her" and "hers."

Erase the movie title *Kiss Me Deadly* from the first paragraph and put *Tiara Tahiti* and *The Magnificent Seven* in its place.

Select the third paragraph and move it between what are now the first and second paragraphs. Do so by dragging the paragraph.

Step 5: Saving and closing

Save the letter and close it.

Deciding on the Look of Documents

Part II

In this part . . .

Part II explains how to change the way documents *look*. Get this stuff down, and you will be well on your way to mastering Microsoft Word for Windows 95. In Part II, you learn how to change the size and appearance of text; embellish text by boldfacing and italicizing it; align text on the page in many different ways; and change line spacing, margin width, and indentations.

Applying Character Styles to Text

Objectives for This Unit

- ✔ Boldfacing words and headings
- ✔ Italicizing words in documents
- ✔ Underlining words and letters
- ✔ Putting superscript and subscript letters and numbers in documents
- ✔ Striking out text passages

Prerequisites
- ▶ Telling Word what you want it to do (Unit 2)
- ▶ Entering and editing text (Unit 3)
- ▶ Selecting text (Lesson 3-2)
- ▶ Moving around in documents (Unit 4)

N o doubt you've envied your friends and colleagues for the large and unusual typefaces, boldfaced letters, italicized letters, and other amenities that they have put in their word processed documents. Now you will learn how to put these character styles in your documents, too.

on the test

Unit 6 explains how to boldface and italicize text. It demonstrates how to underline letters and even how to get superscript and subscript letters. You'll also learn how to draw lines through words to show that they have been struck out of a document. All these special effects are known as *character styles*.

on the disk
- ▶ Bold
- ▶ Italics
- ▶ Underline
- ▶ Effects
- ▶ Character Styles

Boldfacing Headings in Documents

Lesson 6-1

To *boldface* a word means to give it a heavier type so that it looks darker and stands out on the page. When readers first see a page, their eyes travel first to the boldfaced words, which is why headings are almost always boldfaced. Sometimes you see boldfaced words in the text as well. In this book, for example, letters and words that you are supposed to type are boldfaced so that you know exactly what to type.

Figure 6-1: You can apply more than one character style from the Font dialog box.

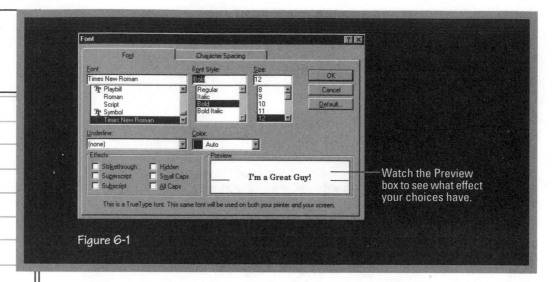

Figure 6-1

Watch the Preview box to see what effect your choices have.

Bold button

Ctrl+B is shortcut key for boldfacing text

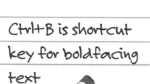

☑ **Progress Check**

If you can do the following, you've mastered this lesson:

❏ Boldface text with the Bold button.

❏ Boldface text by pressing Ctrl+B.

❏ Boldface text by choosing the Format⇨Font command.

on the disk

Word for Windows offers several different ways to boldface text. In this lesson, you try all of them. To complete the exercise in this lesson, open the Bold file in the Practice folder.

on the test

1 **With the cursor at the top of the document, click the Bold button.**

The Bold button has a *B* on it. Notice that the Bold button appears to be pressed down on the toolbar after you click it.

2 **Type** Why You Should Elect Rick Switches!

The text appears in boldfaced type.

3 **Click the Bold button again to turn off boldfacing.**

Now the Bold button on the toolbar is no longer pressed down. You can always tell when boldfacing is on by looking at the Bold button.

4 **Press Enter twice to drop down two lines, and then type** Here are the reasons why you should vote for me:.

The text is not boldfaced because you turned off boldface by pressing the Bold button for the second time in step 3.

5 **Select the first heading, "My Opponent Is a Boldfaced Liar!"**

6 **Press Ctrl+B.**

The headline is boldfaced. Notice how the Bold button on the toolbar is pressed down again, even though you gave the Bold command by pressing Ctrl+B. If you press Ctrl+B a second time, you turn off boldface, and you can enter regular text again.

7 **Select the second heading, "I'm a Great Guy!"**

8 **Choose Format⇨Font.**

The Font dialog box, shown in Figure 6-1, appears. This dialog box lets you change the style, size, and typeface of text.

9 **In the Font Style box, click Bold and then click OK.**

Figure 6-1 shows the Bold option being selected. Take a look in the Preview box. It shows what your Font Style choice will look like in your document.

10 **Boldface the third heading any way you want.**

The fastest way to boldface text is to click the Bold button or press Ctrl+B. However, by choosing Format⇨Font, you can apply several different styles at once, as you will see in the next lesson.

11 **Close the Bold file without saving your changes.**

Italicizing Words

Lesson 6-2

Italicized letters slant upward and to the right, like so: *Hello, I've been italicized!* Conventional wisdom says to italicize words for emphasis, but if you use italics for that purpose, do so sparingly. Only one or two words should be emphasized at a time. Too many italicized words at once, *and you start to get the impression that the author is screaming at you!*

Foreign words and expressions are usually set in italics. When you introduce a technical term in a book or paper and define it for the first time, the convention is to italicize the term. In references to words as words or letters as letters, the word or letter is usually italicized, as in this sentence: To spell the word *kite*, you need a *k*, an *i*, a *t*, and an *e*.

So much for the copy editing lesson. You are here to learn how to italicize words, and you will be glad to know that italicizing is easy in Word 95. For this exercise, open the Italics file and follow these steps:

1 **Select the foreign word *soi-disant* in the first paragraph.**

This word means "so-called" or "self-styled" in French. Better italicize the word so that readers know that they are encountering a foreign term.

2 **Click the Italic button.**

The word is italicized. Notice how the Italic button is pressed down. One way to tell whether text has been italicized is to put the cursor in the text and look at the Italic button to see whether it is pressed down.

3 **Select the word *neo-opportunism* in the first paragraph.**

Neo-opportunism is not a foreign term (although it sounds like one), but the word needs to be italicized because it is being defined for the first time.

4 **Press Ctrl+I.**

In the last lesson, you pressed Ctrl+B to boldface text, and in this lesson, you press Ctrl+I to italicize it. In the next lesson, you will press Ctrl+U to underline text. Do you notice a pattern here?

5 **Select *le neuf opportunisme*, the French term inside parentheses.**

6 **Choose Format⇨Font.**

As in Figure 6-1, the Font dialog box appears. The Font dialog box presents yet another way to italicize text.

7 **In the Font Style box, click Italic and then click OK.**

Now the term is italicized. In the next three steps, you will see how you can italicize and boldface text with one trip to the Font dialog box.

8 **Select "Jean LeBarge (1933–1988)," the first line in the document.**

9 **Choose Format⇨Font.**

10 **Choose Bold Italic in the Font Style box.**

11 **Look in the Preview box to see what italicized, boldfaced text looks like.**

Always look in the Preview box to see the effect of your character style choices.

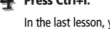

Italic button

Ctrl+I is shortcut key for italicizing text

☑ **Progress Check**

If you can do the following, you've mastered this lesson:

❑ Italicize text by clicking the Italic button.

❑ Italicize text by pressing Ctrl+I.

❑ Italicize text by choosing Format➪Font.

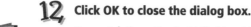

on the test

12 **Click OK to close the dialog box.**

Congratulations. You just killed two birds with one stone. You can also get boldfaced, italicized text by selecting the text and either clicking the Bold button as well as the Italic button or pressing Ctrl+B and then Ctrl+I.

13 **Italicize the word *manqué* in the last paragraph in whatever way works best for you.**

14 **Close the Italics file without saving your changes.**

You can italicize text as you enter it. To do so, simply click the Italic button or press Ctrl+I and start typing. When you want to type regular text again, click the Italic button a second time or press Ctrl+I again to turn off italics. To remove italics from text, select the text and click the Italic button.

Lesson 6-3   # Underlining Words

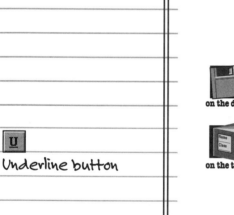

Now that most people have word processors and can get italicized text, you don't see underlines very often. However, underlines still have uses. In the command names in this book, for example, the letters used in shortcut commands are underlined. Sometimes headings are underlined, too.

on the disk

To learn how to underline text, open the Underline file in the Practice folder and follow these steps:

on the test

1 **Click the Underline button.**

This button, found on the Formatting toolbar, is the underlined <u>U</u>.

U

Underline button

2 **Type** I Dare You.

As you type, the text is underlined.

3 **Select the next line, "I Dare You Again."**

4 **Press Ctrl+U.**

Now this line is underlined, too. You can underline text before or after you enter it.

Ctrl+U is shortcut key for underlining text

5 **While the line is still highlighted, press Ctrl+U and then click the Underline button.**

As you do so, notice how the underline disappears and reappears. You can always remove the underlining from text by selecting the text and either clicking the Underline button or pressing Ctrl+U.

6 **Select the third line, "I Dare You Yet Again," and choose For-mat➪Font.**

The Font dialog box appears, offering a handful of underlining options that you can't get by pressing keys or clicking buttons.

7 **Click the down arrow next to the Underline box and choose the Words Only underline option.**

Your screen should look like Figure 6-2. With the Words Only option, the space between words is not underlined.

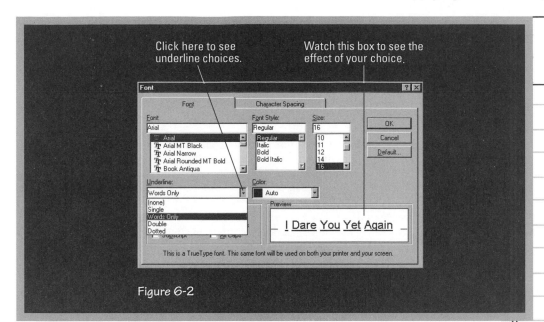

Click here to see
underline choices.

Watch this box to see the
effect of your choice.

Figure 6-2

Figure 6-2: The Font dialog
box offers several
underline options.

Notes:

8 **Click OK to close the dialog box.**

Back in your document, the words themselves are underlined, not the spaces
between them.

9 **Select the next line, "I Double Dare You, In Fact."**

10 **Choose Format⇨Font, open the Underline drop-down list on the
Font dialog box, choose the Double option, and click OK.**

The selected text receives a double underline. To see the double underlining,
though, you have to click in the document to remove the highlighting.

11 **Select "I Double Dare You, In Fact" again and click the Underline
button or press Ctrl+U.**

Doing so doesn't remove the double underline. Instead, it turns the double
underline into a single underline. Who would have thought it? If you ever put a
double underline on text and change your mind about it, you can always select
the text and click the Underline button to get a single underline.

12 **Select the last line in the document, choose Format⇨Font, open
the Underline drop-down list, choose Dotted, and click OK.**

Now you get a dotted underline.

☑ **Progress Check**

If you can do the following,
you've mastered this lesson:

❑ Underline words in a
document with the
Underline button and
Ctrl+U.

❑ Put a double underline
on words.

❑ Put a dotted underline
on words.

Superscript, Subscript,
and Strikethrough

Lesson 6-4

So far in Unit 6, you've learned how to boldface, italicize, and underline
words. In this lesson, you will try three slightly esoteric character styles:
superscript, subscript, and strikethrough.

on the test

A *superscripted* letter or number has been raised up a bit in the text. For example, in the theory of relativity, the 2 is superscripted: $E = mc^2$. Superscript is also used in ordinal numbers (1st, 2nd, 3rd) and for footnote numbers in text (although if you want to use footnotes in Word 95, don't bother with superscript; choose Insert⇨Footnote instead).

A *subscripted* letter or number has been lowered a bit in the text. In the following chemistry equation, for example, the 2 has been lowered to show that two atoms of hydrogen are needed along with one atom of oxygen to form a molecule of water: H_2O.

Strikethrough text has ~~a line running through it~~. Lawyers use strikethrough to show where they have struck text from legal contracts. Sometimes strikethrough is used to show where text has been erased, as in this sentence: The following students have improved their behavior and will get to go on the class field trip: Tad, ~~Suzie~~, Jeremy, ~~David~~.

on the disk

For this exercise, you will use the Effects file in the Practice folder. Open that file now and follow these steps to learn about superscript, subscript, and strikethrough:

1 **Select the 2 in πr2.**

The 2 needs to be superscripted, because the area of a circle equals π times the radius squared.

2 **Choose Format⇨Font.**

The Font dialog box, shown in Figure 6-3, appears.

3 **In the Effects area in the lower-left corner of the dialog box, click the Superscript check box and then click OK.**

Now the 2 is raised off the ground a little bit, and everyone can see that this formula finds the area of a circle.

4 **In the sulfuric acid chemical formula, select the 2.**

This 2 needs to be subscripted.

5 **Choose Format⇨Font, press Alt+B to put a check mark in the Subscript check box, and click OK.**

Instead of pressing Alt+B, you can also click the Subscript check box. Now the 2 in the chemical formula is lowered a bit.

6 **Select the 4 in the formula for sulfuric acid and repeat step 5 to subscript it.**

7 **Select the last line in the document.**

Remember, you can select an entire line by clicking once in the left margin.

8 **Choose Format⇨Font and click the Strikethrough check box.**

Your screen should look like Figure 6-3. Notice the Preview box, where you can see the effects of your choices.

9 **Click OK.**

The last line is struck out on-screen.

10 **Close the document without saving your changes to it.**

☑ Progress Check

If you can do the following, you've mastered this lesson and are ready to move on to the Unit 6 quiz:

❑ Superscript a letter or number in a document.

❑ Subscript a letter or number.

❑ Use the Strikethrough option to show where text should be removed from a document.

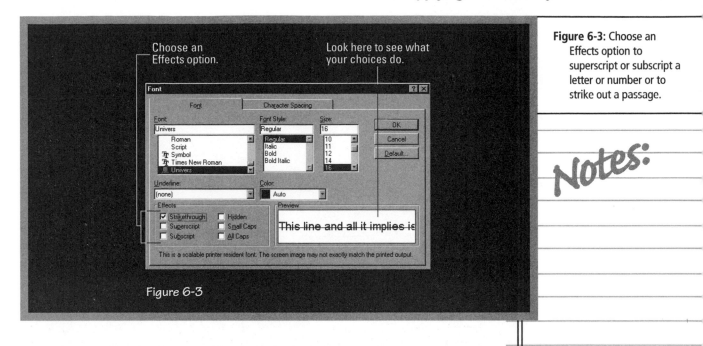

Choose an Effects option.

Look here to see what your choices do.

Figure 6-3

Figure 6-3: Choose an Effects option to superscript or subscript a letter or number or to strike out a passage.

Notes:

Unit 6 Quiz

For the following questions, circle the letter of the correct answer or answers. Each question may have more than one right answer.

1. **This button does which of the following?**

    A. Boldfaces the text you have selected

    B. Turns on boldfacing so that you can enter boldfaced text

    C. Turns boldface text you have selected back into regular text

    D. Releases deadly killer bees into the environment

2. **Besides getting boldfaced, italicized, or underlined text by pressing buttons and clicking keys, you can use which of the following commands?**

    A. Edit⇨Paste

    B. Format⇨Font

    C. View⇨Normal

    D. Format⇨Change Case

3. **Which of the following techniques can you use to see whether text is italicized, boldfaced, or underlined?**

    A. Look at the text.

    B. Put the cursor in the text and see if the Bold, Italic, or Underline button is pressed down on the Formatting toolbar.

    C. Check your digital personal organizer to see when you last formatted text.

    D. Call the reference desk at the local library.

4. **Which is the correct shortcut key for italicizing text?**

   A. Ctrl+U

   B. Ctrl+I

   C. Ctrl+P

   D. Alt+I

5. **Which of the following techniques will get you boldfaced and underlined text?**

   A. Select the text and click the Boldface and Underline buttons.

   B. Select the text and press Ctrl+B and then Ctrl+U.

   C. Select the text, open the Font dialog box, choose Bold in the Font Style box, choose Single in the Underline box, and click OK.

   D. Click the Bold button, press Ctrl+U, and start typing.

   E. All of the above.

6. **Which of the following is an example of subscript text?**

   A. $E = mc^2$

   B. H_2O

   C. ~~...but only in the event of an earthquake~~

   D. You will arrive on time!

7. **A superscripted letter or number is one that has been:**

   A. Lowered a bit

   B. Raised a bit

   C. Tossed overboard

   D. Put in a forgotten corner of the refrigerator

Unit 6 Exercise

on the disk

1. Open the Character Styles file in the Practice folder to test your ability with character styles.

2. Boldface and underline the heading of this document.

3. Italicize all the foreign words in the second paragraph (foreign words have red wiggly lines underneath them).

4. Apply superscript to the 2 in πr2.

Unit 7

• • • • • • • • •

Changing the Appearance of Text

Objectives for This Unit

✓ Changing the size of letters in text

✓ Creating a drop capital

✓ Choosing a font or typeface

✓ Selecting a new default font for newly created documents

✓ Changing the color of text

✓ Highlighting text in different colors on-screen

Prerequisites

▶ Telling Word What You Want It to Do (Unit 2)

▶ Entering and Editing Text (Unit 3)

▶ Selecting Text (Lesson 3-2)

▶ Moving Around in Documents (Unit 4)

on the disk

▶ Type Size

▶ Font

▶ Color

▶ Highlight

▶ Unit 7 Exercise

In Unit 7, you take your first tentative steps in the desktop publishing arena. Unit 7 is where you learn how to change the size and appearance of the letters in your documents. Unit 7 also explains how to put a *drop cap*, also known as a *drop capital*, in a document. You've probably seen drop caps before. They are the large letters at the start of chapters that drop down into the text a few lines.

Besides describing how to change the size and appearance of letters, this unit also teaches how to change the color of text.

You are about to learn a few amazing and very useful things. Fasten your seat belt.

Choosing a Type Size

Lesson 7-1

Besides boldfacing headings to make them stand out on the page, you can enlarge them. Obviously, large words on a page catch the reader's eye faster than small words, which is why headings are usually a few points larger than most of the text in a document.

on the test

Type Size is measured in *points*. A point is ¹/₇₂ of an inch. If you choose 72-point type, your letters are one inch high. The larger the point size, the larger the letters. Business and love letters usually use 10- or 12-point type. For headings, choose a larger point size. You may be interested in knowing that the main headings in this book are 24 points high and the text you are reading is 10 points high.

Word 95 gives you two ways to change the size of type: with the Font Size drop-down list box on the Formatting toolbar and with the Format⇨Font command. You can change Type Size before you enter text or change it afterward by selecting the text and choosing a command.

on the disk

To practice changing type size, open the Type Size file in the Practice folder and read on.

Changing Type Size with the Font Size drop-down list box

The Font Size drop-down list box can be found on the Formatting bar between the Font menu and the Bold button. When you click the Font Size drop-down list box's down arrow, a drop-down list of font size choices appears. With the Type Size file open, follow these steps to learn about the Font Size drop-down list box:

on the test

1 Click the down arrow on the Font Size drop-down list box to see the point size options.

To begin with, the list offers options ranging from 8 to 18 points, but you can get more options. Figure 7-1 shows what your screen looks like.

2 Click the down arrow at the bottom of the list.

When you click, another option — 20 — becomes available.

3 Keep clicking until you see 24.

4 Click 24 to choose a 24-point font size.

Just move the cursor to a new font size in the list and click it to choose a new font size.

You can also type a size directly into the Font Size box. In fact, you may have to type in an odd-numbered font size, because all the settings on the Font Size drop-down list box except for 9 and 11 are even numbers.

5 Type Why You Should Elect Rick Switches.

The text you type is twice as big as the rest of the text. The other text in this document is 12-point text, and this text is 24-points high.

6 Press Enter.

7 Open the Font Size drop-down list box again and choose 12-point type this time.

To get to the 12-point option, you have to click the up arrow on the Font Size drop-down list box.

8 Type Here is why you should vote for me:.

The 12-point type you enter is half as big as the 24-point heading.

9 Select the next line, "My Opponent Is a Boldface Liar!"

Font Size drop-down list box

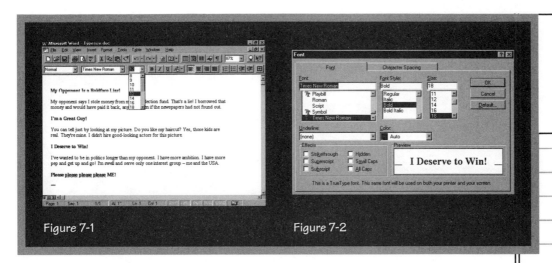

Figure 7-1: Choosing a new point size from the Font Size drop-down list box.

Figure 7-2: Choosing a font size in the Font dialog box.

Figure 7-1   Figure 7-2

10   **Pull down the Font Size drop-down list box and select 18 to change the line to 18-point type.**

You can also change font size by selecting text and choosing a font size option, as this step demonstrates.

11   **Select the line, "I'm a Great Guy!"**

12   **Without pulling down the Font Size drop-down list box, click the 12 in the Font Size box and type** 18.

When you click the 12, it turns a darker color. As soon as you type **18**, the new font size replaces the 12. When you click in the document, you see the letters change size.

Besides opening the Font Size drop-down list, you can enter a point size of your own in the box.

Changing Type Size with Format⇨Font

The other way to change font sizes is to choose Format⇨Font. With the Type Size file still open, follow these steps to check out this command:

1   **Select the line that reads, "I Deserve to Win!"**

2   **Choose Format⇨Font to see the Font dialog box, shown in Figure 7-2.**

3   **Choose 18 in the Size box.**

The Size box is located to the left of the OK button. To choose a point size from this box, you can type in a number, click a number in the list, or click the down arrow on the scroll bar until you see the point-size option you want and click it.

Before you click OK in this dialog box, be sure to look in the Preview box. The Preview box gives you an idea of what your point-size choice will do to the text.

4   **Click OK.**

I Deserve to Win is now 18 points high.

5   **Select the last line in the document.**

6   **Press Ctrl+Shift+> three times to enlarge the type from 12 to 18 points.**

As you use this shortcut, watch the Font Size drop-down list box. Each time you press the key combination, your type gets 2 points larger. To reduce the size of type by 2 points, press Ctrl+Shift+<.

Notes:

Figure 7-3: A drop cap is an elegant way to begin a chapter.

Figure 7-4: The Drop Cap dialog box is where you decide what the drop cap should look like.

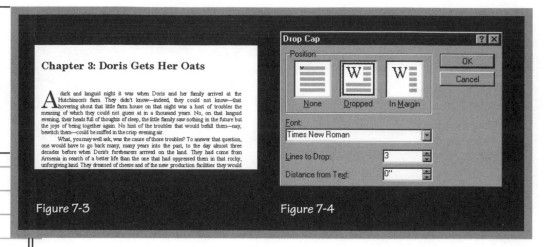

Figure 7-3   Figure 7-4

Ctrl+Shift+> and Ctrl+Shift+< respectively enlarge and reduce the size of type by 2 points

7 Take a look at all the good work you've done on the Type Size file and then close the file without saving your changes.

Changing the size of headings is an important first step in creating a good-looking document. The second step is changing the font. That is the subject of the next lesson.

extra credit

✔ Progress Check

If you can do the following, you've mastered this lesson:

❏ Change the size of type with the Font Size drop-down list box.

❏ Change the size of type by using the Font dialog box.

❏ Create a drop cap.

Creating a drop cap

A *drop cap*, also known as a *drop capital*, is a large capital letter that "drops" into the text. Sometimes drop caps appear at the start of chapters in books, as in Figure 7-3. To create a drop cap:

1. Put the text cursor at the start of the paragraph, to the left of the letter you want to drop.

2. Choose Format⇨Drop Cap.

   The Drop Cap dialog box appears, as shown in Figure 7-4.

3. In the Drop Cap dialog box, choose the drop cap you want by clicking a box.

   Dropped puts the drop cap inside the text. In Margin places all the text in the paragraph to the right of the drop cap. (None removes a drop cap.)

4. Choose a font from the Font drop-down list.

   Choose a font that's different from the text in the paragraph.

5. In the Lines to Drop box, choose how many text lines the letter should "drop on."

6. In the Distance from Text box, keep the 0 unless you're dropping an I, 0, 1, or other skinny letter or number.

7. Click OK.

If you're not in Page Layout View, a dialog box asks whether you want to go there. Click Yes. You see your drop cap in all its glory.

The drop cap appears in a box or *text frame.* To change the size of the drop cap, choose Format⇨Drop Cap again and play with the settings in the Drop Cap dialog box.

Choosing a Font for Text   Lesson 7-2

The surest and easiest way to impress friends and colleagues with your word processing prowess is to include two, three, or four different fonts in your documents. A *font* is a typeface design of a particular size and format. Usually, headings and text are in different fonts. In this book, for example, the text you are reading is in Berkley Book font. The text in the headings is in Tekton Bold font.

Which fonts you can use in your documents depends on which ones have been loaded on your computer. In any case, finding out which fonts you have and experimenting with different fonts is easy. This lesson explains how to choose a font and apply it to text with the Font menu on the Formatting toolbar and with the F<u>o</u>rmat⇨<u>F</u>ont command.

on the disk

For this exercise, you use the Font file in the Pratice folder. Open that file now to experiment with fonts.

Choosing a font from the Font list

To choose a font from the Font drop-down list on the Formatting toolbar, use these techniques:

1 Select "Why You Should Elect Rick Switches," the first line in the document.

2 Click the down arrow on the Font menu to see a list of font choices.

The Font list is on the Formatting bar to the left of the Font Size drop-down list. When you click its down arrow, your screen looks like Figure 7-5.

At the top of the menu are the fonts you used already in the document. Word 95 puts the fonts there to make it easier for you to choose them. You can select other fonts by clicking the down arrow and scrolling down the list.

on the test

Fonts with the letters *TT* next to their names are TrueType fonts. A *TrueType font* looks the same on your computer screen as it does when it is printed on paper. When you choose a TrueType font, you can be absolutely certain of what the text will look like when you print it.

3 Choose Arial from the Font drop-down list box.

To choose the Arial font, click it with the mouse. If it is not listed at the top of the menu, click the down arrow to scroll down the list of fonts.

4 Select the next heading, "My Opponent Is a Boldface Liar!"

5 Click the Font drop-down list box and then choose the Braggado-cio font.

You have to scroll down the Font menu to get to Braggadocio. "Braggadocio" means "braggart" in Italian. You can see why they named this font Braggadocio.

Figure 7-5: You can
choose a font from the
Font drop-down list on
the Formatting toolbar.

Figure 7-6: From the Font
dialog box, you can
choose a font and
much else besides.

Notes:

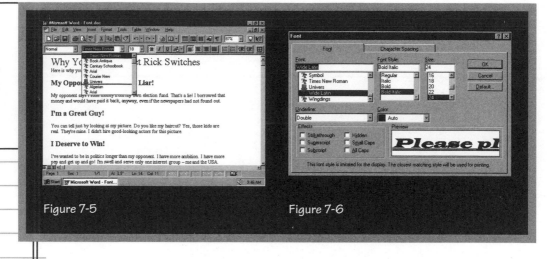

Figure 7-5   Figure 7-6

heads up

You can also change fonts as you type text by choosing the new font from the
Font list (or from the Font dialog box, as the next exercise demonstrates) and
then typing. However, I think it is far better to enter the text before you
experiment with fonts. That way, you can concentrate on the words themselves. It is better to solve all grammar, spelling, and clarity problems before
you start fooling with fonts. After type has been set in an unusual font,
detecting writing problems becomes more difficult.

Leave the Font file open for the next exercise, which explains how to choose
fonts from the Font dialog box. Do not pass Go. Do not collect $200.

Choosing a font with Format⇨Font

You can also select a font by following these steps:

1 **Select the next heading in the Font file, "I'm a Great Guy!"**

2 **Choose Format⇨Font to see the Font dialog box.**

You can also choose fonts with this dialog box (see Figure 7-6).

3 **Click the down arrow in the Font list and click a font with an
interesting name.**

After you click your font, look in the Preview box to see what it looks like. The
advantage of using the Font dialog box rather than the Font list box to choose
fonts is that you can actually view the fonts before you choose them. The
Preview box shows you exactly what your font choice looks like.

4 **Click OK when you find a font you like.**

The heading now appears in the font you chose in step 3.

5 **Select the last line in the document, the plea for a vote.**

6 **Choose Format⇨Font.**

Another advantage of the Font dialog box is that you can change several
settings at once, as the next four steps demonstrate.

7 **Choose a wacky font from the Font list.**

My idea of a wacky font is Desdemona or Wide Latin. What's yours? Experiment with the fonts and look in the Preview box until you find a wacky font.

8 Choose Bold Italic from the Font Style list to boldface and italicize the last line in the document.

9 From the Size menu, choose a large point size.

Choose 24 points or something even larger.

10 From the Underline drop-down list box, choose Double to double underline the last line of the document.

The Font dialog box looks something like Figure 7-6. Look in the Preview box to see what your choices mean in real terms.

11 Click OK to close the dialog box.

The last line in the document is a doozy, is it not? This exercise had you choose weird fonts and go hog-wild so that you could learn about fonts, but you should usually be conservative when choosing fonts.

heads up

Unless you are trying to be funny or wacky on purpose, use only three or four fonts at most in a document. The main thing is to be consistent. Headings of the same type or level should have the same font and be the same point size. All chapter headings should be the same font and point size. Text in numbered steps, for example, should be the same font and point size, as should text in normal paragraphs. Well, you get the idea.

extra credit

Choosing a default font for new documents

When you open a brand-new document and start typing, does the text appear in your favorite font? If it doesn't, you can make the font you use most often the default font:

1. Choose Format⇨Font to open the Font dialog box (see Figure 7-6).

2. Choose a font from the Font drop-down list box.

3. Click the Default button.

4. Click Yes when Word 95 asks you whether this font really should be the default font.

Now when you open new documents and start typing, you will see the font you chose as the default.

Word for Windows makes the default choice automatically

Recess

In the last two lessons, you learned a couple of very important things — how to change the size and appearance of text. You are becoming an expert word processor. Some kind of graduation ceremony is in order. Take a leisurely stroll around the block as you hum "Pomp and Circumstance" under your breath.

☑ **Progress Check**

If you can do the following, you've mastered this lesson:

❑ Choose a font from the Font drop-down list box.

❑ Choose a font with the Format⇨Font command.

❑ Choose a default font for a new document.

Figure 7-7: Choosing a color for text.

Notes:

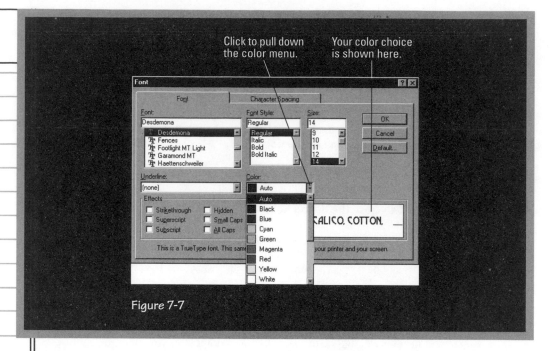

Figure 7-7

Lesson 7-3   Choosing a Color for Text

If you are lucky enough or wealthy enough to own a color printer, you can print documents in color. Even if you don't have a color printer, you can play with different colors — as long as you have a color monitor and can see colors on-screen. Sometimes people make text a different color to call attention to it. For example, if you are proofreading somebody else's work on-screen, you might change the color of the passages that you think should be rewritten.

on the disk

For this exercise in "colorizing" text (also known as "Ted Turner-izing" text), you use the Color file in the Pratice folder. Follow these steps to learn how to change the color of text:

1 Open the Color file.

I have already applied color to most of this document to give you an idea of what you can do with the many colors that are available.

2 Select the last two lines of the document.

You can do so by dragging the mouse cursor in the left margin beside the two lines.

3 Click Format⇨Font to open the Font dialog box.

4 Click the down arrow in the Color text box.

The Color list drops down, as shown in Figure 7-7.

5 Click a color to choose it.

Darker colors can be found at the bottom of the list. To get to these colors, click the down arrow at the bottom of the Color list's scroll bar. Word 95 offers 14 colors, plus black and white.

When you choose a color, don't forget to take into consideration the background color. In other words, if you are printing on white paper, you should choose a dark color for your font because light colors, such as yellow and magenta, do not show up very well on a white background.

6 Click OK to close the dialog box.

The last two lines in the document appear in the color you chose.

7 Select the entire document.

As you may recall from Lesson 3-2, you can select an entire document by triple-clicking in the left margin, pressing Ctrl+A, clicking in the left margin while holding down the Ctrl key, or clicking Edit⇨Select All.

8 Choose Format⇨Font to see the Font dialog box, choose Auto in the Color menu, and then click OK.

The Auto option turns all colorized text into normal text. Use it when you want to remove colors from text.

9 Click the Undo button to reverse what you did in step 8 and get your colors back.

10 Select a word or letter and right-click.

Notice that Font is one of the options.

11 Choose Font on the shortcut menu.

The Font dialog box appears.

12 Choose a new color for the text you selected from the Color list and click OK.

Now you know why they call them "shortcut menus."

Getting a color printer to work right is like driving a high-strung English sports car. When it runs, it runs beautifully, but you have to tinker with it a lot, and it is often in the garage being repaired. If you intend to print with color, be prepared to spend a lot of time adjusting the color in your documents and playing with your color printer.

Undo button

☑ **Progress Check**

If you can do the following, you've mastered this lesson:

❏ Change the color of text in documents.

❏ Remove color from text.

Highlighting Text

Lesson 7-4

Besides choosing colors from the Font dialog box, you can put color in a document by highlighting text. You might, for example, highlight text to call attention to the most important parts of a document. With this method of colorizing text, you give the letters and the background different colors, as if you had drawn over the letters with a fat felt-tip pen.

To highlight text, use the Highlight button on the Formatting toolbar. It's the one to the right of the Underline button. When you click the down arrow next to the Highlight button, a drop-down list of color choices appears. Click a color and start highlighting. As long as you have a color printer, you can print the text you have highlighted with the Highlight button.

Highlight button and pull-down menu

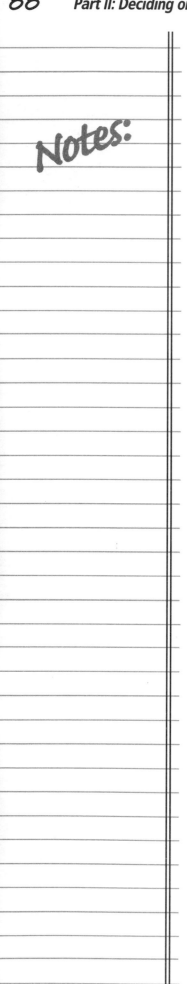

Notes:

on the disk

For this exercise, you use the Highlight file in the Pratice folder. Open the file now. It has two American flags, one without color and one that has been highlighted with red and blue. Each flag has the names of the original Thirteen Colonies on the stripes.

Everybody loves the red, white, and blue, but for this exercise you will suppose that interior decorators have taken control of America. They want something a little less bold for the flag. Something subtle yet forceful. Something elegant and refined, yet full of spirit — like the nation itself. It could happen here!

1 Click the down arrow beside the Highlight button on the Formatting toolbar.

The Highlight pull-down list appears, offering four light colors: yellow, neon green, baby blue, and magenta. Notice that the four colors are light. That's because the idea is to highlight text, not cover it up and make it impossible to read. You can, however, use other colors besides these four.

You can use the None option on the menu to remove highlights. Click the Cancel option, if you pull down the list accidentally and want to get out of it without choosing a color.

2 Click green on the drop-down list and move the cursor on-screen.

The cursor changes into a crayon. This is the highlight cursor. By dragging, you can highlight the text with the color you chose from the Highlight pull-down list.

3 Drag the cursor over the word *Connecticut* on the flag.

The word — and the stripe — turn green.

4 Drag the cursor over every second stripe on the flag to make it green, too.

In other words, the red stripes on the left should turn green on your flag.

As long as you have the highlight cursor, you can keep highlighting text. You don't have to click the Highlight button each time you want to highlight something. If you need to know which highlight color has been chosen, just glance at the Highlight button. The small square on the button shows which color has been chosen from the menu.

5 Click the Highlight button to turn highlighting off.

Click the Highlight button when you want to stop highlighting. Now the Highlight button is not pressed down, and you don't see the highlight cursor.

6 Pull down the Highlight list again and choose magenta.

7 Highlight the second stripe on the flag (Delaware) to make it magenta and then highlight every second stripe after that to fill in the rest of the stripes.

Yikes! A green and magenta flag! What can you do to fix that?

8 Pull down the Highlight list and choose None.

None removes highlights. The little square on the Highlight button should be white.

9 Highlight the magenta stripes to make them white again.

As you highlight each magenta stripe, it turns white.

You can also remove highlights by selecting the text that has been highlighted and then choosing None on the Highlight pull-down list.

10 **Choose Tools⇨Options and click the Revisions tab of the Options dialog box.**

If you want to highlight text with a color not found on the Highlight pull-down list, choose this command. For the flag, you will choose dark green to go with the neon green stripes that are already there.

11 **In the Highlight Color list, choose Dk Green.**

To make this choice, click the down arrow on the Highlight Color list to see a list of colors and then click the down arrow on the scroll bar to get to the Dk Green option. Click the Dk Green option to select it.

12 **Click OK to close the dialog box.**

13 **Drag the highlight cursor over the formerly magenta stripes to make them dark green.**

There you have it — a neon green and dark green flag. The dark green stripes represent America's newfound ecological-mindedness, and the neon green stripes represent the fact that America is an electric, dynamic, forward-looking country that can meet any challenge.

14 **Play with the Highlight feature to your heart's content and then close the Highlight file without saving your changes.**

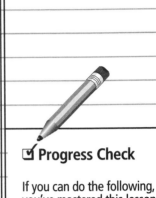

☑ **Progress Check**

If you can do the following, you've mastered this lesson:

❑ Highlight parts of a document.

❑ Remove highlights from the text.

Unit 7 Quiz

For the following questions, circle the letter of the correct answer or answers. This short quiz is meant to help you remember what you learned in Unit 7. Each question may have more than one right answer.

1. **The fastest way to change the size of type is to:**

   A. Select the text and choose a point size from the Font menu.

   B. Retype the text.

   C. Select the text, choose Format⇨Font, choose an option from the Size menu, and click OK.

   D. Ask someone else to do it for you.

   E. Select the text and make a choice from the Font pull-down list box.

2. **The word *font* means the same thing as which of these?**

   A. Fountain

   B. Typeface

   C. Type Size

   D. Elephant

   E. Soda fountain

3. **Which procedure changes the font to Arial?**

   A. Select the text and choose Arial from Font drop-down list.

   B. Select the text, choose Format⇨Font, choose Arial from the Font list in the Font dialog box, and click OK.

C. Choose Arial from the Font drop-down list and start typing.

D. Select the text, right-click it, choose Font from the shortcut menu, choose Arial from the Font list of the Font dialog box, and click OK.

E. All of the above.

4. **You can make the following settings by choosing Format⇨Font and filling in the Font dialog box:**

A. Choose a font.

B. Choose a character style.

C. Choose a Type Size.

D. Choose a color for text.

E. All of the above.

5. **Who said, "Everybody talks about the weather, but nobody does anything about it"?**

A. Horace Greeley

B. Jane Austen

C. Mark Twain

D. Henry James

E. Charles Bukowski

6. **To apply color to text, use which of these techniques:**

A. Use nail polish.

B. Select the text and choose a color in the Font dialog box.

C. Use spray paint.

D. Why would you want to do that, anyway?

E. Press hard on the keys.

Unit 7 Exercise

1. Open the Unit 7 Exercise file in the Pratice folder.

2. Change the size of the boldface headings from 12 to 16 points.

3. Change the font of the headings from Times Roman to Playbill. As you do so, italicize the headings.

4. Change the paragraph text from Times Roman to Bookman.

5. Make the headings red.

Ways of Aligning Text

Objectives for This Unit

✓ Centering and justifying text between the margins

✓ Aligning text on the left and right margins

✓ Using tabs to align text

✓ Indenting paragraphs and first lines

✓ Making a hanging indent

Prerequisites

▶ Opening a document
(Lesson 1-5)

▶ Finding Your Way
Around the Screen
(Lesson 1-6)

▶ Giving commands with
buttons, keys, and menus
(Unit 2)

▶ Selecting Text (Lesson 3-2)

on the disk

▶ Justify
▶ Align
▶ Tabs and the Ruler
▶ Tabs Dialog Box
▶ Indent
▶ Unit 8 Exercise

In Unit 9 you get your first chance to take a bird's-eye view of the page. This is where you take your nose out of the words and start looking at how words are arranged on the page. Half the work of word processing is getting the text to look good on the page. Even if all the words are spelled correctly and the text reads well, a page with a sloppy layout makes a bad impression.

In this unit, you learn how to lay out text between the margins. You will learn how to center text, justify it, right-align it, and left-align it. You will also see how to use tabs to align text in different ways and how to indent paragraphs. Finally, you learn a very elegant trick — how to create a hanging indent.

Centering and Justifying Text   Lesson 8-1

Centering text means to make it an equal distance from the left and right margins. Headings and titles are often centered across the page. In word processing terms, *justify* means to align text so that it butts against both the left and right margins.

Figure 8-1 shows the four ways you can align text in Word 95. You can center text, justify it, right-align it, or left-align it. This lesson explains how to center and justify text. Turn to the next lesson to learn how to right-align or left-align it.

Figure 8-1: Ways of aligning text.

Notes:

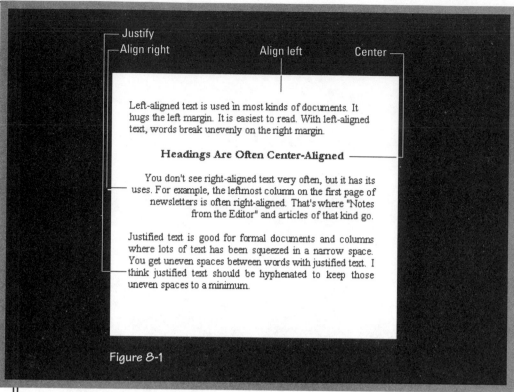

Justify
Align right
Align left
Center

Left-aligned text is used in most kinds of documents. It hugs the left margin. It is easiest to read. With left-aligned text, words break unevenly on the right margin.

Headings Are Often Center-Aligned

You don't see right-aligned text very often, but it has its uses. For example, the leftmost column on the first page of newsletters is often right-aligned. That's where "Notes from the Editor" and articles of that kind go.

Justified text is good for formal documents and columns where lots of text has been squeezed in a narrow space. You get uneven spaces between words with justified text. I think justified text should be hyphenated to keep those uneven spaces to a minimum.

Figure 8-1

heads up

Text is aligned with respect to the left and right *margins,* not the left and right sides of the page. On a page with a two-inch right margin and a one-inch left margin, a centered heading appears not across the center of the page, but a little to the left because of the wider right margin. If text looks odd after you align it, the problem probably lies with the margins.

on the disk

For this exercise in centering and justifying text, open the Justify file in the Practice folder and follow these steps:

1 Put the cursor anywhere in the first line of the document and click the Center button.

The title is centered. When you give a command to change the alignment of a paragraph, you don't have to select the paragraph; you just have to put the cursor in the paragraph.

2 Put the cursor anywhere in the second line and press Ctrl+E.

The byline is centered. Pressing Ctrl+E is another way to center text. Why not Ctrl+C? Because pressing Ctrl+C copies text to the Clipboard. I think I'll put a trick question about this on the test.

3 Place the cursor anywhere in the announcement that begins, "Pay Attention . . . "

4 Choose Format➪Paragraph, click the down arrow in the Align-ment box, choose Centered, and then click OK.

This is the third way to change text alignment. This way is rather longwinded, but you can choose it if you want to change other settings from the Paragraph dialog box at the same time that you change text alignment.

Center button

Ctrl+E is shortcut
for centering text

Justify button

5 Place the cursor on the *P* in "List of Players" and drag down to the *t* in "Lady Capulet."

In the next step, you will center all five lines. In step 1, you learned that you don't have to select an entire line or paragraph to realign it. When you want to realign several paragraphs at once, you don't have to select them in their entirety, either; you just need to select a part of each one.

6 Click the Center button.

All five lines are centered.

on the test

7 Place the cursor anywhere in the last paragraph and click the Justify button.

Now the text butts against both the left and right margins.

8 Go to the top of the document and place the cursor in the first explanatory paragraph, the one that begins, "When should you . . ."

9 Press Ctrl+J.

Now that paragraph is justified. Notice how the Justify button on the Formatting toolbar is "pressed down." If you have any doubts about how text is aligned, put the cursor inside the text and glance at the alignment buttons on the Formatting toolbar.

on the test

10 Close the Justify file without saving the changes you made.

Ctrl+J is shortcut for justifying text

☑ **Progress Check**

If you can do the following, you've mastered this lesson:

❏ Center text by clicking the Center button or pressing Ctrl+E.

❏ Justify text by pressing Ctrl+J or clicking the Justify button.

❏ Twiddle your thumbs quickly enough to generate heat.

Left- and Right-Aligning Text   Lesson 8-2

The last lesson explained how to center and justify text. This one goes a step further and tells you how to right-align and left-align text.

The text in this book is left-aligned. Left-aligned text sticks to the left margin and breaks unevenly on the right margin. If you look along the right margin of this paragraph, you will see that the lines end in different places to create what typesetters call a *ragged* right margin. (I always thought that it looked more jagged than ragged.)

Right-aligned text, on the other hand, hugs the right-margin and breaks words unevenly on the left margin. Right-aligned text looks very good in columns and tables, as you will learn later in this book.

on the disk

For this exercise, open the Align file in the Practice folder and follow these steps:

on the test

1 Place the cursor anywhere in the second paragraph and click.

Now look at the alignment buttons on the Formatting toolbar. The Justify button is pressed down because this paragraph has been justified.

2 Click the Align Left button.

The paragraph is left-aligned. Notice how the Align Left button on the Formatting toolbar is now pressed down.

The first and second paragraphs are identical except for their alignment. This is your chance to compare left-aligned text with justified text. In justified text, a lot of empty space appears between words. In left-aligned text, that empty space is shoved to the right end of the line.

Align Left button

Ctrl+L is shortcut for left-aligning text

Align Right button

Ctrl+R is shortcut for right-aligning text

Center button

☑ Progress Check

If you can do the following, you've mastered this lesson:

❑ Left-align a paragraph by clicking the Align Left button or pressing Ctrl+L.

❑ Right-align a paragraph by pressing Ctrl+R or clicking the Align Right button.

on the test

3 **Move the cursor into the first paragraph and press Ctrl+L.**

Now that paragraph is left-aligned as well.

4 **To experiment with right-aligned text, press Page Down or the down arrow key several times to move the cursor past the page break and select these lines in the song: "'Tis the gift to come down where we ought to be."**

You will right-align these lines in the next step.

5 **Click the Align Right button.**

Now the two lines butt against the right margin rather than the left.

6 **Place the cursor anywhere in the second-to-last line and drag down to select a part of the last line of the song.**

When you give alignment commands, you don't have to select all the text you want to realign. Alignment commands apply to whole paragraphs, so you only have to select a part of the paragraph you want to realign.

7 **Press Ctrl+R.**

You can also right-align text by pressing this shortcut key combination.

8 **Press the Page Down key to cross the next page break and bring the Wins-Losses table into view.**

The team names in the left-hand column of the table would look better if they were right-aligned in the column.

9 **Select the left-most column of the table by dragging the cursor from the top of the column to the bottom.**

If you do this successfully, the rectangles with the team names in them turn black and the names themselves turn white.

10 **Click the Align Right button.**

That looks better, don't you think? It helps distinguish the first column, which has team names in it, from the other columns, which present information about the teams.

11 **Select the second, third, and fourth columns by dragging from the rectangle with "Wins" in it down to the one with "0" (0 ties, that is) in it.**

While you're sprucing up this table, you may as well fix the other columns, too.

12 **Click the Center button on the Formatting toolbar.**

Now the table looks even better. You can have hours of fun with the alignment buttons.

13 **Look back at all the amazing work you did in this exercise and close the Align file without saving it in case you want to try this exercise again later.**

The next lesson explores yet another way to align text in documents — with tab stops.

Aligning Text with Tabs   Lesson 8-3

In Lessons 8-1 and 8-2, you learned how to center, justify, right-align, and left-align text. Suppose that you want to do everything at once. In other words, suppose that you want to have a line of text in which words are left-aligned, right-aligned, and centered. To do that, you need to use tabs.

on the test

To see how tabs work, press the Tab key a few times. Each time you press this key, you advance the text cursor by a half-inch. In a new document, tab stops are left-aligned and are set at half-inch intervals, but you can change that if you want to. Besides left-aligned tabs, Word 95 offers right-aligned, center-aligned, and decimal tabs. Figure 8-2 shows how the tabs work. This list describes what they do:

Tab	What It Does
Left-aligned	Aligns the left side of text with the tab stop. In Figure 8-2, you can see how the left side of the months and numbers line up.
Center-aligned	Centers the text so that it straddles the tab stop. Notice how the months and numbers are centered under the tab stop in Figure 8-2.
Right-aligned	Aligns the right side of text with the tab stop. In Figure 8-2, notice how the right side of the months and numbers line up evenly.
Decimal	Aligns text on the decimal point. Numbers to the right of the decimal point appear on the right side of the decimal tab stop, as Figure 8-2 shows. Everything else appears on the left side. Use the Decimal tab to line up numbers.

Lesson 8-3 shows you how to create and work with tabs. For this lesson, you will use the Tabs and the Ruler file in the Practice folder. Open that file now to prepare for the exercises. You can work with tabs from the ruler or from the Tabs dialog box. You will try out the ruler first. If your ruler isn't on-screen, choose View➪Ruler now to see it.

Working with tabs and the ruler

In the Tabs and the Ruler file, I have already set up tab stops in various places. I'll show you how to set up tab stops shortly, but follow these steps for now to see how tabs on the ruler work:

1 **Press the Tab key once to get to the first tab stop.**

If you look at the ruler, you will see that this is a left tab stop. You can tell because the Left-aligned tab symbol, shaped like an L, appears above the cursor on the ruler.

2 **Type** Left.

Notice what the text does — its left side aligns with the tab stop.

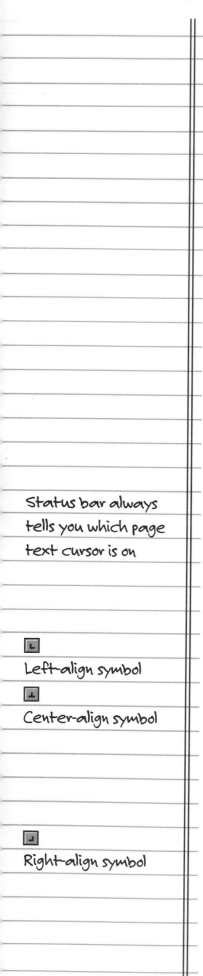

Status bar always
tells you which page
text cursor is on

Left-align symbol

Center-align symbol

Right-align symbol

on the test

3 Press Tab to get to the Center tab stop and type Center.

See how the text is centered under the tab stop. The Center-align tab symbol looks like an upside-down T. You can see it on the ruler. Text is centered at this tab stop as you enter it on-screen.

4 Press Tab again to get to the Right tab stop and type Right.

The right side of the text lines up under the tab stop, almost as if you had clicked the Align Right button. The Right-align symbol looks like a backwards L, which makes sense, seeing how a Right-align tab does the opposite of what a Left-align tab does.

5 Press tab to get to the Decimal tab stop and type Decimal.001.

This tab stop works just like the Right tab stop until you get to the decimal point. Everything past the decimal point works like the Left tab stop. The Decimal tab symbol is an upside-down T with a decimal point on it.

6 Select all the text and numbers above the first page break.

7 Move the mouse pointer onto the ruler, click one of the tab alignment symbols, and then drag it a short distance on the ruler.

As you drag the symbol, the text that is aligned with the symbol moves as well. Notice the dotted line running down the screen. This line is meant to help you align text on the screen and adjust tab stops. You can change tab stop positions on the ruler at any time by dragging a tab alignment symbol.

8 Move the mouse cursor past the first page break, to the start of page 2, for the next exercise.

Now that you have some experience with how tabs work, you can try entering a few tab stops of your own. In this exercise, you will place tab stops in roughly the same places that they are on page 1 of the Tabs and the Ruler file:

1 With the cursor on the first line of page 2, click the Tab selector box four times.

The tab selector box is located on the far left side of the ruler. To start with, you see the Left-align symbol in the box, but each time you click, the symbol changes. You see the Center-align symbol, the Right-align symbol, the Decimal symbol, and then the Left-align symbol again.

The next four steps show how to use the Tab selector box to create tab stops.

2 Click the .5-inch mark on the ruler.

The Left-align symbol — the one in the Tab selector box — appears at the half-inch mark.

3 Click the Tab selector box again to see the Center-align symbol and then click on the 2-inch mark on the ruler.

This creates a Center tab stop at the 2-inch mark. Meantime, the Left-align tab stops that were at the 1- and 1.5-inch marks are removed.

Until you create tab stops of your own, Left-align tab stops appear at half-inch intervals on the ruler. But after you create a new tab stop, all tab stops between the one you created and the beginning of the ruler are removed.

heads up

4 Click the Tab selector box to see the Right-align symbol and then click the 3.5-inch mark on the ruler.

Now you've created a Right-align tab stop. Notice the Right-align tab symbol at the 3.5-inch mark on the ruler.

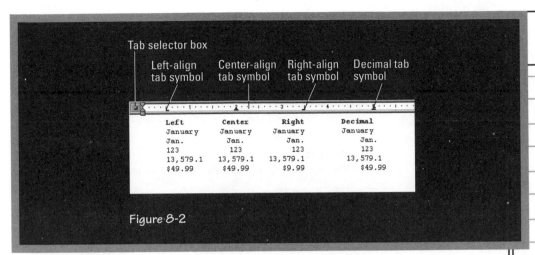

Figure 8-2

Figure 8-2: Tabs on the ruler.

Notes:

Decimal tab symbol

5 **Click the Tab selector box one more time to get the Decimal tab symbol and then click on the 5-inch mark on the ruler.**

I think you get the idea. You just entered a Decimal tab stop. Notice that the Decimal tab symbol looks like the Center-align symbol but with a decimal point.

6 **To test out your new tab stops, press Tab and enter** Left, Center, Right, Decimal.001, **pressing Tab after you've entered each word.**

These are the same words you entered in the preceding exercise. The results should be the same. This time, however, *you* entered the tab stops instead of me.

7 **Press Enter to get to the next line.**

If you glance at the ruler, you will see that the tab stops you created are still in force. You don't have to re-enter tab stops for each new line.

8 **Select the line you entered in step 6 and copy it lower on page 2.**

When you copy the text, you copy the tab settings as well.

Leave the Tabs and the Ruler file open for the next exercise, in which you will learn how to change tab settings and remove tab stops.

What happens if you decide, for example, that a left-align tab should be a right-align tab? Changing tabs is as easy as adjusting them. Removing tabs is also very easy, as this exercise demonstrates:

1 **Scroll to page 3 of Tabs and the Ruler and select names of actors and the roles they play (don't select the line that reads, "List of Players").**

If you glance at the ruler, you will see that the two lists of names are aligned with Left-align tabs. In the next six steps, you will center-align and right-align the list of actors' names on the right.

2 **Drag the second Left-align tab symbol, the one above the actors' names, off the ruler.**

To drag a tab symbol off the ruler, click the symbol with the mouse, hold down the mouse button, and then drag it down. The tab symbol disappears.

When you remove the Left-align tab, the actors' names move leftward to the nearest available tab stop. Tab stops, you remember, are set by default at half-inch intervals. How far the names move to the left depends upon the length of the corresponding role name in the first list.

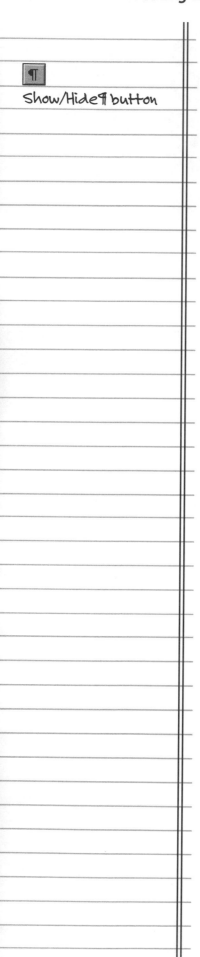

¶

Show/Hide¶ button

on the test

3 Click the Show/Hide¶ button on the Standard toolbar to see where the Tab key was pressed in this document.

Arrows appear where the Tab key was pressed (the arrow next to Juliet's name is quite small). Click the Show/Hide¶ button whenever you have doubts about where the Tab key was pressed and where text will move or has moved when you adjust tab settings.

4 Click the Tab selector button to get the Center-align tab symbol, and then click the 2.5-inch mark on the ruler.

The actors' names are centered on the 2.5-inch mark.

5 Click the Show/Hide¶ button again to get rid of the arrows and remove the highlighting.

Now you can get a good look at your alignment change. What do you think? Suppose that you right-aligned the actors' names instead of centering them.

6 Select the players' names and roles again and remove the Center-align symbol by dragging it from the ruler.

7 Click the Tab selector box to get the Right-align symbol (the backwards L), and then click the 2.5-inch mark.

It doesn't work because the actors' names don't have enough room. You can adjust the tab stop, however.

8 Drag the Right-align symbol on the ruler to the 3.5-inch mark.

Be careful not to drag the symbol off the ruler because that removes the tab stop. At 3.5 inches, the actors' names look pretty good.

9 Click the "List of Players" line and drag the Center-align tab stop on the ruler until this line is centered above the other lines.

You don't have to select the entire line because you are only dealing with one line.

10 Select the list on page 4 of the Tabs and the Ruler file and put a Decimal tab stop at about the 1.5 inch mark.

I trust you know how to do this. The Decimal tab is great for aligning numerals and monetary figures with decimal points. To create the Decimal tab stop, click the Tab selector box until you see the Decimal tab symbol, and then click on the 1.5-inch mark on the ruler.

11 Close the Tabs file and the Ruler file without saving your changes.

Working with the Tabs dialog box

The other way to set tab stops is to use the Tabs dialog box. The Tabs dialog box offers one important setting that the ruler doesn't offer — leaders. In word processing terms, a *leader* is a series of identical characters, usually periods, that run from one place to another on the page. Period leaders almost always appear in tables of contents, where they connect the heading names in the left column with the page numbers in the right column.

on the disk

To learn how to work with tabs from the Tabs dialog box, you will use the Tabs Dialog Box file in the Practice folder. Open it now. It is nearly identical to the Tabs and the Ruler file you saw in the first half of this lesson.

1 **Select the text on page 1 and choose Format⇨Tabs.**

The Tabs dialog box appears, as shown in Figure 8-3. Below the Tab Stop Position box are the tab stop settings that are in the text you selected. You would have to click the scroll bar to see more than ten tab stops.

2 **Click 0.5", 2", and so on down the line and notice how the selections change in the Alignment radio buttons.**

The 0.5" tab stop is a left-aligned tab stop, the 2" tab stop is center-aligned, and so on. The Tab Position box shows, from the start of the line to the end, where all the tab stops are.

To change the alignment of a tab stop, click the tab stop in the Tab Stop Position scroll box and then click a new Alignment option. To change the position of a tab stop, you have to remove the tab stop and reenter it at a new position. The next two steps show how.

3 **Click 5" in the Tab Stop Position box and click the Clear button.**

Now the 5" tab stop — the Decimal tab stop — is removed. You have to reenter it at a new position.

4 **In the Tab Stop Position text box, enter 5.5.**

However, Word 95 thinks that you are entering a Right-align tab stop because the previous tab stop, the one at 3.5", is a Right-align tab stop.

5 **Click the Decimal radio button to make your 5.5" tab stop a Decimal tab stop.**

6 **Click OK to close the dialog box.**

The right-most column of words and numbers has moved further to the right.

7 **Move the mouse cursor past the first page break, to the start of page 2, for the next exercise.**

Clear All button removes all tab stop settings from Tab Stop Position box

on the disk
You can also enter tab stops with the Tabs dialog box. Whether you set tab stops with the Tab selector box or the Tabs dialog box is up to you. With the ruler, you get to "eyeball it" and see how your choices affect text. For precision, however, the Tabs dialog box is the better choice because it tells you exactly where you are creating tab stops on the ruler. To enter tab stops with the Tabs dialog box:

1 **With the cursor on the first line of page 2, choose Format⇨Tabs.**

The Tabs dialog box appears. The Tab Stop Position settings are blank. First you will create a Left-aligned tab stop at the half-inch mark on the ruler.

2 **Enter .5 in the Tab Stop Position text box.**

3 **Click the Set button.**

You don't have to choose the Left alignment button before you click Set because Left has already been chosen.

4 **Enter 2 in the Tab Stop Position box, click the Center radio button, and click Set to create a center-align tab stop on the ruler.**

When you finish creating a tab stop, click the Set button, not the OK button. Click OK only after you've finished creating all the tab stops.

5 **Create a right-align tab stop at 3.5 inches and a decimal tab stop at 5.5 inches.**

To do so, click the appropriate Alignment radio buttons and enter number settings in the Tab Stop Position text box.

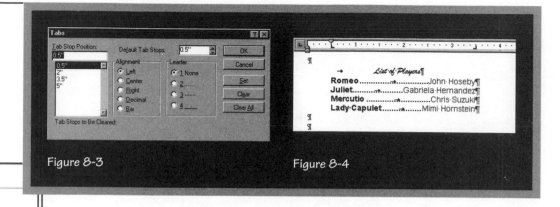

Figure 8-3: The Tabs dialog box.

Figure 8-4: Click the Show/Hide¶ button when you need to see formatting characters, including the arrows that show where Tab was pressed.

Figure 8-3

Figure 8-4

Notes:

¶

Show/Hide¶ button

✓ **Progress Check**

If you can do the following, you've mastered this lesson:

❑ Change tab stops with the ruler and with the Tabs dialog box.

❑ Remove tab stops.

❑ Adjust tab stops.

6 **Click OK to close the Tabs dialog box.**

7 **To test out your new tab stops, press Tab and enter** Left, Center, Right, Decimal.001**, pressing Tab after you've entered each word.**

When you're done, the line you just entered should look like the one at the top of the Tabs Dialog Box file.

Leave the file open so that you can try out the next exercise.

In this, the final exercise in Lesson 8-3, you will learn how to change a tab stop and how to add a leader to a tab:

1 **Scroll to page 3 of Tabs Dialog Box and select the list of actors and role names (don't select the line, "List of Players").**

2 **Choose Format⇨Tabs to see the Tabs dialog box.**

Two left-aligned tab stops are here, one at 1" and one at 2.5". You will change the second one to a right-aligned tab stop at 3.5". However, to do so, you have to delete the 2.5" tab stop first.

3 **Click on the 2.5" in the Tab Stop Position box and click the Clear button.**

4 **Enter** 3.5 **in the Tab Stop Position text box and click the Right alignment radio button.**

5 **Under Leader, click the 2 radio button to place a dot leader between the tab stop you are creating now and the one that comes before it.**

You can also choose a dash leader (3) or a line leader (4). The leader you choose will appear between the tab stop you are creating and the previous tab stop on the ruler.

6 **Click the Set button and then click OK to close the dialog box.**

The leader shows you precisely which role is being played by which actor. Leaders make reading reference material like this much easier.

7 **Click the Show/Hide¶ button on the Standard toolbar to see where the Tab key was pressed in this document.**

The arrows show you where Tab was pressed, as Figure 8-4 demonstrates. The paragraph symbols (¶) tell you where the Enter key was pressed, and dots appear where blank spaces are. At some point in your word processing career, you will see a bunch of periods and you won't be able to tell how they got there until you click the Show/Hide¶ button and notice the tab arrows. You can click the Show/Hide¶ button whenever you are in doubt about how a document was laid out.

Indenting Paragraphs and First Lines   Lesson 8-4

Indenting means to put more distance between the left or right margin and the text. Often the first line of a paragraph is indented by a half-inch, or one tab stop. In this book, notice how the numbered lists are indented. They are farther from the left margin than the explanatory text is. You may find plenty of good reasons to indent text. If you have a long quotation, for example, you will probably want to put it in separate, indented paragraphs so that readers know that they are reading quoted text, not original text.

heads up

When you indent text, you indent it from the margins, not from the left or right edge of the page. The indent commands you will learn about in this lesson all move the text away from the margins. If you've come here looking for a way to change the margins in your document, turn to Lesson 9-2.

on the disk

This lesson covers all three ways that you can indent text in Word 95. You can use the Increase and Decrease Indent buttons on the Formatting toolbar, drag markers on the ruler, or use the Format⇨Paragraph command. For this lesson, you will use the Indent file in the Practice folder. Open that file now. To do these exercises, the ruler should be on-screen. If it is not, choose View⇨Ruler.

Indenting paragraphs from the margins

Follow these steps to indent paragraphs from the left or right margin:

1 **Move the cursor into the second paragraph, which is single-spaced.**

This paragraph is a quoted passage and should be indented to set it off from the rest of the text.

2 **Click the Increase Indent button.**

on the test

When you click this button, you move the entire paragraph away from the left margin by a half-inch (one tab stop). You can press Ctrl+M to indent by a half-inch. When you press Ctrl+M in step 3, watch the ruler to see what happens.

3 **Press Ctrl+M.**

All the markers on the left side of the ruler move inward a half-inch. Later in this exercise you will use these markers to change the margin.

Meantime, the passage has moved 1 inch from the left margin, but not any distance at all from the right margin. The paragraph looks odd.

4 **Click the Decrease Indent button twice to move the paragraph back to the left margin.**

on the test

You can also decrease the indent by pressing Ctrl+Shift+M. When you click the Decrease Indent button, you move the paragraph or selected paragraphs a half-inch toward the left margin, not away from it.

5 **With the cursor still in the passage from *MacBeth,* drag the left indent marker on the left side of the ruler to the right by a half-inch.**

As you do, a vertical line appears to help you indent the paragraph.

Increase Indent button

Ctrl+M is shortcut for increasing indent by 1/2 inch

Decrease Indent button

Figure 8-5: Indenting paragraphs with the ruler.

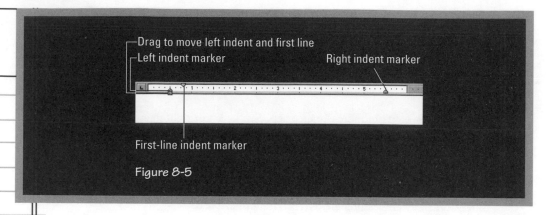

Figure 8-5

Notes:

By dragging markers on the ruler, you can "eyeball it" and choose exactly how far to indent text. Figure 8-5 describes the markers on the ruler. When you drag the box on the left side, you move the entire paragraph, including the first line, away from the right margin. Drag the *first-line indent* marker — the triangle that points down — to indent the first line in the paragraph only. Drag the left indent marker to indent all but the paragraph's first line.

6 Drag the right indent marker to the left to indent the paragraph a half-inch from the right margin.

The right indent marker is the triangle that points up on the right side of the ruler. As you drag, a dotted line appears on-screen to help you see how far you are indenting text from the right margin.

Now your passage is indented a half-inch from both margins. Readers will know that it is a quoted passage.

7 Place the cursor in the last paragraph of the document.

This paragraph is also a quoted passage and needs to be indented. This time, you will indent it with the Paragraph dialog box.

8 Choose Format⇨Paragraph to see the Paragraph dialog box.

9 In the Indentation area, click the up arrow in the Left scroll box five times to enter .5" in the box.

Each time you click, you change the setting by .1". The Left and Right boxes control how far text is indented from the left and right margins.

The Preview box at the bottom of the dialog box shows you the paragraph you are indenting so that you can see the effect of your choices.

10 Enter .5 in the Right scroll box.

You can also change settings by typing numbers directly into the box.

11 Click OK or press Enter to close the Paragraph dialog box.

Now the passage at the bottom of the document is also indented from the left and right margins by a half-inch.

12 Just for fun, press Enter and start typing.

Your next paragraph is indented the same way as the preceding one. It is also single-spaced. Remember, when you press Enter, you carry forward all the formatting from the preceding paragraph to the next paragraph.

Leave this document open. You will use it to experiment with first-line indents in the next section of this lesson.

Indenting the first line of a paragraph

You can indent the first line of a paragraph independently of the other lines. In many documents, the first line of each paragraph is indented by a half-inch. With Word 95, you can make that half-inch indentation by pressing the Tab key. But you can also indent the first line with the first-line indent marker on the ruler or with the Paragraph dialog box. You might use either of these techniques instead of Tab, for example, when you want to indent the first line of several paragraphs. All you have to do is select the paragraphs first.

on the disk

To practice indenting the first line of several paragraphs, do the following in the Indent file that you opened in the last exercise:

1 **Press Ctrl+Home to move the cursor to the first paragraph.**

2 **Drag the first-line indent marker on the ruler to the half-inch mark.**

The first-line indent marker is the triangle that points down on the left side of the ruler. As you move the marker, a dotted line appears on your document to help you see where you first line will start.

3 **To practice with the indent markers, drag the box on the left side of the ruler to the right.**

When you drag the box, you move both the first-line indent and the left indent.

4 **Drag the left indent marker to a position directly below the first-line indent marker.**

The left indent marker is the triangle that points up. If you grab it just right, you can move the left margin without disturbing the first-line indentation. If you accidentally grab the box, however, you will move both the left indentation and the first-line indentation. (Click the Undo button if that happens.)

Now the first paragraph is indented way too far from the left margin. In the next five steps, you will fix that with the Paragraph dialog box and enter a new first-line indentation as well.

5 **Choose Format⇨Paragraph to see the Paragraph dialog box.**

6 **Under Indentation, change the Left option to 0" and the Right option to 0".**

You changed left and right indentations in steps 9 and 10 of the preceding exercise. Go there if you've forgotten how to do it.

7 **Click the down arrow in the Special box and choose the First Line option.**

Figure 8-6 shows you how.

8 **Enter a figure in the By box to tell Word 95 how far you want to indent the first line of the paragraph.**

Word 95 suggests .5", but you can enter another figure by clicking the up or down arrow or typing in a number yourself.

9 **Click OK or press Enter to close the Paragraph dialog box.**

Now the first line of the paragraph is indented. It would have been easy enough to do this by pressing the Tab key, but the first-line indent marker on the ruler and the Paragraph dialog box let you decide exactly how far you want to indent the first line. Besides, you can indent the first line of many, many different paragraphs at once by first selecting the paragraphs and then using the ruler or the Paragraph dialog box.

10 **Close the Indent file without saving the changes you made.**

Figure 8-6: Creating a first-line indentation.

Figure 8-7: Hanging indents work well in headings.

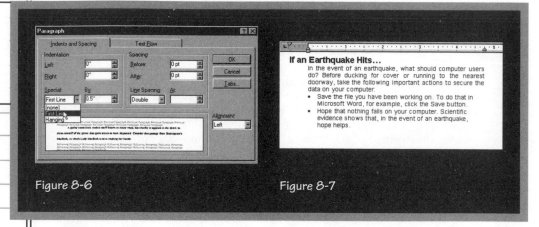

Figure 8-6   Figure 8-7

Creating a hanging indent

What Word 95 calls a *hanging indent* may better be described as an "outdent." When you indent the first line of a paragraph, you move it away from the left margin. When you create a hanging indent, you move every line but the first *toward* the right margin so that the first line "hangs" over the other lines in the paragraph.

Three hanging indents appear in Figure 8-7. The first is in the heading, which hangs into the margin. The other two hanging indents can be seen in the bulleted list. The bullets hang. The sentences attached to the bullets wrap in such a way that the bullets are clearly visible on the left side.

This book also has hanging indents. Lesson titles hang into the left margin, and the numbers in instruction lists also hang. Hanging indents are a good way to make text stand out, because the text appears by itself in or near the margin.

To experiment with hanging indents, follow these steps:

1. Type a heading, press Enter, and type a few lines of text.

2. Put the cursor in the heading and drag the first-line indent marker on the ruler into the left margin.

    The indent markers on your ruler look something like those in Figure 8-7.

    You can also create hanging indents with the Paragraph dialog box. But if you want to make a heading hang into the margin, you have to do it with the first-line indent marker.

    If you printed your page, the heading would hang into the left margin and no one would fail to notice it.

3. Select the lines of text you entered in step 1.

4. Choose Format⇨Paragraph to see the Paragraph dialog box.

5. In the Special drop-down list, choose Hanging.

6. In the By box, click an arrow or enter a number to tell Word 95 how far the second and subsequent lines should fall to the right of the paragraph's first line.

    The number you enter determines how far the first line hangs. Subsequent lines will be moved to the right by the distance you enter in the By box.

7. Click OK to close the Paragraph dialog box.

Word 95 creates hanging indents automatically for bulleted and numbered lists.

☑ Progress Check

If you can do the following, you've mastered this:

❏ Indent paragraphs with the Increase and Decrease Indent buttons.

❏ Indent paragraphs and first lines with the markers on the ruler.

❏ Use the Paragraph dialog box to indent paragraphs and first lines.

Unit 8 Quiz

For the following questions, circle the letter of the correct answer or answers. This short quiz is meant to help you remember what you learned in Unit 8. Each question may have more than one right answer.

1. **To *justify* text means to do which of the following?**

   A. Show that what it says is right and reasonable

   B. Lay out text so that it butts against the left and right margins

   C. Make the text hug the left margin

   D. Make the text stick to the right margin

   E. Center the text between the margins

2. **Clicking this button does which of the following?**

   A. Right-aligns the text

   B. Centers the text

   C. Indents the paragraph by one tab stop

   D. Creates newspaper-style columns

   E. Puts bar codes on a product

3. **Which of the following statements is wrong?**

   A. Press Ctrl+L to line up text on the left margin.

   B. Press Ctrl+R to line up text on the right margin.

   C. Press Ctrl+J to justify text.

   D. Press Ctrl+C to center text.

   E. Press Ctrl+C to copy text to the Clipboard.

4. **A *tab* is which of the following?**

   A. A bill you run up at a bar

   B. A thing to align words and numbers on the computer screen

   C. A kind of soft drink

   D. A kind of cat

   E. Short for *tabular*, as in relating to or like a table

5. **If you click the ruler when this symbol is in the Tab selector box, what kind of tab stop do you create?**

   A. A right-aligned tab stop

   B. You don't create a tab stop at all. *Na-ah,* you don't.

   C. A left-aligned tab stop

   D. A hanging indent

   E. A thorny dilemma

6. **Which of the following does *not* indent a paragraph?**

    A. Press Ctrl+M.

    B. Click the Increase Indent button.

    C. Drag the box on the left side of the ruler.

    D. Open the Paragraph dialog box and change the Left indentation setting.

    E. Keep hitting the Coke machine until a can falls out or you get your money back.

7. **A hanging indent does which of the following?**

    A. Lets it all hang out

    B. Pulls the first line of a paragraph toward the left margin

    C. Hangs its head and cries

    D. Hangs by a thread

    E. Hangs fire

Unit 8 Exercise

Open the Unit 8 Exercise file in the Practice folder and do the following:

1. Center the heading at the top.

2. Justify the two paragraphs (not the lists).

3. Use tabs to left-align the part names on the list in the center of the document and right-align the actors' names.

4. Place a leader between the part names and actors' names.

5. Indent the two paragraphs by 1 inch on each margin.

6. Center the address at the bottom, first by clicking a button and then by using the Center-align tab.

Unit 9

Laying Out the Page

Objectives for This Unit

✓ Determining the amount of space between lines of text

✓ Setting up the margins for a document

✓ Making room on the margin to bind a document

✓ Starting a fresh new page

✓ Creating landscape documents and documents of unusual sizes

✓ Silencing all car alarms permanently in your neighborhood

Prerequisites

▶ Creating a document (Lesson 1-2)

▶ Opening a document (Lesson 1-5)

▶ Finding Your Way Around the Screen (Lesson 1-6)

▶ Giving commands with buttons, keys, and menus (Unit 2)

▶ Filling In Dialog Boxes (Lesson 2-5)

▶ Selecting Text (Lesson 3-2)

on the disk

▶ Line Spacing
▶ Unit 9 Exercise

At the start of Part II, you had your nose to the page as you applied styles such as bold and italics to characters. Then you leaned back a bit and saw how to change the size and font of text. After that, you leaned even farther away from the page and learned how to arrange, or align, text in different ways.

In Unit 9, you will learn how to arrange lines, not words, on the page. You will step even farther back to see what the page looks like if you hold it at arm's length. How big are the margins? Should the text be double- or single-spaced? Suppose you turn the page on its side and print it in landscape mode instead of in portrait mode, as is usually done?

Unit 9 explains the basics of laying out the page in Word 6. This unit is short and won't take you long to complete, but what you learn here is very important. This unit could save your life if, for example, you become lost in a blizzard with only a pen knife and a can of refried beans.

Handling Line Spacing   Lesson 9-1

No doubt a teacher ordered you at some time or other to "double-space all term papers. I simply cannot read a hundred single-spaced papers, boys and girls." Double-spacing the text is very, very easy in Word 95. When you open a new document and start typing, the lines are single-spaced, but you can double-space lines with a flick of the wrist.

Figure 9-1: Choosing
line-spacing options
from the Paragraph
dialog box.

Figure 9-2: Four line-
spacing options:
Exactly, Single, At
Least, and Double.

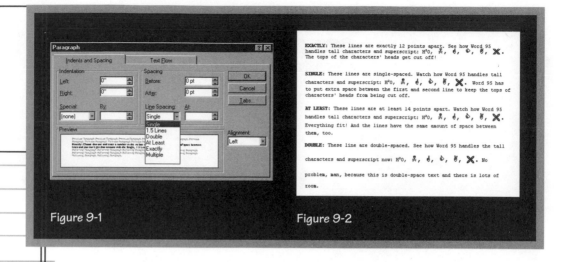

Figure 9-1   Figure 9-2

Besides the single- and double-space options, you can tell Word 6 to put a
specific amount of space between lines or even get triple- and quadruple-
spaced lines. Line spacing can become a problem when tall characters or
special characters appear in the text, so Word 95 offers line-spacing options to
handle that problem.

on the disk

For this brief lesson in handling line spacing, open the Line Spacing file in the
Practice folder. Then follow these steps to get acquainted with Word 95's line-
spacing options:

**1 Click the cursor in the middle of the first paragraph, hold down
the mouse button, and drag to the middle of the third paragraph.**

In step 2, you will change the line spacing of the first, second, and third
paragraphs. You don't have to select them in their entirety, however, because
line spacing commands apply to the entire paragraph that the cursor is in. In
this case, you've selected parts of three paragraphs, so the cursor is in effect in
three paragraphs at once. Any line-spacing command that you use will affect
all three.

on the test

2 Press Ctrl+2.

The text in the first three paragraphs is double-spaced.

3 Click anywhere in the first paragraph.

In the next step, you will give a command to single-space the paragraph, but
you don't have to select the paragraph first. Just click inside it.

4 Press Ctrl+1.

Now the text in the first paragraph is single-spaced. Notice how more space
is between the first and second line than is between the second and third.
Word 95 put that extra space in to accommodate the tall characters in the
second line. Having different amounts of space between lines looks odd. How
can you fix that?

5 Choose Format⇨Paragraph to open the Paragraph dialog box.

The Line Spacing options are in the middle, above the Preview area. As you
make line-spacing choices, look in the Preview box to see what effect your
choices have.

**6 Pull down the Line Spacing list, as shown in Figure 9-1, and choose
the Exactly option.**

This option puts a specific amount of space between lines and tells Word 95 to
make no adjustments whatsoever to accommodate tall characters.

Notes:

*Ctrl+2 is
shortcut for double-
spacing text*

*Ctrl+1 is
shortcut for single-
spacing text*

In the At box, Word 95 suggests putting exactly 12 points between lines (it does that because the characters are 10 points high; 2 points are added to put extra space between the lines). You could type another point-size measurement in the At box, but leave the 12 in to see what happens.

7 **Click OK to close the Paragraph dialog box.**

At exactly 12 points, tall characters don't have enough room. That's because tall characters are 16 points high. Of course, you could solve this problem by shrinking the tall characters, but no matter. You're here to experiment with the line-spacing options.

8 **Click in the third paragraph, the one that begins with "AT LEAST," and choose Format⇨Paragraph.**

9 **Choose At Least from the Line Spacing drop-down list, enter 16 in the At box, and then click OK.**

Word 95 will now put 16 points between lines of text (or more, if necessary) to accommodate characters taller than 16 points. One way to solve the problem of having large characters in text is to use this option and enter the point size of the tallest character in the At box. This way, you get a uniform space between lines, as your screen and Figure 9-2 both show.

10 **Click in the last paragraph and choose Format⇨Paragraph.**

This paragraph is double-spaced. "Double" appears in the Line Spacing box, and you can see double-spaced text in the Preview box.

11 **Choose Single in the Line Spacing box and then 1.5 Lines (look in the Preview box each time).**

Always look in the Preview box to see what your choices do before you click OK to close the Paragraph dialog box.

12 **Choose Multiple in the Line Spacing box, enter 4 in the At box, and then click OK.**

You've just quadruple-spaced the last paragraph. The Multiple option lets you make line-spacing choices above and beyond the Single, 1.5 Lines, and Double options in the Line Spacing box.

13 **Click the Undo button to reverse what you did in step 12.**

Before you close this file, take one last look at the line-spacing choices you made and what they did to the text on your screen. Line spacing is an important thing to know about, as any student whose teacher is nearsighted can tell you.

a point is 1/72 of an inch

Undo button

☑ **Progress Check**

If you can do the following, you've mastered this lesson:

❑ Change the line spacing by pressing Ctrl key combinations.

❑ Change line spacing in the Paragraph dialog box.

❑ Know how to select paragraphs before you give line-spacing commands.

Setting Up and Changing the Margins

Lesson 9-2

Margins are the empty space between the text and the left, right, top, and bottom edges of a page. When you open a new document, Word 95 gives you the following margins: 1 inch for the margins along the top and bottom of the page, and 1.25 inches for the left and right margins.

Figure 9-3: Changing the size of the margins.

Figure 9-4: Change the Gutter setting to make room in the margin for binding a document.

Notes:

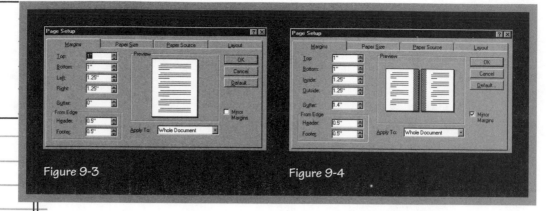

Figure 9-3   Figure 9-4

You may find plenty of reasons to change the size of the margins. If you need more blank space to the side of text so that readers can jot down notes there, you can widen the margin. If a wide table doesn't work in the present margins, you can make the margins narrower to make room for the table. If you're frugal, you can shrink the margins to fit more text on the page and save money on paper.

on the test

Don't confuse margins with indentations. Text is indented from the margin, not from the edge of the page. If you want to change how far a paragraph is indented, see Lesson 8-4. Don't change the margins every time you want to change how far a paragraph is indented.

Word 95 is very touchy about letting you change margins. You can't change the size of the margins midway in a document unless you create a new section, although the program does give you a chance to create a new section at the same time you change margin sizes, as you will see in step 7 of the next exercise.

To learn how to set up and change margins, follow these steps:

1 Open a new document.

2 Choose File⇨Page Setup.

The Page Setup dialog box appears, as shown in Figure 9-3. Notice the margin settings in the Top, Bottom, Left, and Right boxes.

3 To experiment, enter new margin settings in the Top, Bottom, Left, and Right boxes.

Type settings directly into the boxes or click the up or down arrows to change the settings. The larger the numbers, the wider the margins. As you enter new settings, keep your eye on the Preview box. It gives you a picture of what your page will look like.

4 Click OK to close the Page Setup dialog box.

5 Type some gibberish and press the Enter key a few times to enter a few lines on the page.

Suppose you want to change the margin settings for your entire document or change margin settings in the middle of a document. How do you do that?

6 Choose File⇨Page Setup and change the Top, Bottom, Left, and Right settings.

7 Click the down arrow in the Apply To drop-down list.

Two options are available, Whole Document and This Point Forward. (If your sample document has more than one section, you have a third option called This Section.)

If you choose Whole Document, the new margin settings will be applied to your entire document. Page breaks, indentations, and everything else that is affected by the margin will change throughout your document.

If you choose This Point Forward, Word 95 creates a new section at the location of the cursor and applies your new settings to all text from the cursor to the end of the document or from the cursor to the next section, if one exists.

8 **Choose This Point Forward from the <u>A</u>pply To list and click OK to close the Page Setup dialog box.**

A line and the words "End of Section" appear above the text cursor in your document. You just created a new section for your margin settings. Notice the words *Sec 2* on the status bar. You are in the second section.

9 **Type some gibberish.**

If you changed the Le<u>f</u>t margin setting, the text you type in this step should not line up under the text you typed at the top of the document.

10 **Marvel at how easy it is to change margin settings, and then close this document without saving it.**

extra credit

Making room to bind a document

If you intend to bind the document you are working on, you need to make room for the binding. Big plastic bindings eat into page margins and make the text beside the binding difficult to read. Lucky for you, Word 95 makes handling bindings easy. After you've made room for the binding, you can adjust the margin sizes accordingly.

To make room to bind a document:

1. Choose <u>F</u>ile⇨Page Set<u>u</u>p.

2. On the <u>M</u>argins tab, click the up arrow beside the G<u>u</u>tter box and watch the Preview box as you do so (see Figure 9-4).

   The Preview box shows how the binding eats into your document. The longer the document, the more gutter space you need for binding.

3. If yours is a two-sided document with text printed on both sides of the paper, click the Mi<u>r</u>ror Margins check box and adjust the gutter accordingly.

   If you click Mi<u>r</u>ror Margins, the Le<u>f</u>t margin setting changes to <u>I</u>nside, and the Right margin setting changes to <u>O</u>utside. Two-sided documents have no left and right margin, only the inside margin (the side of the page closest to the binding) and the outside margin (the side farthest away).

4. Adjust the margin settings now that you can see what the binding does to your pages.

   As you adjust the settings, compare the number in the G<u>u</u>tter box with the numbers in the four margin setting boxes. The number in the Le<u>f</u>t box (or the <u>I</u>nside box if your document is double-sided) should be larger than the number in the G<u>u</u>tter box.

5. Click OK to close the Page Setup dialog box.

status bar appears along the bottom of the screen

gutter is part of page that binding eats into

☑ **Progress Check**

If you can do the following, you've mastered this lesson:

❑ Change the margin settings for an entire document.

❑ Change the margins midway through a document.

❑ Make room in a document for plastic bindings.

Figure 9-5: When you enter a page break, a horizontal line and the words *Page Break* appear on-screen.

Figure 9-6: Besides pressing Ctrl+Enter, you can enter a page break with the Break dialog box.

Figure 9-5   Figure 9-6

Lesson 9-3   Starting a New Page

This is the shortest lesson in this book. I thought of squeezing instructions for starting a new page in one of the other lessons, but starting a new page is important enough to have a lesson of its own. You will probably complete this lesson in two minutes, five seconds.

As you know, Word gives you another page so that you can keep going when you fill up one page. But what if you need to start a new page right away? Whatever you do, *don't* press Enter over and over until you fill up the page. A faster, better way exists.

For this exercise, pretend that you have just thought of a perfect title for the great American novel, *Earth Make Way*. You now need to write the title page and then go immediately to the next page so that you can start this magnificent work of literature. Follow these steps to see how to start a new page:

1 **Open a new document.**

2 **Press Enter a few times to get to the middle of the page, click the Center button, and type** Earth Make Way.

How do you get to the next page right away to begin writing your definitive Maileresque masterpiece about the essence of the American soul?

3 **Press Ctrl+Enter.**

As shown in Figure 9-5, a horizontal line and the words *Page Break* appear immediately on your screen. You have entered a page break. Now you are at the top of the next page and the status bar says *Page 2*.

You can also enter a page break by choosing Insert⇨Break to see the Break dialog box shown in Figure 9-6. Make sure that the Page Break radio button is selected, and click OK.

4 **Press the Backspace key to erase the page break you just entered.**

To erase a page break, either backspace over it or put the cursor right before it and press the Delete key.

Good luck with that novel!

Center button

☑ **Progress Check**

If you can do the following, you've mastered this lesson:

❏ Enter a page break by pressing Ctrl+Enter.

❏ Delete a page break.

❏ Dance the rumba until the wee hours of the morning.

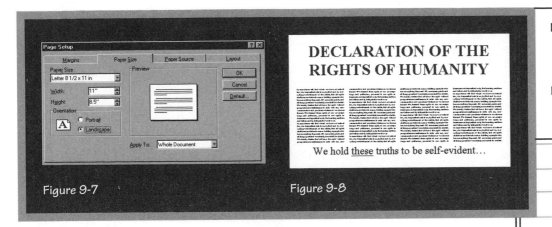

Figure 9-7

Figure 9-8

Figure 9-7: Click the Landscape button to print landscape mode documents.

Figure 9-8: Some kinds of documents look better in landscape mode.

Creating a "Landscape" Document

Lesson 9-4

In a *landscape* document, the page is wider than it is long, like a painting of a landscape. Most documents are printed in portrait style, with the short sides of the page on the top and bottom. However, creating a landscape document is sometimes a good idea because a landscape document stands out from the usual crowd of portrait documents.

This lesson explains how to set up a document so that it prints in landscape mode. Before you print a landscape document, though, make sure that your printer can handle it. You will find instructions for printing on unusual-size paper at the end of this lesson. If your printer can handle strange paper sizes, go for it. A 'zine or newsletter with an unusual shape gets people's attention.

To turn the page on its side and create a landscape document, open a new document and follow these steps:

1 **Choose File⇨Page Setup.**

2 **Click the Paper Size tab.**

You see the Page Setup dialog box shown in Figure 9-7. The Orientation settings are in the lower-left corner.

3 **In the Orientation area, click the Landscape button.**

The piece of paper in the Preview box turns on its side.

4 **Click OK.**

Some documents look better in landscape mode. The pamphlet in Figure 9-8 wouldn't look as bold or important if it had been printed the usual way in portrait mode.

Notes:

before you create documents in landscape mode, make sure that your printer can handle them

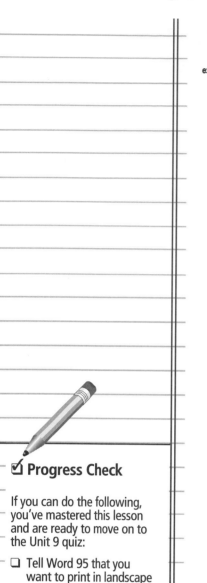

Progress Check

If you can do the following, you've mastered this lesson and are ready to move on to the Unit 9 quiz:

❑ Tell Word 95 that you want to print in landscape mode.

❑ Tell Word 95 that you want to print on paper other than the standard 8.5 x 11.

❑ Tell it like it is.

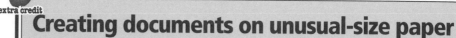

Creating documents on unusual-size paper

You don't have to print exclusively on standard 8.5 x 11 paper; you can print on legal-size paper and other sizes of paper as well. However, before you start playing around with weird paper, make sure that your printer can handle it.

To change the size of the paper on which you will print a document, take note of the paper size you will be using and follow these steps:

1. Choose File⇨Page Setup.

2. Click the Paper Size tab.

   The Paper Size tab is shown in Figure 9-7. To print on nonstandard paper, you use the Paper Size settings.

3. Choose a setting from the Paper Size drop-down list.

   On the list are Legal, Executive, and a European standard. If none of these suits you, choose Custom Size at the bottom of the list. You have to scroll down the list to get to Custom Size.

4. Look at the settings in the Width and Height text boxes and, if necessary or if you chose Custom Size in step 3, enter settings of your own.

   You can type settings directly in the Width and Height text boxes or click the up and down arrows.

5. Click OK to close the Page Setup dialog box.

If you keep legal-size paper in one tray of your printer and standard-size paper in another, for example, click the Paper Source tab in the Page Setup dialog box and change settings there before you print your document.

Recess

Unit 9 wasn't very difficult, was it? I think you will find that the lessons in this book get easier and easier as you go along — and not because the subject matter gets easier, either. The lessons will get easier because you are becoming a better word processor. You are becoming comfortable with Word 95. You are comfortable. You are comfortable and sleepy. You are getting sleepy. Sleepy. Sleepy.

While you're in this hypnotic trance, take a break before the test at the end of this unit.

Unit 9 Quiz

For the following questions, circle the letter of the correct answer or answers. This short quiz is meant to help you remember what you learned in Unit 9, not to bother you in any way. Each question may have more than one right answer.

1. **Which of the following shortcuts double-spaces a paragraph?**

   A. Press Ctrl+1.

   B. Double-click the paragraph.

   C. Select the paragraph and press 2.

   D. Press Ctrl+2.

   E. Hold your finger in front of your nose and stare intently at it with both eyes.

2. **Which of these commands gets at the line-spacing options?**

   A. Format⇨Font

   B. File⇨Page Setup

   C. Format⇨Tabs

   D. Format⇨Paragraph

   E. View⇨First Row Center

3. **You can tell which section of a document the cursor is in by doing which of the following?**

   A. Asking the usher

   B. Looking at the Sec reading on the status bar

   C. Looking for an "End of Section" break on the computer screen

   D. It doesn't matter, because you don't need to know that anyway, okay?

   E. Looking in Word 95's Help program

4. **Which of these commands changes the margin settings?**

   A. File⇨Save

   B. Edit⇨Paste

   C. File⇨Properties

   D. Eat⇨Toast

   E. File⇨Page Setup

5. **Which of the following entertainment acts starred in the movie *Duck Soup*?**

   A. Hootie and the Blowfish

   B. The Marx Brothers

   C. The Lennin Sisters

   D. The Brothers Karamazov

   E. The Brothers Grimm

6. **To start a brand-new page in a document, you do which of the following?**

   A. Keep pressing Enter until that dotted line shows up to tell you that you're on a new page.

   B. Press Ctrl+Pause Break.

Notes:

C. Press Ctrl+Enter.

D. Click Insert⇨Break.

E. Click Insert⇨Gas Pump.

7. **Printing in *Landscape mode* means:**

A. Printing a picture of a big, ugly seascape with a wave crashing at night on a lonely beach

B. Printing on legal-size paper

C. Printing on a page that is wider than it is long

D. Writing the initials of your high school on a hillside in giant letters

E. Printing on a long, narrow page

Unit 9 Exercise

1. Open the Unit 9 Exercise file in the Practice folder.

2. The lines are 1.5 lines apart throughout the document. Single-space the quotations and double-space the other paragraphs.

3. Change the left and right margins of the document from 1.25 inches to 1.5 inches.

4. Put the title and byline on one page and move the start of the essay to page 2.

5. Arrange to print this document on legal-size paper instead of the standard 8.5 x 11.

Unit 6 Summary

▶ **Boldface:** To boldface text, click the Bold button, press Ctrl+B, or choose Format⇨Font and then choose the Bold Font Style option.

▶ **Italics:** To italicize text, click the Italics button, press Ctrl+I, or choose Format⇨Font and then choose the Italics Font Style option.

▶ **Underlines:** To underline text, click the Underline button, press Ctrl+U, or choose Format⇨Font and then choose an Underline option.

▶ **Special effects:** To get superscript, subscript, or strikethrough text, choose Format⇨Font and then click an Effects option in the dialog box.

Unit 7 Summary

▶ **Type size:** To change the size of type, select it and click an option on the Font Size drop-down list or choose Format⇨Font and a Size option.

▶ **Fonts:** To choose a font, click the Font drop-down list and choose a font name, or choose Format⇨Font and then select a font in the dialog box.

▶ **Colors for text:** To make text appear in a color, select the text, choose Format⇨Font, and then choose a color from the Color drop-down list.

▶ **Highlight colors:** To highlight a color, click the Highlight drop-down menu and choose a color, and then drag the highlight cursor over the text.

Unit 8 Summary

▶ **Centering and justifying text:** To center text, select it and click the Center button or press Ctrl+E. To justify text, click the Justify button or press Ctrl+J.

▶ **Left- and right-aligning text:** To left- or right-align text, select it and click the Align Left or Align Right button, or else press Ctrl+L or Ctrl+R.

▶ **Using tabs to align text:** To create tab stops for aligning text, click the Tab selector box on the ruler until you see the type of tab you want, and then click on the ruler where you want the tab to be. You can also create tab stops and tab settings with the Format⇨Tabs command.

▶ **Indenting paragraphs:** To change paragraph indentations, click the Increase or Decrease Indent buttons, press Ctrl+M or Ctrl+Shift+M, drag markers on the ruler, or choose Format⇨Paragraph and make choices in the Indentation area of the Paragraph dialog box.

Unit 9 Summary

▶ **Changing line spacing:** Press Ctrl+1 to get single spacing, press Ctrl+2 to get double-spacing, or choose Format⇨Paragraph and choose Line Spacing options.

▶ **Setting up margins:** To set the margins, choose File⇨Page Setup and fill in the margin settings in the dialog box.

▶ **Starting a new page:** To begin a new page, place the cursor where you want the new page to start and press Ctrl+Enter.

▶ **Printing a landscape document:** To print in landscape mode, choose File⇨Page Setup, click the Paper Size tab, and then click the Landscape option button in the Orientation area.

Part II Test

This test will make you. Or it will break you. This test will make your knees quiver. It will ruin your whole day and make you feel inadequate. It will make you yank out handfuls of your hair. This test will make you sigh. It will make sweat pour down your brow. It will make you wish that you were 20 years younger, like these kids today, who pick up on computers as if they were just playthings.

Actually, this test will do nothing of the kind. It is meant to help you find out what you learned well in Part II and what you need to go back to and review. All the questions asked here are flagged with "On the Test" icons on the pages of Part II so that you can go back and find the answer to a question if you miss it. You'll also find the answers in Appendix A.

True False

T F 1. Computers are our friends and want to help us.

T F 2. Bold, italics, and underline are character styles.

T F 3. Italicized letters slant upward and to the right.

T F 4. The following has a subscript number: $E = mc^2$.

T F 5. Type size is measured in something called *points*.

T F 6. Fonts on the Font menus with the letters *TT* next to their names are TrueType fonts that look the same on your computer screen as they do when printed.

T F 7. Ctrl+E is the shortcut for centering text.

T F 8. A center-aligned tab stop centers text across the middle of the page.

T F 9. After you press the Show/Hide¶ button, you can see arrows that show where in the document the Tab key was pressed.

T F 10. You can press Ctrl+1 to single-space a paragraph.

Multiple choice

For these questions, circle the right answers. Each question may have more than one right answer.

11. **To tell which character styles, if any, have been applied to text, you can do which of the following?**

    A. Choose Help⇨Answer Wizard.

    B. Choose View⇨Normal.

    C. Select the text and look at the align buttons on the Formatting toolbar to see which are pressed down.

    D. Look closely at the text.

    E. Press Ctrl+B or Ctrl+I.

12. **You can boldface and italicize text at the same time by selecting it and doing which of the following?**

    A. Pressing Ctrl+B

    B. Choosing a new font from the Font menu

    C. Clicking the Align Right button

    D. Pressing Ctrl+B *and* Ctrl+I

    E. Choosing Format⇨Font and then Bold Italic from the Font Style drop-down list in the Font dialog box

Part II Test

13. **To change the size of type, you select the text and do which of the following?**

    A. Choose a font size from the Font Size drop-down list.

    B. Type a new font size in the Font Size drop-down list.

    C. Choose a bigger font from the Font list.

    D. Choose 200% from the Zoom Control menu on the Standard toolbar.

    E. Choose Format⇨Font, enter a number in the Size text box, and click OK to close the Font dialog box.

14. **If you can do it, the fastest way to change fonts is to select the text and do which of the following?**

    A. Choose Format⇨Font, make a choice from the Font scroll list, and click OK to close the Font dialog box.

    B. Click a font from the top of the Font list on the Formatting toolbar, where the fonts you used already are on display.

    C. Click the Bold button or press Ctrl+B.

    D. Type much faster than usual.

    E. Open the Font list on the Formatting toolbar, scroll down the list, and choose a font.

15. **When you open a new document, the tab stops are set as follows:**

    A. Center-aligned, with one tab stop in the middle

    B. Who said to stop the tabs? I didn't. I told them to keep going.

    C. Left-aligned, with one tab stop every half inch

    D. There are no tab stops when you open a document. You have to put them in.

    E. Right-aligned, with one tab stop on the right margin

16. **To indent several paragraphs at once, you select them and do the following:**

    A. Click the Increase Indent button.

    B. Choose File⇨Page Setup and change the margins.

    C. Drag the left indent marker on the ruler.

    D. Press the Tab key.

    E. Press Ctrl+I.

17. **To double-space a paragraph, you do which one of the following?**

    A. Select the paragraph and choose a bigger font size from the Font Size list.

    B. Select the document and press Ctrl+2.

    C. Click in the paragraph and press Ctrl+2.

    D. Click in the paragraph, choose Format⇨Paragraph, choose Double from the Line Spacing menu, and click OK.

    E. Press Ctrl+Shift+> with the cursor in the paragraph.

18. **Computer nerds like *Star Trek* so much for which of the following reasons?**

    A. The high-tech stuff is so exciting.

    B. The gadgets are really neat, and you don't have to open doors because they open for you automatically.

    C. Girls in other galaxies are foxy, wear miniskirts, and even know how to speak English.

    D. Those jumpsuits they wear are cool.

    E. All the episodes have tidy moral conclusions that you can talk about later with your friends.

Part II Test

Matching

19. **Match the button to its name:**

A. [icon]   1. Align Left

B. [icon]   2. Undo

C. [icon]   3. Center

D. [icon]   4. Justify

E. [icon]   5. Align Right

20. **Match the button to its name:**

A. [icon]   1. Decrease Indent

B. [icon]   2. Bold

C. [icon]   3. Italic

D. [icon]   4. Underline

E. [icon]   5. Increase Indent

21. **Match the keyboard shortcut with its description:**

A. Ctrl+E   1. Italicizes text

B. Ctrl+M   2. Centers text

C. Ctrl+J   3. Increases the indent by one tab stop

D. Ctrl+I   4. Left-aligns text

E. Ctrl+L   5. Justifies text

22. **Match the following actresses with the movies in which they starred:**

A. Eva Marie Saint   1. *Tiara Tahiti*

B. Joan Crawford   2. *The Postman Only Rings Twice*

C. Sofia Loren   3. *On the Waterfront*

D. Rosenda Monteros   4. *Johnny Guitar*

E. Lana Turner   5. *Two Women*

Part II Lab Assignment

In Part II, you learned how to boldface, italicize, and underline text. You learned how to change the size and look of text and how to align the text in many different ways. You also learned how to change the margin of pages and indent text, as well as print in landscape mode and print on unusual-size paper. In this lab assignment, you will get the chance to try out what you learned in Part II, but I won't tell you exactly what to do. Instead, you will be given a document to work on and you will decide where text-formatting and page-formatting changes need to be made. Then you will make those changes yourself.

In the last lab assignment, you put together a letter to Sidney Bloom, an ex-Hollywood gossip columnist. You wrote Sidney Bloom to ask about an actress named Rosenda Monteros. Monteros was a big star in the 1950s and 1960s, but she has disappeared from view, and an editor at *Silver Screen* magazine has asked you to write a "Where Are They Now?" article about the talented and beautiful Hispanic actress.

Where is Rosenda Monteros? While you are waiting for Sidney Bloom to reply to your letter, you get on the Internet to see whether you can find out anything. After searching for a while, you find something called "Ruckner's Movie Database" and run a search for movies with Rosenda Monteros. What luck! Eight Rosenda Monteros movies are in the database.

You copy the information into a Word 95 file that you call Rosenda Monteros Movies. Like most things copied from the Internet, the file appears in a monotype font and has almost no formatting whatsoever. Better format this file and make it look really good. You may want to include this information in a sidebar for your article about Rosenda Monteros.

on the disk

I have done you the favor of putting the Rosenda Monteros Movies file in the Practice folder. Open Rosenda Monteros Movies now to do the lab assignment for Part II.

Step 1: Changing the font and font size

Select the entire document and change the font to a font that is easy to read. Increase the font size as well so that you can see what you're doing.

If you read this document, you will notice that it includes many different elements: movie titles, listings of the actors and directors, and descriptions of the movies. Should the entire document have the same font? Maybe you should use different fonts for the different elements.

Step 2: Changing character styles

Do you want to use some character styles in this document? You should definitely boldface the title at the top of the document, and I would boldface the movie titles in the document as well. What about italics? Besides the titles of movies with Rosenda Monteros in them, several other movie titles and book titles are mentioned. Usually, book and movie titles are italicized. Do you want to underline anything?

Step 3: Centering and aligning

How do you want to align the text? You might center the title at the top of the document. Do you want the movie descriptions to be left-aligned? Justified? How about the actors' names? You could use tabs to align the actors' names and maybe run a tab leader from the role name to the actor's name. How do you want to handle directors' names and screenwriters' names?

Part II Lab Assignment

Step 4: Indenting paragraphs

Maybe the movie descriptions should be indented a bit. Or you could create hanging indents for the movie titles. It's up to you.

Step 5: Line spacing

What about line spacing? Should the whole document be double- or single-spaced? Do you want to put a specific amount of space between the lines?

Printing Documents, Envelopes, and Labels

Part III

In this part . . .

Part III guides you through everything you need to know about printing. You learn how to preview a file before you print it so that you can catch mistakes before they make it to the printer. You also learn how to tell Word 95 how your printer handles files and how to print documents in various ways. For example, you can print more than one copy of a file, print a part or all of a file, and even print an address on an envelope. All of it is explained here for your learning pleasure.

Getting Ready to Print

Objectives for This Unit

✓ Telling Word 95 which printer you are using

✓ Previewing documents before you print them

Prerequisites

▶ Saving and Naming a Document (Lesson 1-3)

▶ Opening a Document (Lesson 1-5)

▶ Giving commands with buttons, shortcut keys, and menus (Unit 2)

▶ Filling In Dialog Boxes (Lesson 2-5)

▶ Moving Around in Documents (Unit 4)

on the disk

▶ Print Preview

▶ Unit 10 Exercise

Until you print a document, it doesn't amount to much. A document that hasn't been printed is like an idea that you have not communicated in any way. It sits in your head, and whether it is brilliant or inconsequential doesn't matter at all because nobody knows about it.

In Part III, you will learn how to print the marvelous documents that you have been creating with Word 95. You will learn how to send them through the printer so that you have something concrete and three-dimensional at which your friends and colleagues can marvel.

This part explains how to print all or part of a document and how to tell the printer to print on both sides of the paper. It tells how to print more than one copy of a document. You'll also learn how to print addresses on envelopes and get a "sneak preview" so that you can get a good look at your work before you send it to the printer. Part III also explains how to make sure that your printer and Word 95 understand each other, and that is the subject of Lesson 10-1.

Telling Word 95 How You Want to Print   Lesson 10-1

To print documents successfully, Word 95 and your printer have to be on speaking terms. They have to understand one another. Word 95 has to know what kind of printer you are using and which shelf in your printer the paper is to come from if your printer has more than one shelf for paper.

heads up

on the test

When you installed Word 95, the installation program was supposed to have investigated which type of printer you use. It was supposed to have set up your printer to work correctly, but sometimes the installation program doesn't do a good job of sussing out printers, and it tells Word 95 to print to the wrong type of printer. When that is the case and you try to print something, you usually see a dialog box that tells you that Word 95 is unable to print your document.

This lesson explains how to tell Word 95 which kind of printer you are using. It also explains how to tell Word 95 which paper tray to get paper from when it prints a document.

To do the exercise in Lesson 10-1, open a new document and follow these steps:

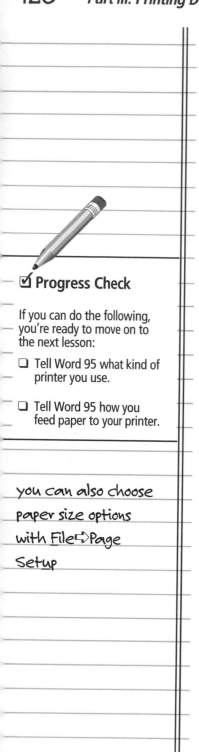

☑ Progress Check

If you can do the following, you're ready to move on to the next lesson:

❏ Tell Word 95 what kind of printer you use.

❏ Tell Word 95 how you feed paper to your printer.

you can also choose paper size options with File⇨Page Setup

1 **Choose File⇨Print to open the Print dialog box.**

You can also press Ctrl+P to open the Print dialog box. Look in the Name box to make sure that your printer is listed there. If the wrong printer is listed, go on to step 2; otherwise, move on to step 3.

2 **Click the down arrow in the Name box to see a list of printers, and choose the one on which you want to print your document.**

Figure 10-1 shows what the list of printers looks like when it is pulled down. Your list is likely different from mine.

3 **Click the Properties button.**

The Properties dialog box appears. You use this dialog box to tell Word 95 which tray to get paper from and what size paper or envelope on which you intend to print the document. (Lesson 11-4 explains how to print on an envelope.)

4 **If necessary, choose a Paper size (or envelope size) option by clicking on one of the icons.**

5 **If necessary, click the Paper source down arrow and tell Word 95 how or where you feed paper to your printer.**

Figure 10-2 shows the Paper source options. Choose a tray or choose the feeding method by which you stuff paper in the maw of your printer. You know your printer better than I do. How do you feed paper to it? On the end of a hook?

6 **Click OK to close the Properties dialog box.**

7 **Click OK to close the Print dialog box.**

heads up

Be careful how you change the properties of your printer in the Properties dialog box. The settings that you choose in this dialog box become your default settings. In other words, if you tell Word 95 that your printer gets paper from the upper tray, your printer will try to get its paper there each time you print a document. The properties settings have to be accurate — no ifs, ands, or buts.

If you start fooling around in the Properties dialog box and regret having done so, click the Restore Defaults button. This action gives you back your original settings.

Lesson 10-2   *Getting a Sneak Preview of a Document*

Every day, 10,000 or so people print documents, look at them, and realize that they made glaring errors that need correcting. So they correct the errors, print their documents again, and toss the flawed first drafts in the garbage.

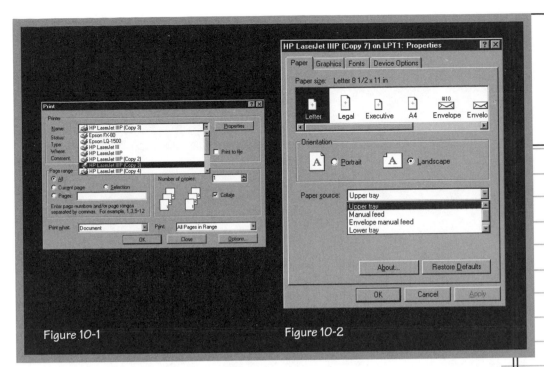

Figure 10-1   Figure 10-2

You don't have to be one of those 10,000 wasteful people because you can *preview* documents before you print them. That way, you can catch errors before you run them through the printer and waste 1, 2, or 20 sheets of paper.

Previewing documents before you print them is the subject of this lesson. Word 95 has a special screen for previewing documents. From this screen, you can zoom in and examine the parts of a document that look odd and may need correcting. You can see several pages at once or only one page. You can even shrink a document that is running a few lines onto the last page so that it has no stray lines and fills the last page to the brim.

To learn how to preview documents, you will use the Print Preview file in the Practice folder. Open that file now and follow these steps:

1 Click the Print Preview button on the Standard toolbar.

The Print Preview button is located to the right of the Print button. When you click it, you see the Preview screen, as shown in Figure 10-3. You can also open the Preview screen by choosing File⇨Print Preview.

At first, only the first page of the document appears on the Preview screen, but you can make more than one appear. In this document, there are four pages. You can tell how many pages are in the document by glancing at the status bar, which also appears on the Preview screen. The status bar says 1 / 4. In the next step, you will see all four pages on the Preview screen.

2 Click the Multiple Pages button, and when the menu with page icons appears, hold the mouse button down and drag until you select four page icons.

If you do this correctly, the bottom of the menu with page icons says 2 x 2 pages. Now you can see all four pages of the document. Do you notice any errors? I think I see one on the first page.

3 Click the One Page button.

Now only one page is on the Preview screen again — the first page. The error is in the paragraph just above the middle of the page. That paragraph is supposed to be justified like the paragraph near the bottom of the page, not left-aligned. (If you didn't notice the error, don't worry about it. I noticed it only because I know this document far better than you. I laid it out.)

Print Preview button

Multiple Pages button

One Page button

Figure 10-3: The Preview screen is your last and maybe your best chance to catch errors before you print a document.

Notes:

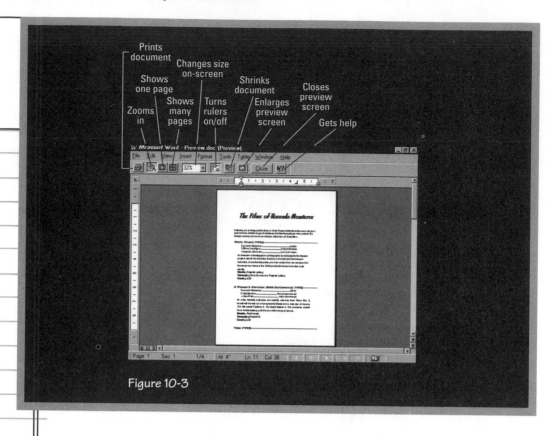

Prints document
Changes size on-screen
Shows one page
Shrinks document
Shows many pages
Turns rulers on/off
Closes preview screen
Enlarges preview screen
Zooms in
Gets help

Figure 10-3

Magnifier button

View Ruler button

Full Screen button

Zoom Control box

on the test

You can get a close look at a document with the Magnifier button. When you first open the Preview screen, the Magnifier button is pressed down. The next step explains what you can do when this button is pressed down.

4 **Glance at the Magnifier button to make sure that it is active (if it isn't active, click it) and then move the mouse onto the page.**

As you move the mouse onto the page, the mouse pointer changes into a magnifying glass with a plus sign in it, as shown in the margin.

5 **Click in the paragraph above the middle of the page that should be justified, not left aligned.**

When you click, the document enlarges to 100% on the Preview screen (notice that the Zoom Control box now says 100%).

6 **Click the View Ruler button to remove the rulers and see more of the document on-screen.**

7 **Click the Full Screen button to see even more of the document.**

Hmmmm. You still can't see the other paragraph at the bottom of the screen to see whether it is left-aligned or justified. You want to compare that paragraph to the one you can see to find out whether they are different and one should be corrected.

8 **Click the down arrow on the Zoom Control list and choose the 50% setting from the drop-down list to shrink the page and get a bird's-eye view of it.**

The Zoom Control settings do not affect the size of text in the document. They determine only how the page looks on the Preview screen. Besides choosing a setting from the list, you can type a setting of your own in the Zoom Control box.

By choosing or entering a Zoom Control setting, you can enlarge the page (to 200 percent, or twice its size) or shrink it way down to see "the big picture."

At 50 percent, you can see how the paragraphs differ. No doubt about it, one of the paragraphs has been laid out incorrectly. The one above the middle of the document should be justified. You will have to fix that problem when you get out of the Preview screen.

9 **Click in the right margin next to the paragraph that has been laid out incorrectly to see whether it is indeed left-aligned.**

Once again, the mouse pointer changes into a magnifying glass with a plus sign in it as you move the mouse pointer onto the document. However, after you click, notice that the magnifying glass has a minus sign in it.

10 **Click the Full Screen button again to get the status bar, ruler, and menu back.**

11 **Click the mouse pointer in the document again.**

Now you see the one-page view of the document again. If you click the magnifying glass when it has a minus sign inside it, you "zoom out," or move away from the document and make it look smaller. If you click the magnifying glass when it has a plus sign in it, you "zoom in," or move closer to the document and make it look bigger.

Close

Close button

12 **Click the Close button to get out of the Preview screen and return to your document.**

Leave the Print Preview file open. You can use it as you read the Extra Credit instructions that follow.

on the test

If Print Preview were a real document, you would go to the paragraph on page 1 that should be justified and fix it by clicking the Justify button on the Formatting toolbar. But never mind that, because the purpose of this exercise was to show you how the Preview screen and its buttons work. If you like what you see on the Preview screen and don't have to correct anything, you can print your document directly. To do so, click the Print button on the toolbar in the Preview screen.

☑ **Progress Check**

If you can do the following, you have mastered this lesson and are ready to move on to the Unit 10 quiz:

❑ Open the Preview screen to examine a document.

❑ Zoom in on a document with the magnifying glass.

❑ Change the size of a document on the Preview screen.

extra credit

Preventing stray lines

Murphy's Law says that if something can go wrong, it will. Murphy's Law of Printing says that if you want to print an important letter or resume, one or two extra lines will stray onto the last page and you will be forced to cut lines on previous pages to make everything fit tidily. It is uncanny, but when you write a letter, the last line always seems to fall on the last page all by itself. That looks bad, of course, so you have to fix the problem by shortening the letter a bit.

I have good news: Word 95 can fix the stray lines by pulling them back onto the preceding page. On the Preview screen is a button called Shrink to Fit. When you click it, Word 95 does its best to eliminate stray lines and often succeeds.

To experiment with the Shrink to Fit button, open the Print Preview file (if it is not already open), choose File➪Print Preview to open the Preview screen (if you haven't done so already), and follow these steps:

1. Click the Multiple Pages button and drag the cursor over the page icons to select four pages.

   Step 2 in the preceding exercise explains how to do this, in case you need to review it.

   Notice that the fourth page has a stray line on it. You can fix that.

2. Click the Shrink to Fit button.

   Before your very eyes, the last line is tucked onto page 3.

3. Click Close to close the Preview screen.

If you go to the end of the document, you will see that the last line is indeed on page 3. Way to go, Word 95!

Shrink to Fit button

Recess

I put you through the wringer with that exercise about the Print Preview screen. All those buttons to click! All that weird stuff about plus and minus magnifying glasses! I'm sorry, I really am, and to make it up to you, here's what I'm going to do: I'm giving you a raise and telling you right now to take the rest of the day off. No, take the rest of the week off! If anybody deserves a raise and a week's vacation, it's you.

Unit 10 Quiz

For the following questions, circle the letter of the correct answer or answers. This short quiz is meant to help you remember what you learned in Unit 10. Each question may have more than one right answer.

1. **Which of these commands tell Word 95 what kind of printer you are using?**

    A. Clicking the Print button

    B. File⇨Page Setup

    C. File⇨Print

    D. File⇨Properties

    E. Edit⇨Bookmark

2. **To preview a document before you print it, you do which of the following?**

    A. Click the Print Preview button.

    B. Get to the theater early so that you can see the previews of coming attractions.

    C. Choose View⇨Page Layout.

    D. Choose File⇨Print Preview.

    E. Choose a setting from the Zoom Control menu.

3. **To see more than one page on the Preview screen, you do which of the following?**

    A. Select a number of pages before you preview them.

    B. Click the Multiple Pages button and drag the cursor over the page icons.

    C. Choose a high percentage on the Zoom Control menu.

    D. Click the One Page button several times.

    E. Why would you want to see more than one page? One is enough for me.

4. **On the Preview screen, what happens when you click the cursor on a page and the mouse cursor is a magnifying glass with a plus sign in it?**

   A. The page shrinks down.

   B. I don't know, but you can kill bugs with a magnifying glass if the sun is shining bright.

   C. The page blushes.

   D. You can see all the warts and irregularities on the page.

   E. The page enlarges to 100% — in other words, its actual size.

5. **The Shrink to Fit button on the Preview screen does which of the following?**

   A. Makes it hard to fit into your new blue jeans.

   B. Makes you wonder why you didn't buy the preshrunk jeans.

   C. Makes you think that maybe you're putting on weight because you can't fit into these jeans.

   D. Makes you jump up and down and flex your legs to try to stretch out your jeans.

   E. Squeezes stray lines at the end of a document onto the previous page.

Unit 10 Exercise

1. Open the Unit 10 Exercise file in the Practice folder.

2. Open the Preview screen.

3. Display the first two pages of the document.

4. Zoom in on a paragraph.

5. Change a Zoom Control setting.

6. Close the Preview screen.

Notes:

Printing in Word 95

Objectives for This Unit

- ✓ Printing all or part of a document
- ✓ Printing several copies of a document
- ✓ Printing on both sides of the paper
- ✓ Printing on an envelope

Prerequisites

- ▶ Saving and Naming a Document (Lesson 1-3)
- ▶ Opening a Document (Lesson 1-5)
- ▶ Giving commands with buttons, shortcut keys, and menus (Unit 2)
- ▶ Filling In Dialog Boxes (Lesson 2-5)
- ▶ Moving Around in Documents (Unit 4)

on the disk
- ▶ Print
- ▶ Envelopes

Unit 10 explained how to get documents ready to print. It explained how to introduce Word 95 to your printer and how to preview documents so that you can correct all errors before you run your work through the printer.

In this unit, you get down to the nitty-gritty. This is where you actually print documents. You will see how to print all or part of a document, how to print on both sides of the paper, how to print more than one copy, and even how to print an address on an envelope.

Is your printer plugged in and turned on? If it isn't, plug it in and turn it on. You are about to print some documents and become a published author.

Printing an Entire Document   Lesson 11-1

This lesson shows you how to print an entire document. Nothing is easier in Word 95 than printing an entire document. Word 95 offers all kinds of options for printing this, that, or the other part of a document, but if you want to go whole hog and print the whole thing, you can do it with the flick of a wrist.

Print button

hard copy is the
printed version, not
the electronic
version, of a
document

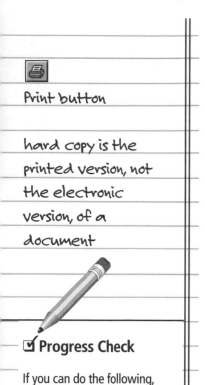

☑ **Progress Check**

If you can do the following,
you are ready to move on to
the next lesson:

❑ Print a document from
start to finish by clicking
the Print button.

❑ Click the Print button from
inside the Preview screen.

❑ Open the Print dialog box
and give the command for
printing an entire document.

---

on the disk

For the exercises in this unit, you will use the Print file in the Practice folder.
Open that file now and follow these steps to learn how to print a document:

on the test

1 Click the Print button.

That's all there is to it. To print an entire document from start to finish, click
the Print button on the Standard toolbar.

If you blindly and boldly did what step 1 said to do, you should hear whatever
sound your printer makes and very shortly see the four pages of the Print file.
Click the Print button when you are absolutely certain that your document is
ready to be printed or if you are one of those people who prefers to proofread
the hard copy of a document rather than proofread what is on the computer
screen (I'm one of those people).

2 Choose File⇨Print Preview to see the Preview screen.

Notice the Print button on the left side of the toolbar. You can print a
document directly from the Preview screen by clicking this button, too.

3 Click the Close button to close the Preview screen.

4 Choose File⇨Print to see the Print dialog box.

By clicking OK in this dialog box, you can print an entire document. Notice that
the Print what box says Document and that the All radio button is selected in
the Page range area. As long as both of those options are selected, clicking OK
in this dialog box prints the entire document from start to finish.

5 Click Cancel to close the Print dialog box.

on the test

To sum up, you can print a document in three ways: click the Print button on
the Standard toolbar, click the Print button on the Preview screen, or choose
File⇨Print (or press Ctrl+P) and simply click the OK button in the Print
dialog box.

The other lessons in Unit 11 explore the many options in the Print dialog box.
Leave the Print file open if you want to go on to the next lesson.

Lesson 11-2   Printing Part of a Document

The last lesson explained how to print an entire document lock, stock, and
barrel. But more often than not, you want to print part of a document,
perhaps to review some troublesome pages you have been working hard to get
right or to reprint a page on which you had to fix an error.

This lesson explains how to print part of a document. You can print text you
have selected, the page that the text cursor is on, a range of pages, or several
different page ranges.

To experiment with printing part of a document, open the Print file if it is not
already open and follow these steps:

1 Select a word or two in the document.

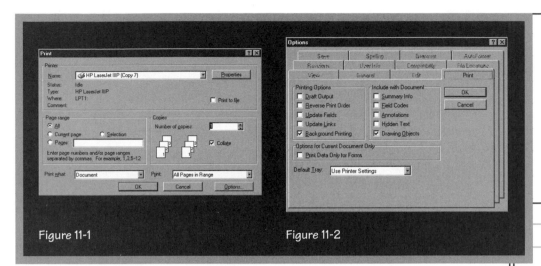

Figure 11-1

Figure 11-2

Figure 11-1: To print parts of a document, print a single page, or print more than one copy, choose options in the Print dialog box.

Figure 11-2: The Print tab in the Options dialog box offers many sophisticated printing options.

2 **Press Ctrl+P to open the Print dialog box.**

You can also choose File⇨Print to open this dialog box, which is shown in Figure 11-1.

Ctrl+P is shortcut
for opening Print
dialog box

3 **Click the Selection radio button in the Page range area of the dialog box.**

If you click OK now, Word 95 prints the one or two words that you selected in step 1.

on the test

4 **Click the Current page radio button.**

If you click OK now, Word 95 prints one entire page — the one that the cursor is on. You can quickly print one page in a document by putting the cursor on the page and clicking the Current page radio button in the Print dialog box.

on the test

5 **Click the Pages radio button.**

With this option, you can print only certain pages by entering pages and page ranges in the text box. Enter hyphens to designate the page range and commas, too, if you want to print more than one page range. For example, entering **1-4** prints pages 1 through 4, but entering **1,4** prints only pages 1 and 4.

You can enter combinations of ranges. For example, entering **1, 3-4** prints all of the Print file except page 2.

6 **Enter** 1-2,4 **in the Pages text box.**

In a moment, you will click OK and print these pages.

7 **Click the down arrow in the Print what box to see the options.**

on the test

This book does not cover annotations, summary info, and the other options on this drop-down list, but you should know that they are there. Quite soon, you will become a wiz with Word 95 and might find a need to print these parts of a document along with the main text.

8 **Click the Options button to see the Print tab of the Options dialog box.**

The Print tab is shown in Figure 11-2. In the same vein as the items on the Print what drop-down list, you can print the Include with Document items shown here along with the main text.

☑ **Progress Check**

If you can do the following, you've mastered this lesson:

❑ Tell Word 95 to print the page the cursor is on.

❑ Tell Word 95 to print a range of pages in a document.

❑ Tell Word 95 to print selected text in a document.

9 **Click the Cancel button to back out of the Options dialog box.**

Now you are safely in the Print dialog box again, where you told Word 95 to print pages 1, 2, and 4.

10 **Click OK to close the dialog box and send an order to the printer for pages 1-2 and 4.**

So ends Lesson 11-2. In the next lesson you will learn how to print more than one copy of a document. Keep the Print file open to continue this daring adventure.

Lesson 11-3

Printing More Than One Copy

on the test

No, you don't have to stay in the office during lunch to print 100 copies of the annual report. To print copies, you don't have to sit at your computer and give the Print command over and over. You can tell Word 95 to print 100 copies and go to lunch — as long as your printer can handle that much work.

This lesson explains how to print more than one copy of a file. It is a short lesson and can be completed in 3 minutes and 14 seconds. For this lesson, you will use the Print file you opened in Lesson 11-1. If you closed that file, open it now and follow these steps:

1 **Choose File⇨Print to open the Print dialog box.**

Figure 11-1 shows this dialog box. You can also press Ctrl+P to open it.

2 **Click the up arrow in the Number of copies scroll box twice to enter a 3 in the text box.**

Rather than clicking the up or down arrow, you can type the number of copies you want in the Number of copies text box.

3 **Click the Collate check box to remove the check mark.**

Notice what happens to the three sample pages when you click the Collate check box. The sample pages show the order in which pages are printed when the copies are not collated. The four pages of the Print file will be printed in this order: 111, 222, 333, 444.

4 **Click the Collate check box again.**

With the check mark back in the box, the copies will be collated, as shown by the sample pages in the dialog box. Now the file will be printed in this order: 1234, 1234, 1234.

5 **Click OK to print three copies of the Print file.**

Leave the Print file open a little longer. You will need it for another 3 minutes and 14 seconds as you learn how to print on both sides of the paper.

extra credit

Printing on both sides of the paper

Theoretically, you can cut the amount of money you spend on paper in half by printing on both sides of the paper, and you can cut the amount of clutter around your desk in half, too. To print on both sides of the paper, you run the paper through the printer twice, first printing the odd pages and then the even.

Follow these steps to print on both sides of the paper:

1. Press Ctrl+P to open the Print dialog box.
2. Click the down arrow in the Print drop-down menu and choose Odd Pages.
3. Click OK.
4. When the printer has printed and spit out the odd pages, turn them upside-down and put them back in the printer.
5. Choose File⇨Print to open the Print dialog box.
6. Click the down arrow in the Print drop-down menu, but this time choose Even Pages.
7. Click OK.

If all goes according to plan, you end up with a double-sided document with the odd pages on one side and the even pages on the other.

☑ **Progress Check**

If you can do the following, you've mastered this lesson:

❑ Tell Word 95 to print more than one copy of a document.

❑ Print collated and uncollated copies.

❑ Print on both sides of the paper.

Printing Addresses on Envelopes   Lesson 11-4

You don't have to address envelopes by hand, although doing it that way is often easier. Lesson 11-4 explains how to print addresses and return addresses on envelopes. Before you try to print an address on an envelope in this exercise, you will probably have to consult the dreary manual that came with your printer to find out how your printer takes envelopes. Go and do that now. I'll wait here for you.

on the disk

To experiment with envelope printing and see whether you want to go to the trouble, open the Envelopes file in the Practice folder. Then follow these steps:

1 **Select the name and address of the person to whom you want to send the letter.**

In this case, you should select Sidney Bloom's name and address.

2 **Choose Tools⇨Envelopes and Labels.**

As shown in Figure 11-3, the Envelopes and Labels dialog box appears with the address you selected in the Delivery Address box. Your address should appear in the Return Address box. If it isn't there, click Cancel to close the dialog box, click Tools⇨Options, click the User Info tab, and enter your name in the Name box and your address in the Mailing Address box. Then start all over with step 1.

For this exercise, the delivery and return addresses are correct, but if you needed to change them, you could do so by entering new addresses in the Envelopes and Labels dialog box now.

click Omit button if you don't want return address on envelope

Figure 11-3: The Envelopes and Labels dialog box.

Figure 11-4: Getting ready to feed the printer.

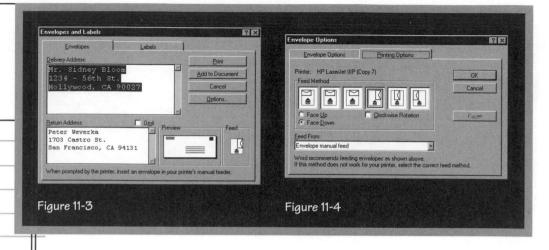

Figure 11-3   Figure 11-4

Notes:

☑ **Progress Check**

If you can do the following, you've mastered this lesson and are ready to move on to the Unit 11 quiz:

❏ Enter the correct delivery and return address in the Envelopes and Labels dialog box.

❏ Tell your printer what size envelope to print on.

❏ Tell Word 95 how you feed envelopes to your printer.

3 **Click the envelope icon in the Feed area to tell Word 95 how envelopes are fed to your printer.**

The Envelope Options dialog box appears, as shown in Figure 11-4. Get ready to wrestle with this dialog box.

4 **Choose the Feed Method icon that most closely resembles the way in which you feed envelopes to your printer.**

5 **If you need to, click the Face Down or Face Up radio button and the Clockwise Rotation check box to make the envelope in the picture resemble the way in which you feed envelopes into your printer.**

6 **Click the down arrow on the Feed From drop-down list, and choose which printer tray the envelope is in or how you intend to stick the envelope in your printer.**

7 **Click OK to return to the Envelopes and Labels dialog box.**

8 **Click the envelope in the Preview box.**

The Envelope Options tab of the Envelope Options dialog box appears.

9 **Pull down the Envelope Size menu and select the size of the envelope on which you want to print.**

10 **Click OK to close the dialog box.**

11 **Click Print in the Envelopes and Labels dialog box to give your printer the order to print.**

Don't forget to stick an envelope in the printer before you click OK.

Don't forget to put a stamp on the envelope, either.

Recess

That does it for Unit 11. I suggest that you get a good night's sleep before going any further. Lie on your back, read a good book, and drift into the Land of Nod. You can't look at a computer screen while lying on your back. That is yet one more reason why computers will never replace books.

Unit 11 Quiz

For the following questions, circle the letter of the correct answer or answers. This short quiz is meant to help you remember what you learned in Unit 11. Each question may have more than one right answer.

1. **This button does which of the following?**

    A. Opens the Print dialog box.

    B. Sends a fax.

    C. Prints the open document from start to finish.

    D. Opens the Preview screen.

    E. Saves the document.

2. **If you enter 3-4 in the Pages text box of the Print dialog box and click OK, which pages will print?**

    A. Page 34

    B. Pages 1 and 2

    C. Pages 3 and 4

    D. Everything but pages 3 and 4

    E. Your guess is as good as mine.

3. **What is the keyboard shortcut for opening the Print dialog box?**

    A. Ctrl+P

    B. Alt+P

    C. Ctrl+E

    D. Ctrl+Q

    E. Ctrl+V

4. **Which Page range option in the Print dialog box prints only the page that the text cursor is on?**

    A. All

    B. Current page

    C. Selection

    D. Pages

    E. None of 'em

5. **If you print three copies of a three-page document with the Collate option, the pages will come out of the printer in which order?**

    A. 111, 222, 333

    B. A 1 and a 2 and a 3 . . .

    C. 123, 123, 123

    D. Scoo-bee doo-be do

    E. 321, 321, 321

6. **What is the fastest way to print an address on an envelope?**

   A. Write it yourself by hand.

   B. Select the name and address on the letter, click Tools⇨Envelopes and Labels, click the envelope icon in the Feed area to tell Word 95 how envelopes are fed to your printer, choose a Feed Method icon and the Face Down or Face Up radio button, choose which printer tray the envelope is on, click OK to get back to the Envelopes and Labels dialog box, click the envelope in the Preview box, pull down the Envelope Size menu and select the size of the envelope you will print on, and click Print in the Envelopes and Labels dialog box to give your printer the order to print.

   C. Get somebody else to do it.

   D. Consult the manual that came with your printer.

   E. Click the Print button.

Unit 11 Exercise

1. Open the Print file in the Practice folder and print the entire thing.

2. Print page 3 only.

3. Print pages 1, 2, and 4 by giving a single command in the Print dialog box.

4. Print the odd pages in the document.

5. Print two copies of pages 1 and 2.

Unit 10 Summary

▶ **Setting up your printer:** Press Ctrl+P to open the Print dialog box. Click the down arrow in the Name box to see a list of printers and choose the one on which you want to print your document, and then click OK.

▶ **Previewing a document:** Click the Print Preview button on the Standard toolbar or choose File⇨Print Preview and use the buttons on the Preview screen to examine your document closely. Click Close to get back to your document, or click the Print button to print it.

Unit 11 Summary

▶ **Printing a whole document:** Open the document and click the Print button on the Standard toolbar.

▶ **Printing part of a document:** Press Ctrl+P to open the Print dialog box and then choose a Page range option: All, Current page, Selection, or Pages. If you choose Pages, enter a page range in the text box.

▶ **Printing several copies:** Open the Print dialog box and enter the number of copies you want to print in the Number of copies box. Then click OK.

▶ **Printing on both sides of the paper:** Choose File⇨Print to open the Print dialog box, choose Odd Pages from the Print drop-down menu, and click OK to print the odd pages. Then turn the paper over and feed it to the printer, press Ctrl+P to open the Print dialog box, and choose Even Pages from the Print drop-down menu to print the even pages.

▶ **Printing on envelopes:** In the letter document, choose the name and address of the person to whom the letter is being sent and choose Tools⇨Envelopes and Labels. Then choose the appropriate options in the Envelopes and Labels dialog box and click OK.

Part III Test

This test will tell you once and for all what the future holds. If you do well on this test, you will make yourself more employable. You will take your first steps toward financial security and riches and a life of ease and spiritual fulfillment. If you fail this test, you will lose confidence in yourself. You will start believing that computers can't be mastered and that all is lost, and you will sink into a deep despair from which you will never emerge. This test will tell you what kind of a human being you are and whether you are tough enough to make it in the competitive, cutthroat Twenty-First Century. This test is the turning point in your life.

Actually, this test won't do much of anything except tell you what you learned in Part III. The answers to the questions asked here can be found next to the "On the Test" icons found throughout Part III. If you have trouble with a question, go back to the lesson in Part III that covers the topic you are having trouble with. You can also find the answers in Appendix A.

True False

T   F   1. Someday, all jobs will be done by computers.

T   F   2. All printers are alike, so Word 95 doesn't need to know anything about your printer to print documents.

T   F   3. You can spot errors in documents before you print them from the Preview screen.

T   F   4. You should plant seeds during the full moon.

T   F   5. You can print a document from the Preview screen.

T   F   6. To print an entire document, all you have to do is click the Print button on the Standard toolbar.

T   F   7. You can print annotations in documents, summary info, and the other things with the Print what pull-down menu in the Print dialog box.

T   F   8. You can print several copies of a document by clicking the Print button over and over.

T   F   9. Printing on both sides of the paper saves trees.

T   F   10. Even a man who says his prayers by night can become a werewolf when the moon is full and bright.

Multiple Choice

11. **On the Preview screen, what happens when you click the cursor and the cursor is a magnifying glass with a plus sign in it?**

    A.   The Preview screen gets larger.

    B.   The Preview screen disappears.

    C.   The document shows at 100 percent size so that you can read it easily.

    D.   Everything looks bigger all of a sudden.

    E.   You print the document.

12. **You can determine how big the document looks on the Preview screen by doing which of the following?**

    A.   Clicking the icon when it is a magnifying glass with a minus sign in it

    B.   Entering a new percentage in the Zoom Control menu box

    C.   Clicking the Full Screen button

    D.   Closing the Preview screen and looking at the real document

    E.   Clicking the Print button

Part III Test

13. **Use which of these commands to print an entire document?**

    A. Click the Print button on the Standard toolbar.

    B. Click the Print Preview button.

    C. Click the Print button on the Preview screen.

    D. Choose File⇨Close.

    E. Choose File⇨Print (or press Ctrl+P) and click the OK button in the Print dialog box.

14. **To print pages 1, 3, 12, 13, 14, 17, and 20 of a document, you enter which of the following in the Print dialog box's Pages text box?**

    A. 1-3,12-14,17-20.

    B. I'm not into numbers.

    C. 1,3,12-14,17,20.

    D. 2, 4-11,16-16,28,19.

    E. I can't deal with this right now.

15. **The keyboard shortcut for opening the Print dialog box is which of the following?**

    A. Ctrl+O

    B. Ctrl+P

    C. There isn't such a shortcut.

    D. Ctrl+D

    E. Alt+F+P

Matching

16. **Match the buttons on the Preview screen with their names:**

    A. [icon] 1. Shrink to Fit

    B. [icon] 2. One Page

    C. [icon] 3. Print

    D. [icon] 4. Multiple Pages

    E. [icon] 5. Magnifier

17. **Match the correct buttons to the correct function:**

    A. [icon] 1. Prints the entire document

    B. [icon] 2. Creates a new document

    C. [icon] 3. Pastes what is on the Clipboard to the document

    D. [icon] 4. Opens the Preview screen

    E. [icon] 5. Saves the document

18. **Match the Page range option in the Print dialog box with its function:**

    A. Pages   1. Prints the entire document

    B. Selection   2. Prints the page that the text cursor is in

    C. All   3. Lets you print a range of pages

    D. Current Page 4. Prints the selected text in the document

Part III Lab Assignment

Now comes your third lab assignment. If you did the previous two lab assignments at the ends of Parts I and II, you know that lab assignments give you practice with the techniques that you learned in each part. In this lab assignment, you will preview a document and print it in various ways.

I won't tell you exactly how to do each task. By now, you have enough experience with the program to know either how to do a task or, in cases where Word 95 offers more than one way to do a task, which way is best for you.

In the lab assignment at the end of Part II, you formatted a four-page document that listed and described the movies that the elusive Rosenda Monteros appeared in. You have been given an assignment by *Silver Screen* magazine to write a "Where Are They Now?" story about Rosenda Monteros, the famous Hispanic actress. Looking over the list of her movies, you decide that the editor of *Silver Screen* would probably like to see the list. In fact, it would probably be good to publish the list along with your article.

on the disk

I guess it goes without saying, but the editor can't see your list until you print it. And that is the object of this lab assignment — to preview and print the list. For this lab assignment, open the Part III Lab Assignment file in the Practice folder and complete the following steps.

Step 1: Previewing the entire document

Open the Preview screen and display all four pages of the document.

Step 2: Looking for and fixing errors

Examine the document to see whether you can find any errors. If you find any, close the Preview screen and fix them. You have to use the Magnifier button and cursor to do so. Can you squeeze this whole document onto three instead of four pages? Give it a try. (The "Extra Credit" instructions at the end of Units 10 and 11 explain how.)

Step 3: Printing part of a document

Print the pages on which you found errors to get a better idea of whether or not you fixed them correctly. (**Hint:** The errors have to do with whether paragraphs are aligned correctly, and they are on pages 1 and 3.)

Step 4: Print an entire document

Print the document on both sides of the paper.

Streamlining Your Work

Part IV

In this part . . .

In Part IV, you take command of Word 95. Here, you learn how to change the look of the screen itself, use windows to get a different view of your documents, check for spelling errors, use the Thesaurus, number the pages of a document, create numbered and bulleted lists, and create headers and footers, among other things. This is where you take Word 95 by the collar and give it a good shake!

Deciding How the Screen Should Look

Objectives for This Unit

✓ Adding and removing toolbars from the screen

✓ Adding and removing the ruler

✓ Changing the unit of measurement on the ruler

✓ Switching to Full Screen view

✓ Switching to Page Layout view

Prerequisites

▶ Finding your way around the screen (Lesson 1-6)
▶ Giving commands with buttons, menus, and shortcut keys (Unit 2)
▶ Using the scroll bars to move around (Lesson 4-1)

on the disk   ▶ Page Layout

When you first see the Word 95 screen, it looks a bit like Tokyo's busy Ikebukoro subway station: It is daunting. Do you need all those buttons, menus, and symbols to get your work done? Do you need all that clutter? Not necessarily.

Unit 12 explains how to remove some of the clutter from the Word 95 screen. It also explains how to get the clutter back when you need it. In this unit, you'll find out how to remove the toolbars and get more toolbars when you need them (Word 95 offers eight different toolbars in all). You will also learn how to work in Full Screen view and change to Page Layout view.

Removing and Adding Toolbars   Lesson 12-1

As you use Word 95, only the tools you really need should be on-screen. You can temporarily chuck the other tools and call them back into service when you need them. In this lesson, you will learn how to add and remove toolbars from the screen. To complete this lesson, all you need to do is open a new document and follow these steps:

Figure 12-1: This shortcut menu appears when you right-click on a toolbar.

Figure 12-2: The Toolbars dialog box.

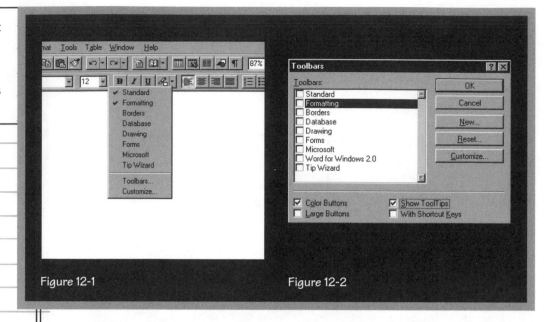

Figure 12-1   Figure 12-2

Notes:

Appendix B shows buttons on toolbars and explains what each button does

on the test

1 Right-click on the Standard toolbar or the Formatting toolbar.

When you right-click on a toolbar, a shortcut menu appears with the names of several toolbars on it, as Figure 12-1 shows. Notice the check marks next to Standard and Formatting. The check marks tell you that these toolbars have been selected and are already on-screen.

2 Click Formatting on the shortcut menu.

The Formatting toolbar disappears from the screen. If you are working on a document and don't need any of the commands on the Formatting toolbar, you can remove that toolbar to make more room on-screen.

3 Right-click on the Standard toolbar and choose Standard from the shortcut menu.

Now the Standard toolbar is removed as well. Look how much room you have on-screen to work. Suppose, however, that you want the toolbars back.

4 Choose View⇨Toolbars to see the Toolbars dialog box.

Figure 12-2 shows the Toolbars dialog box, which offers the same toolbars as the shortcut menu, plus a toolbar called Word for Windows 2.0. You can add and remove toolbars from this dialog box as well as from the shortcut menu.

Another way to open the Toolbars dialog box is to right-click on a toolbar and choose Toolbars from the shortcut menu.

on the test

5 Click Standard and Formatting to put those toolbars on-screen again, and click OK to close the dialog box.

Now you're back where you started. In the next two steps, you will see how to put toolbars on-screen by pressing buttons.

6 Click the Drawing button on the Standard toolbar.

When you click this button, the Drawing toolbar appears along the bottom of the screen. You use this toolbar to draw things in Word 95.

7 Click the Borders button on the Formatting toolbar.

Yet another toolbar appears. The Borders toolbar is for putting borders around paragraphs and tables. You can put as many toolbars as you want on-screen.

8 Click anywhere on the Borders toolbar (except on a button or a menu), hold down the mouse button, and drag the Borders toolbar onto the screen.

Drawing button

Borders button

When you do so, the toolbar changes into a rectangle and is ripped away from the other toolbars along the top of the screen. You can move a toolbar on-screen if you are going to use it often and want to get at it quicker. If you were putting borders around a large table, for example, you might drag the Borders toolbar on-screen to make your work go faster.

heads up

When you drag a toolbar on-screen, don't click on a button or menu. You have to find a spot on either end of the toolbar or between the buttons on which to click.

Now that the Borders toolbar is on-screen, it has a title bar. You can move a toolbar by dragging its title bar. You can also change a toolbar's shape, as the next step demonstrates.

9 **Move the cursor to the right edge of the Borders toolbar. When it changes into a double-headed arrow, click and drag to the right, and then release the mouse button.**

As you drag, you see the outline of a rectangle. That rectangle shows you the shape the toolbar will take when you release the mouse button.

10 **Click on the title bar of the Borders toolbar, drag it to the top of the screen, and then release the mouse button.**

As you drag the title bar, you move the toolbar. Now the Borders toolbar appears right below the menu bar. You can put a toolbar just about anywhere on-screen. With some toolbars, you can even drag the bottom edge down to make a long, skinny rectangle that fits nicely along the left or right side of the screen.

Before you move on to step 11, glance at the Drawing and Borders buttons. They are "pressed down."

11 **Right-click on any toolbar on-screen and choose Drawing from the shortcut menu.**

12 **Right-click on a toolbar again and choose Borders.**

Now you are back to your original toolbars, Standard and Formatting, and the Drawing and Borders buttons are not pressed down.

Word 95 offers many different toolbars — and not just the ones listed in the Toolbars dialog box. For example, Lesson 10-2 introduced you to the buttons along the top of the Preview screen. You can drag the buttons on the Preview toolbar onto the screen, too. As you get good at using Word 95, you will encounter many different toolbars. Use the techniques from this lesson to put them on-screen, remove them, and move them around.

Appendix B explains what the buttons on the toolbars do.

Sidebar notes

title bar is strip along top of a window, dialog box, or toolbar

↔

☑ Progress Check

If you can do the following, you've mastered this lesson:

❏ Add and remove toolbars from the screen with the shortcut menu.

❏ Add and remove toolbars with the Toolbars dialog box.

❏ Move and change the shape of toolbars on-screen.

Removing the Ruler   Lesson 12-2

Having the ruler on-screen isn't always necessary. When you are indenting text, putting a graphic in a document, setting up page margins, creating tab stops, or doing some other task in which size plays a part, you need the ruler. The rest of the time, you don't need it. You don't need to see the ruler to type a letter to Aunt Enid or Uncle Bert, for example.

Notes:

Lesson 12-2 explains how to make the ruler disappear and also how to get it back. This lesson would be the shortest in the book had I not thrown in some instructions for changing the unit of measurement on the ruler. Even then, completing this very short lesson takes two minutes and 24 seconds or less.

To complete Lesson 12-2, all you need to do is put a document on-screen. Then do the following:

1 Choose View to pull down the View menu.

If you started this exercise with the ruler on-screen, a check mark appears next to the Ruler menu item. Otherwise, the check mark is not there.

2 Choose Ruler from the View menu.

If the ruler was there before, it disappears. If you started without the ruler, you have one now.

3 Pull down the View menu again.

Either the check mark is there or it isn't. I think you get the idea. If the check mark isn't there, you can choose Ruler to get the ruler back. If you see a check mark and choose Ruler, you remove the ruler from the screen.

4 Choose Ruler again.

You are back to where you started when you began this exercise, with the ruler either on or off your screen.

heads up

Get used to removing the ruler and bringing it back. By removing the ruler when you don't need it, you get more room to work with text, and you make the Word 95 screen look less claustrophobic.

extra credit

Changing the unit of measurement on the ruler

Back in 1975 I think it was, President Gerald Ford declared that the United States would convert to the metric system by the year 1988. It didn't happen, which is not to say that it won't happen. In the spirit of cosmopolitanism, here are instructions for changing the unit of measurement on the ruler from inches to centimeters, as well as to points or picas:

1. **Choose Tools⇨Options.**

2. **Click the General Tab in the Options dialog box.**

3. **At the bottom of the dialog box, click the down arrow beside Measurement Units to see which units of measurement are available.**

4. **Choose Centimeters if you are metric minded.**

   You can also choose Points or Picas. A *point* is the standard unit for measuring type size, and it represents 1/72 of an inch. The Font Size menu on the Formatting toolbar already lists point sizes. A *pica* is a measurement that typographers use. One pica equals 1/6 of an inch.

5. **Click OK to close the Options dialog box.**

   The ruler along the top of the screen displays measurements in the unit you chose.

In the metric system, all units have a uniform scale of relation based on the decimal system. Ten millimeters equal a centimeter, 10 centimeters equal a decimeter, 10 decimeters equal a meter, and so on and so on. Europeans think that this uniformity of scale is wonderful, but I think it's square, man. I prefer the poetic *verst* and the Biblical *cubit*.

☑ Progress Check

If you can do the following, you've mastered this lesson:

❑ Remove the ruler from the screen.

❑ Put the ruler on-screen.

Working in Full Screen View

One of my favorite ways to work is in Full Screen view. In that view, absolutely everything except the document window, the ruler, and a button that says `Full` is cleared from the screen, so concentrating on entering text is easy.

Of course, the toolbars, scroll bars, status bar, and menu bar are gone, which makes giving menu commands and moving around on-screen difficult. You can, however, press keyboard shortcuts and press Alt and a letter to pull down menus and give commands. To get back to Normal view from Full Screen view, you click the Full button or press Esc.

For Lesson 12-3, open a new document and follow these steps to get Practice working in Full Screen view:

on the test

1 **Choose View⇨Full Screen.**

All the clutter is removed from the sides, top, and bottom of the screen, as shown in Figure 12-3. You are now in Full Screen view. As you will learn in the next lesson, you can switch to other views by clicking buttons in the lower-left corner of the screen, but the only way to get to Full Screen view is by choosing View⇨Full Screen.

Speaking of commands, what if you have to give a command in Full Screen view?

2 **Press Ctrl+B and type a few words.**

The words appear in boldface. You have to rely on keyboard presses now that you are in Full Screen view.

3 **Press Alt+O to open the Format menu.**

Remember, you can press Alt in combination with different letters — F, E, V, I, O, T, A, W, or H — to pull down the menus on the menu bar.

4 **Choose Font, select a new font in the Font dialog box, click OK, and type a few more words.**

In this way, you can get to dialog boxes and give commands in Full Screen view.

5 **Press Ctrl+Home to get to the top of the document.**

You have to press keys instead of using the scroll bars to move around.

6 **Right-click anywhere on-screen and choose Font from the shortcut menu.**

Here's another way to get to the Font dialog box. In Full Screen view, you can display a shortcut menu by right-clicking, just as you can in Normal view.

7 **Click Cancel to close the Font dialog box.**

8 **Drag the title bar of the Full Screen button to a new place on-screen.**

You can drag the Full button to move it out of the way as you work.

heads up

When you drag the button around, be sure to click on the title bar and not on the X that appears on the right side of the title bar. If you click on this *X*, the Full Screen button will disappear, and you will never see it again! The only way you will be able to get out of Full Screen view is to press Esc. (Actually, it doesn't disappear forever. To get it back, press Alt+V to see the View menu, press T to open the Toolbars dialog box, click the check box next to Full Screen, and click OK.)

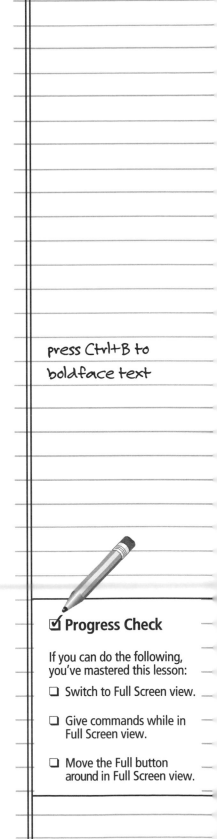

press Ctrl+B to boldface text

☑ **Progress Check**

If you can do the following, you've mastered this lesson:

❑ Switch to Full Screen view.

❑ Give commands while in Full Screen view.

❑ Move the Full button around in Full Screen view.

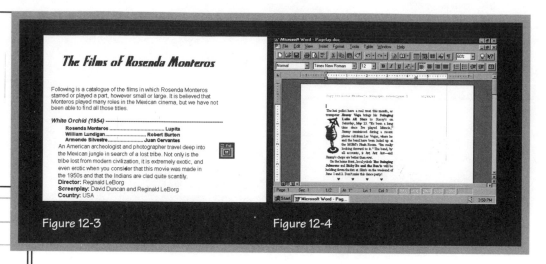

Figure 12-3: In Full Screen view, you can concentrate on the text because all the clutter is removed from the screen.

Figure 12-4: In Page Layout view, you get a good look at the page as a whole.

Figure 12-3   Figure 12-4

Notes:

9 **Click the Full button to get back to Normal view.**

You can also press Esc to get back to Normal view.

I hope that this exercise demonstrated how useful Full Screen view can be. When you want to focus on the text, one of the best ways to do so is in Full Screen view. And Full Screen view gives you a better idea of what your documents will look like when you print them. After all, the people who read your documents won't see all that clutter — the toolbars, scroll bars, menu bar, and status bar.

Lesson 12-4   Working in Page Layout View

When you start Word 95, the first document you see is in Normal view. Normal view is fine for entering text, but Word 95 offers other views as well. In the last lesson, you learned about Full Screen view, in which a lot of the clutter that clings to the sides of the document window is hidden. Word 95 also offers Page Layout view.

Page Layout view shows you more clearly where text appears relative to the sides of the page. Figure 12-4 shows a document in Page Layout view. In this view, you can see graphics, headers, and footers. In fact, you can see only columns in Page Layout view.

on the test

For this lesson in working with Page Layout view, open the Page Layout file in the Practice folder and follow these steps:

on the disk

1 **If you don't see the rulers on-screen, choose View⇨Ruler.**

In Page Layout view, two rulers appear on-screen instead of one. Besides the horizontal ruler at the top of the screen is a vertical ruler on the left side. The vertical ruler is there to help you place graphics and see where you are on the page as you work.

I saved this document in Page Layout view. When you save and close a document in a certain view, it appears in that view when you reopen the document.

2 **On the bottom of the vertical scroll bar, click the double arrows that point down.**

At the bottom of the scroll bar, in the lower-right corner of the screen, is an extra pair of scroll buttons. You use these buttons to "page through" a document. In other words, each time you click one of these double arrows, you move forward or backward by an entire page.

Having clicked the double arrows that point down, you are on page 2. Notice the header at the top of the page. In Page Layout view, you can see headers and footers on-screen.

3 **Click the single arrow at the top of the vertical scroll bar a few times to move up a few lines.**

The top of the second page and the bottom of the first one come into view. In Page Layout view, you can see very clearly where one page ends and the next begins.

4 **Click the Normal View button in the lower-left corner of the screen.**

Word 95 offers three View buttons on the left side of the horizontal scroll bar along the bottom of the document window. When you click the leftmost button, you switch to Normal view. You can also switch to Normal view by choosing View⇨Normal.

on the test

In Normal view, you have only one ruler. Notice how page breaks appear in Normal view — with a line and the words Page Break. (If you don't see the page break, click the up arrow on the vertical scroll bar a few more times.)

5 **Press Ctrl+Home to get to the top of the document.**

What has happened here? The cocktail glass is above the text — it is not embedded in the first paragraph. In Normal view, Word 95 can't show graphics that appear beside text. It has to keep the graphics and the text separate.

6 **Click the Page Layout View button to get back to Page Layout View.**

You can also switch to Page Layout view by choosing View⇨Page Layout. In Page Layout view, the graphic appears beside the text once again, and you can see the header. You can also see the margins of the page very clearly because the ruler is gray where the margins are in Page Layout view.

7 **Double-click on the gray text of the header ("Copy for Oscar Wedlman's . . .").**

As soon as you double-click, the header appears in a box, and the Header and Footer toolbar comes on-screen. Lesson 15-4 explains headers and footers. For now, all you need to know is that you can edit a header or footer in Page Layout view simply by clicking it.

8 **Click the Close button on the Header and Footer toolbar.**

9 **Close the Page Layout file without saving your changes.**

Page Layout view is the way to go when you want to get a better idea of "the big picture" and see how your document will look to readers after you print it.

Recess

So ends Unit 12. By now, you should have a firm grasp of how to control what appears around the borders of the screen and how to switch from Normal view to Page Layout view and back again. It's time for a break. Sit quietly at the rear window of your house or apartment, watch for birds, and see how many you can identify.

"page-turning" buttons on Page View scroll bar

Normal View button

Page Layout View button

☑ **Progress Check**

If you can do the following, you've mastered this lesson and are ready to move on to the Unit 12 quiz:

❑ Switch to Page Layout view.

❑ Switch back to Normal view.

❑ Go from page to page in Page Layout view.

Unit 12 Quiz

Notes:

For the following questions, circle the letter of the correct answer or answers. You may find more than one right answer to each question.

1. **To put a new toolbar on-screen, you do which of the following?**

   A. Right-click and choose the toolbar from the shortcut menu.

   B. Right-click, choose Toolbars from the shortcut menu, choose the toolbar in the Toolbars dialog box, and click OK.

   C. Drag the toolbar onto the screen.

   D. Choose View⇨Toolbars, choose the toolbar from the dialog box, and click OK.

   E. Choose View⇨Page Layout.

2. **To remove a toolbar, you do which of the following?**

   A. Choose View⇨Toolbars, choose the toolbar from the dialog box, and click OK.

   B. Kindly ask it to go away.

   C. Drag it off the screen.

   D. Right-click, choose Toolbars from the shortcut menu, choose the toolbar in the Toolbars dialog box, and click OK.

   E. Right-click and choose the toolbar from the shortcut menu.

3. **Which of the following toolbars can you get by clicking buttons on the Standard or Formatting toolbar?**

   A. The Borders toolbar

   B. The Preview toolbar

   C. The Forms toolbar

   D. The Drawing toolbar

   E. The Microsoft toolbar

4. **To move a toolbar around on-screen, you do which of the following?**

   A. Drag it from the top of the screen into the window.

   B. Choose View⇨Toolbars.

   C. Drag it through the mud.

   D. Drag its title bar.

   E. Drag it by the tail.

5. **To remove the ruler from the screen, you do which of the following?**

   A. Right-click it and choose Ruler from the shortcut menu.

   B. Remove the ruler? But why?

   C. Choose View⇨Ruler.

   D. Choose Ruler⇨Subjugated.

   E. Drag it off the screen.

6. **This button, found in the lower-left corner of the Word 95 screen, does which of the following?**

   A. Turns on the TV.

   B. Creates a decimal tab stop.

   C. Switches to Page Layout view.

   D. Makes your computer weep.

   E. Puts a dimple on your chin.

Unit 12 Exercise

on the disk

For the following exercise, open the Page Layout file in the Practice folder and do the following:

1. Remove the Standard and Formatting toolbars; then bring them back.

2. Display the Borders toolbar and drag it onto the screen; then drag it back again.

3. Switch to Page Layout view.

4. Remove the rulers from the screen.

5. Switch to Full Screen view.

6. Press Alt+V to pull down the <u>V</u>iew menu, and then choose <u>N</u>ormal to get back to Normal view.

7. Close the document without saving it.

Different Ways of Working on Documents

Prerequisites
- Opening a document (Lesson 1-5)
- Finding your way around the screen (Lesson 1-6)
- Giving commands with buttons, menus, and shortcut keys (Unit 2)
- Selecting text (Lesson 3-2)
- Copying and pasting text (Lesson 3-4)

Objectives for This Unit

✓ Working on more than one document at once

✓ Splitting the screen to work in two places in the same document

✓ Opening a second window for a document

✓ Moving from place to place by using bookmarks

✓ Using the Zoom Control menu to change how a document looks on-screen

✓ Inserting one document into another

on the disk
- Article
- Source
- Window
- Zoom
- Insert Document
- Print Preview

In the last unit, you learned how to make the Word 95 document window work for you. This unit goes a step further and explains the commands on the Window menu. These commands can come in very, very handy. For example, you can work in more than one place at once in a document by splitting the screen or by getting two different windows on the same document. You can also do your eyes a big favor by zooming in on text to enlarge the letters on-screen. Finally, this unit demonstrates a very neat technique for recycling old documents and putting them to work in the documents you are writing now.

Working with More Than One Document

Lesson 13-1

In Word 95, working on more than one document at the same time is fairly easy. I can think of many reasons for doing so. If you are working on a cover letter to send with a report, for example, you can open the report and the cover letter and copy text from the report to the letter as you compose the letter. If a passage from the cover letter would work well in the report, you can copy it from the letter to the report. These days, most people have more than one resumé. If I apply for a writing job, I use my Writer resumé, but that doesn't mean that I can't open my Editor resumé and copy material from it to my Writer resumé to boost my image and increase my chances of appearing indispensable.

Notes:

to copy text, select
it and press Ctrl+C

text is entered in
and commands
applied to active
document, not other
open documents

Undo button

✓ **Progress Check**

If you can do the following,
you've mastered this lesson:

❑ Switch from open
document to open
document.

❑ Display more than one
document on-screen.

❑ Minimize and restore
documents in their
windows.

on the disk

on the test

To work on more than one document at once, you use commands on the Window menu. In Lessons 13-1 and 13-2, you will explore these commands. For this lesson, you will use the Article file in the Practice folder. The Article file is the start of an article about Rosenda Monteros, the skillful and talented actress. In this exercise, you will open a second file and use it for inspiration as you write the article.

Follow these steps to practice with the commands on the Window menu:

1 Open the Article file in the Practice folder.

If you scroll to the last line of the article, you see that it begins to offer an example. A good "for example" is never easy to come up with in writing, so you decide to get an example from another file that you've already worked on.

2 Open the Source file in the Practice folder and copy the blue text to the Clipboard.

For the purposes of this exercise, I have colored the text that you need to copy from Source to Article blue. Normally, you would have to search for text to "cannibalize" yourself, of course.

3 Click Window on the menu bar.

As shown in Figure 13-1, both Article and Source appear on the Window menu. All open documents appear at the bottom of the Window menu. The one that is currently active has a check mark next to its name.

4 Click Article to switch to that document.

You can also press 1, the number beside Article on the Window menu, to switch files.

5 With the cursor at the end of the article about Rosenda Monteros, choose Edit⇨Paste to paste the text from the source document, Source, to the article, Article.

With a little cleaning up, you have a perfectly usable description for the last paragraph in the Article file.

6 Click the Undo button to remove the text that you just copied.

7 Go back to Source by choosing it from the Window menu.

In the next seven steps, you will copy the text again, but this time you will do so with both documents displayed on-screen.

8 Choose Window⇨Arrange All.

When you choose this command, Word 95 does its best to put all open documents on-screen. In this case, you only have two open documents, so both fit nicely on-screen, as shown in Figure 13-2. Notice that each has its own scroll bar and that Source is the active document. You can tell because its title bar has color on it, whereas Article's title bar is grayed out.

The blue text should still be highlighted in Source.

9 Scroll to the blue text to make sure that it is still highlighted, and then click the Copy button to copy the text to the Clipboard.

10 Click in the Article window, scroll to the end of the file, and click the Paste button.

When you click in a new window, its toolbar gets "colorized," and that window becomes the active document.

11 Move the cursor over the border between the two windows. When it changes into a two-headed arrow, click and drag to make the Article window bigger and the Source window smaller.

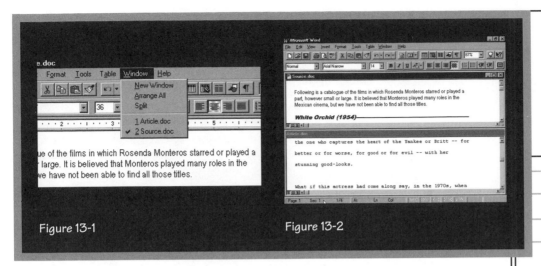

Figure 13-1   Figure 13-2

Figure 13-1: The names of all open documents appear on the Window menu.

Figure 13-2: Choose Window⇨Arrange All to see all open documents on-screen at once.

You can make the windows as large or small as you like by dragging their borders this way. Suppose that you decide that you want the Article file to fill the entire screen again.

12 Click the Maximize button on the Article title bar.

You can also choose Maximize from the Control menu to make the file fill the entire screen. Now the window is maximized. What happened to the Source window?

13 Click Article's Restore button.

Now the two windows are back on-screen again. In the next step, you will copy text from Source to Article by dragging it.

14 Click in the Source file where the text is still highlighted, and hold down the Ctrl key as you drag the highlighted text across the divide and into Article.

You already copied the text twice with the Clipboard. As this step demonstrates, you can also copy or move text directly from open document to open document when both documents are placed side by side on-screen with the Window⇨Arrange All command.

Maximize button

Restore button

heads up

Working with two open documents on-screen is not necessarily easy. Neither window is large enough to get any work done. But you can play with the Maximize and Restore buttons to shrink and enlarge windows as you need them. Go through the exercise in Lesson 13-1 again to get a better feel for the admittedly complex Window⇨Arrange All command.

Working in Two Places in the Same Document

Lesson 13-2

I can think of many, many reasons to work in two places in the same document at once. For example, if you are writing a long report and want the conclusion to fulfill all the promises that the introduction makes, you can open the document to both places to compare them and make sure that they pony up the same information. A report that promises on page 1 to prove that rodents killed the dinosaurs by eating their eggs but concludes by saying that freezing temperatures killed the dinosaurs would not convince anyone that you are a dinosaur expert.

Word 95 offers two ways to open a document to two different places. One way is to split the screen so that one part of the document appears in the top half and the other part appears in the bottom half, as in Figure 13-3. The other way is to open two different views of the same document by using the Window menu, as shown in Figure 13-4. When you choose one view, you go to one place in the document, and when you choose the other, you go to the other place. When you work with two views, you are still working with one document, not two. Changes you make to either view are made to a single document, not two documents.

on the disk

For this lesson about opening two views on a document, open the Window file in the Practice folder. First, you'll see how to split the screen. Lesson 13-2 explains how to open a second view on a document.

Splitting the screen with Window⇨Split

To get some practice in splitting the screen, follow these steps:

1 Choose **Window⇨Split.**

A gray line appears on-screen with the double-arrowed "split cursor" in the middle.

2 Move the split cursor down the screen to just below the opening paragraph of the Window file; then click.

Now a gray line runs across the screen (if you have the ruler turned on, a second ruler runs across the screen as well). You have divided the screen into north and south halves.

3 Click in the southern half of the screen and press Ctrl+End to move to the end of the document.

Your screen should look something like that in Figure 13-3. Does the conclusion make good on the promises made by the introduction? (You may have to scroll up a few lines to see the entire conclusion.) If the conclusion and introduction don't match, you can edit them while both are on-screen.

4 Choose **Window⇨Remove Split** to see only one part of the document.

You are left with the conclusion. If you had chosen Window⇨Remove Split with the cursor on the introduction side of the screen, you would have been left at the start of the document instead of at the end.

5 Press Ctrl+Home to go to the start of the document.

This time, you will learn a second way to split the screen.

Splitting the screen by dragging the split cursor

The Window⇨Split command isn't the only way to split the screen. You can also use the slot at the top of the vertical scroll bar.

1 Move the mouse cursor to the top of the vertical scroll bar along the right side of the screen, to the black "slot" just above the up arrow, and gently lay the cursor there.

If you do so correctly, you see the split cursor again.

"Split" cursor

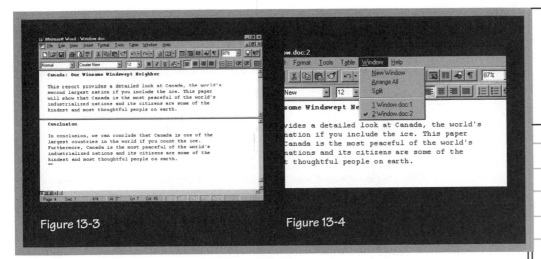

Figure 13-3

Figure 13-4

Figure 13-3: Splitting
the screen.

Figure 13-4: The Window
menu with two different
"outlooks" on the
same document.

2 **When the split cursor appears, hold down the left mouse button and drag the cursor onto the document; then release the mouse button when the gray line is just below the introductory paragraph.**

Once again, the document is divided in half.

3 **Press Ctrl+End to go to the end of the document; then click in the northern half of the screen.**

This time, you'll try another technique for "unsplitting" the screen.

4 **Move the mouse pointer to the split, feel around until you see the split cursor again, and then click and drag the split to the bottom of the screen.**

Sort of like lowering a curtain on the southern half of the screen, isn't it? Now the southern half is gone, and you're left with the introduction.

You can also remove a split by dragging the line to the top of the screen. If you drag the line to the top, you are left with the bottom half of the split screen; if you drag the line to the bottom, you are left with the top half of the split screen.

To sum up, you can split a screen by choosing Window⇨Split or by dragging the split cursor away from the black slot at the top of the vertical scroll bar. To "unsplit" a screen, either choose Window⇨Remove Split or drag the divider to the top or to the bottom of the screen.

Leave the Window file open so that you can do the next exercise.

Opening a window on two places in a document

The other way to work in two different places is to open two different windows on the same document. Follow these steps to practice this method of being in two places at once:

1 **With the cursor at the top of Window, choose Window⇨New Window.**

Notice that the title bar at the top of the screen says `Window.doc:2` rather than `Window.doc`.

Notes:

Notes:

Ctrl+W is shortcut for closing "new window"

☑ **Progress Check**

If you can do the following, you've mastered this lesson:

❏ Split the screen by choosing Window➪Split or by dragging the split cursor.

❏ Use the Window➪New Window command to open two different windows on a document.

2 **Press Ctrl+End to go to the end of the document.**

3 **Click Window on the menu bar to pull down the Window menu.**

As shown in Figure 13-4, two Window.docs are on the menu, one called Window.doc:1 and the other called Window.doc:2.

4 **Click Window.doc:1 on the menu.**

Now you are back at the start of the document. If you enter some text and save the document, the text is saved to Window.doc, not to Window.doc:1. Only Window.doc is on disk; although the Window menu offers you two different views, or outlooks, only one file actually exists. All editorial changes that you make to either version are recorded in Window.doc.

5 **Choose Window➪New Window to see the Window menu.**

Now you see three windows for the file. Yikes! Better start closing some of these "new windows."

6 **Pull down the Control menu and choose Close to close Window.doc:3.**

You can also close a window by pressing Ctrl+W. The Control menu is located to the left of File on the menu bar. Pull down this menu by clicking it.

7 **Click the Close button to close Window.doc:1.**

You can also close a document window by clicking its Close button (the button with an *X* on it). Just be sure to click the document window's Close button, not the program's Close button. If you click the program's Close button, Word 95 will think that you are trying to shut down the program.

8 **Pull down the Window menu and see what it says.**

You'll no longer see a 2, 1, or 3 after Window.doc. You are back where you started, with one window.

heads up

The Window➪New Window command has an important advantage over the other methods of viewing a document in two places or viewing more than one document. When you split the screen or choose Window➪Arrange All to see all the open documents at once, you are left with little room in which to work, whereas the Window➪New Window command gives you a panoramic, full-window look at different parts of a document.

Leave Window.doc open if you care to read the extra credit sidebar. These instructions describe another way to work in more than one place in a document: by using bookmarks.

Lesson 13-3 # Zooming In and Zooming Out

on the test

The eye, as nature invented it, is not meant to stare at a computer screen all day, and that makes the Zoom command all the more valuable. Instead of enlarging the type size of text, you can enlarge (or shrink) text with the Zoom command. The Zoom command doesn't alter type sizes in any way, shape, or form. All it does is change the size of the letters that appear on-screen.

on the disk

This short lesson explains how to use the commands on the Zoom Control menus. To practice using the Zoom command, open the Zoom file in the Practice folder and follow these steps:

extra credit

Marking your place with a bookmark

Yet another way to be in more than one place in a document is to use *bookmarks.* All you do is put a bookmark in an important spot in your document that you plan to return to many times. When you want to return to that spot, choose Edit⇨Bookmark and double-click the bookmark name in the Bookmark dialog box. By creating and using bookmarks, you can hop from place to place quickly in documents.

I put several bookmarks in the Window.doc file. To go to them, follow these steps:

1. **Choose Edit⇨Bookmark.**

   The Bookmark dialog box appears. Notice that the bookmark names are in alphabetical order. If you want to, you can click the Location radio button in this dialog box to make the bookmarks appear in the order in which they appear in the document.

2. **Double-click History in the dialog box.**

   You go to the discussion of Canadian history on page 3. You can also go to a bookmark by clicking it in the dialog box, clicking the Go To button, and then clicking Close.

3. **Scroll down a few lines.**

   In the next two steps, you will create a bookmark of your own.

4. **Choose Edit⇨Bookmark and type your own bookmark name in the Bookmark Name text box.**

   Bookmark names cannot include blank spaces, but you can get around that limitation by using capital letters. For example, if you want to mark the place in a document where you discuss the gross national product, you can call the bookmark GrossNationalProd. Be sure to choose a descriptive name.

5. **Click the Add button to add your bookmark to the list.**

6. **Choose Edit⇨Bookmark to open the Bookmark dialog box again.**

   You see your bookmark name in the list. If this list was long, you may have to click the scroll bar to see the name of the bookmark to which you wanted to go.

7. **Double-click Conclusion to get to the bookmark at the end of the document.**

1 **Click the down arrow to display the Zoom Control menu.**

The Zoom Control menu is on the right side of the Standard toolbar. It offers percentage settings ranging from 200% to 10%. At 200 percent, the document looks twice as large as it is when printed.

2 **Choose 50% from the Zoom Control menu.**

To do so, click on 50%. You started at 100%, so the letters shrink to half their real size.

3 **Click the down arrow on the Zoom Control menu again and choose 200%.**

The letters get quite large. You would have little trouble reading these letters on an eye exam. Likewise, you can keep from straining your eyes by choosing a high percentage on the Zoom Control menu.

100%

Zoom Control menu

☑ **Progress Check**

If you can do the following, you've mastered this lesson:

❑ Change the size of letters on-screen with the Zoom Control menu.

❑ Use the View⇨Zoom command to make working with Word 95 easier.

4 **Type 125 directly in the Zoom Control text box and then click anywhere in the document.**

You don't have to choose from the percentages on the Zoom Control menu. You can choose your own percentage by typing it in the text box.

When you click to complete step 4, the text shrinks from 200 percent to 125 percent of its real height. These letters are still large and easy to read, too.

5 **Choose View⇨Zoom to display the Zoom dialog box.**

As far as I can tell, you have no reason to go to the trouble of choosing this command when choosing Zoom settings from the Zoom Control menu is so easy. Nevertheless, you can go this route if you want to.

6 **Choose the 75% radio button and click OK.**

The Zoom Control commands are simple and easy to get at. Use them often to enlarge the text on-screen and make your work easier. By the way, sometimes you may want to shrink the text way down with the Zoom Control menu. Do so after you lay out a table to see what it looks like from a bird's-eye view, for example.

Lesson 13-4

Inserting One Document into Another

One of the great things about word processing is that you can recycle your work. If you've written something that would fit well in a document you're working on at present, or you've written something that would nearly fit, for example, you can insert the old document directly in the new one and take it from there. Lesson 13-4 explains how to do so.

on the disk

For this exercise, you need the Insert Document file in the Practice folder. Open that file now and follow these steps to complete this very short lesson:

1 **Press Ctrl+End to go to the end of the document.**

You can insert a file anywhere in a document. When you choose Insert⇨File, the file is inserted wherever the text cursor is. You don't have to insert files at the end of documents, although in this case you are going to do just that.

on the test

2 **Choose Insert⇨File.**

The Insert File dialog box appears. You see this same dialog box when you open a file that you have been working on. In this dialog box, you choose the file you want to insert in the same way you choose a file you want to open in the Open dialog box. For this exercise, you will insert the Print Preview file.

3 **In the Look in box, click the Practice folder.**

The file you are going to insert is in the Practice folder.

4 **Click on Print Preview and then click OK.**

The entire file is inserted in the document.

☑ **Progress Check**

If you can do the following, you've mastered this lesson and are ready to move on to the Unit 13 quiz:

❑ Insert one file into another.

❑ Find the file that you want to insert in the Insert File dialog box.

heads up

More than likely, you'll have to make a few changes when you insert a file this way. Usually, the transition from the file you are working on to the file you inserted is abrupt, so you have to write a paragraph to smooth over the transition and edit the inserted file to make it fit with the original. Nevertheless, the Insert⇨File command is a good one to know about. Bottles, cans, and paper aren't the only things that you can recycle.

Unit 13 Quiz

For the following questions, circle the letter of the correct answer or answers. You may find more than one right answer to each question.

1. **To display *different* documents at the same time on-screen, you choose which of these commands?**

   A. Window⇨New Window

   B. Window⇨Arrange All

   C. Window⇨Open

   D. Window⇨Split

2. **To open two different windows for the *same* document, you use which of the following commands?**

   A. Window⇨New Window

   B. Window⇨Arrange All

   C. Window⇨Split

   D. File⇨Open

3. **How can you tell which is the active document on the Window menu?**

   A. It has the number 1 after its name.

   B. It has a check mark next to its name.

   C. It is the first one on the menu.

   D. It is the one that fate has chosen.

4. **To divide the screen in order to view two different parts of a document, you do the following:**

   A. Choose Window⇨New Window.

   B. Choose Window⇨Split.

   C. Move the cursor to the top of the vertical scroll bar, and when the split cursor appears, drag it into the document window.

   D. Choose Banana⇨Split.

5. **Where is the Zoom Control menu located?**

   A. On the Font Size pull-down menu

   B. Two doors down and to your left

   C. On the shortcut menu that appears when you right-click a toolbar

   D. On the right side of the Standard toolbar

Notes:

6. **You use which of these techniques to copy one file into another?**

   A. Copy the text to the Clipboard, and then open the other file and paste the text.

   B. Choose Insert⇨File.

   C. Choose File⇨Open.

   D. Open both documents on-screen.

7. **Who said, "Most men lead lives of quiet desperation?"**

   A. Bob Dylan

   B. Madonna

   C. Sigmund Freud

   D. Sonny Bono

Unit 13 Exercise

on the disk

Open the Window file in the Practice folder and follow these steps to practice the techniques that Unit 13 introduced:

1. Split the screen to see two different parts of the document.

2. Remove the split and then open a second window for the document.

3. Close the second window and go to the conclusion of the document by going to its bookmark.

4. Change the size of the letters on-screen by using commands in the Zoom Control menu.

5. Insert any old document into the Window file.

Writing Aids

Objectives for This Unit

✓ Catching and correcting spelling errors

✓ Finding the right word with the Thesaurus

✓ Finding and replacing words and phrases

✓ Undoing mistakes — and "redoing" your "undos"

✓ Entering text quickly

Prerequisites

◗ Finding your way around the screen (Lesson 1-6)

◗ Giving commands with buttons, menus, and shortcut keys (Unit 2)

◗ Filling in dialog boxes (Lesson 2-5)

◗ Selecting text (Lesson 3-2)

on the disk

◗ Spelling

◗ Find and Replace

◗ Unit 14 Exercise

In this unit, you'll learn ways to improve your writing with Word 95. First and foremost, a word processor's job is to make you a better writer. No matter how the different fonts, splashy colors, and layouts may bedazzle you, when you get down to it, Word 95 was invented to help you communicate with other people. As such, the program has tools to make you a better communicator.

Unit 14 explains how to use the spell-checker to catch and correct embarrassing spelling mistakes. It shows you how to use the Thesaurus to track down the perfect word for whatever you are trying to describe. It also tells you how to find a text in a document — perhaps a name that you entered incorrectly or a phrase that you would like to rewrite. Besides finding words and phrases, you can also find and replace them, and this unit explains how to do that, too.

You'll also learn how to fix mistakes quickly with the Undo and Redo commands and enter text that you use often, such as an address, in a document with a flick of your wrist.

Fixing Spelling Mistakes   Lesson 14-1

Probably four out of ten Word 95 users would say that the neatest thing about the program is its spell-checker. Most people are not good spellers. Words like *accomodate* and *commitee* are easy to misspell (I just misspelled them, did you notice?). The English language, which sounds beautiful to the ear, does not have hard-and-fast spelling rules, unlike most other languages.

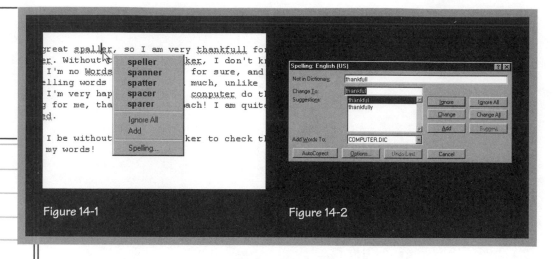

Figure 14-1: The shortcut menu for correcting misspellings.

Figure 14-2: Finding and correcting misspelled words with the spell-checker.

Figure 14-1   Figure 14-2

As you may have noticed, Word 95 puts a red squiggley line under words that are misspelled, as shown in Figure 14-1. Thanks to that red line, you can fix spelling errors as you make them. You can also check spelling errors by running the spell-checker over your documents. This lesson explains how to do both.

To find spelling errors, Word 95 compares the words in your document to the words in its dictionary. When it comes across what it thinks is a misspelled word, it gives you the opportunity to fix it, ignore it, or do one or two other things, as the next exercise demonstrates.

on the disk

For this exercise in spell-checking a document, open the Spelling file in the Practice folder and follow these steps:

1 Right-click on the first misspelled word in the document, *spaller*.

You can tell which words are misspelled because they are underlined with a squiggley red line. As shown in Figure 14-1, a shortcut menu with some suggestions for spelling the word correctly appears when you right-click a misspelled word. Also on the menu are options called Ignore All, Add, and Spelling. You will see what those options do later. For now, just correct the misspelling.

2 Click *speller* on the shortcut menu.

The word is changed to *speller,* and the red line disappears.

3 Press Ctrl+End to go to the end of the document and type your last name.

Later in this exercise, you will add your last name to the Word 95 dictionary so that the spell-checker knows that your last name is not a misspelling. (If your last name is Smith or Green or another name that a dictionary would recognize, type some gibberish for the purpose of this exercise.)

4 Click the Spelling button on the Standard toolbar.

You can also start the spell-checker by choosing Tools⇨Spelling, pressing F7, or right-clicking a misspelled word and choosing Spelling from the shortcut menu.

The spell-checker goes to the top of the document and stops on the first misspelled word it finds, *thankfull,* as shown in Figure 14-2. When you tell Word 95 to spell-check a document, it starts wherever the cursor is and goes to the end of the document, then back to the beginning, and then around to where the cursor was when you gave the command to check for misspellings.

Spelling button

In the Spelling dialog box, the word *thankfull* appears in the Not in Dictionary box, the word *thankful* appears in the Change To box, and the words *thankful* and *thankfully* appear in the Suggestions box.

You want the word *thankful,* so all you have to do is click the Change button to enter the correctly spelled word in the document. If you wanted the word *thankfully,* you would click it in the Suggestions box to make *thankfully* appear in the Change To box and then click the Change button.

5 **Click the Change button.**

The spell-checker goes to the next misspelled word, *clacker.* It should be *checker.*

6 **Type the correct word** checker **in the Change To box and click the Change button.**

If none of Word 95's suggestions will do the job, you can type your own word in the Change To box.

The spell-checker stops on the next misspelled word, *clacker.* But notice how the word *checker* appears this time in the Change To box. Word 95 remembers how you fixed this problem last time, so it offers the word *checker* on the assumption that you'll want to fix this problem the same way you fixed it before.

7 **Click the Change All button.**

This button tells Word 95 to change all occurrences of the word in the document. In this case, you click Change All on the idea that the misspelling *clacker* appears throughout your document and you want to change it wherever it occurs to *checker.*

Next, the spell-checker stops on *Wordsworth.* Wordsworth, a name, is not misspelled, so you should ignore this one. The spell-checker stops on most proper names and all other words that are not in its dictionary.

on the test

8 **Click the Ignore button.**

The spell-checker stops on another *Wordsworth* later in the document. Suppose that the name Wordsworth appears throughout your document. How can you get the spell-checker to quit stopping on it?

9 **Click the Ignore All button.**

Ignore All tells the spell-checker not to stop on the word anymore during this spell-check and all other spell-checks that you run on this document until you close it.

The next word that the spell-checker stops on is *conputer.* Obviously, this should be *computer.* You could click the Change button easily enough to fix it, but suppose that you often misspell *computer* by typing the word with an *n*: *conputer.* If you want, you can have Word 95 "autocorrect" this word — that is, fix *conputer* at the same time that you type it incorrectly — by clicking the AutoCorrect button.

10 **Click the AutoCorrect button.**

Now Word 95 corrects *conputer.* However, it won't correct the word if you spell it *comuter* or *computar.* Choose AutoCorrect when you habitually misspell a word in the same way.

Next, the spell-checker stops on something really strange: the letters *dis.* What's going on here?

11 **Click the down arrow on the scroll bar in the Suggestions box to look at all the suggestions.**

Word offers a ton of suggestions, but none of them works. This calls for radical surgery.

Notes:

click Undo Last to reverse a spelling correction

you can also get Ignore All option when you right-click on a misspelled word

12 **Click in the document to get out of the dialog box, delete the letters *dis,* and type happy in their place.**

You can click outside the Spelling dialog box and fix spelling errors that way, as this step demonstrates.

In the Spelling dialog box, notice that the Re**s**ume button appears where the **I**gnore button used to be.

13 **Click the Re**s**ume button to start the spell-check again.**

The spell-checker stops on the repeated word *indeed.* Besides checking for misspellings, the spell-checker also looks for repeated words. Notice that the **D**elete button appears where the **C**hange button was.

14 **Click the **D**elete button to get rid of the second *indeed.***

The spell-checker stops on the last word in the document, your last name. I presume that your last name will appear in many of your documents. You don't want the spell-checker to stop on your illustrious name, do you?

15 **Click the **A**dd button.**

The **A**dd button adds the word in the Not in Dictionary box to the Word 95 dictionary. Your name is now in the dictionary. Not only will the spell-checker not stop on your name again, but it will also make sure that your name is spelled correctly.

A message box appears to tell you that the spell-check is complete.

16 **Click OK or press Enter to close the message box.**

17 **Type conputer to see how autocorrect works.**

The invisible hand of Word 95 changes the *n* to an *m* because you clicked the AutoCo**r**rect button back in step 10 of this exercise.

You don't have to spell-check an entire document each time you want to check your spelling. To spell-check part of a document, select it before you give the command to start the spell-check.

heads up

Before you close the Spelling file (close it without saving the changes you made), notice the two grievous spelling errors in the last sentence. Instead of *spell* and *spelling,* it says *smell* and *smelling.* The moral is that the spell-checker cannot catch all misspelled words. It recognizes only words that are not in its dictionary. If you mean to type *waddle* and type *twaddle* instead, for example, the spell-checker won't catch the error, because *twaddle* is a legitimate word. When you're working on an important document, proofread it carefully. Don't rely on the smell-checker to catch all your smelling errors.

Add option is also available on Spelling shortcut menu

☑ **Progress Check**

If you can do the following, you've mastered this lesson:

❑ Give the command to spell-check a document.

❑ Correct and ignore misspellings in the Spelling dialog box.

❑ Correct misspellings by clicking in the document and correcting them there.

❑ Tell Word 95 to autocorrect a misspelling that you habitually make.

Lesson 14-2   Choosing Words with the Thesaurus

Finding the right word to describe something is a huge part of writing. To help you, Word 95 offers the Thesaurus. The Thesaurus presents synonyms for words and gives you the opportunity to replace a word with one of its synonyms. A *synonym* is a word that has the same or a similar meaning as another word.

To get some practice using the Thesaurus, open a new document and type **nonsense**. Then do the following exercise:

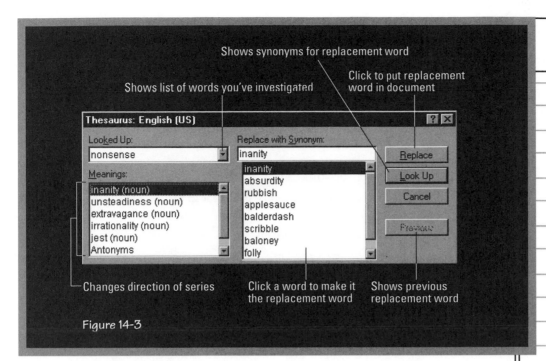

Shows synonyms for replacement word

Shows list of words you've investigated

Click to put replacement word in document

Changes direction of series

Click a word to make it the replacement word

Shows previous replacement word

Figure 14-3

Figure 14-3: The Thesaurus dialog box.

 *Notes:*

on the test

1 With the cursor in the word *nonsense,* choose Tools⇨Thesaurus.

The Thesaurus dialog box appears, as shown in Figure 14-3. You can also get this dialog box by pressing Shift+F7.

Nonsense appears in the Looked Up box. Word 95 puts what it thinks is the synonym you are most likely to want in the Replace with Synonym box, *inanity* in this case. Notice the many different shades of meaning for *nonsense* in the Meanings box. By clicking a word in the Meanings box, you can turn your search for the right synonym in a different direction.

For some words, you can even see a list of *antonyms* — words that have an opposite meaning. If you are having trouble thinking of the right word to use and know its antonym, try choosing Tools⇨Thesaurus and see whether the Thesaurus dialog box lists an antonym for the antonym. You can sometimes find the word you're looking for this way.

2 Click *irrationality* in the Meanings box.

Irrationality appears in the Replace with Synonym text box, and a new set of synonyms appears in the scroll box.

3 Click *stupidity* and then click the Look Up button.

To see synonyms for a word in the Replace with Synonym box, select the word and click the Look Up button. Now a new set of words appears in the Replace with Synonym box, but you've strayed pretty far from the original word in your document, *nonsense.* Can you go back?

4 Click the down arrow on the Looked Up box to see the list of words that you've looked up so far, and click *nonsense* to get back to your original word.

Now you're back where you started. Last time you were here, you chose *irrationality* in the Meanings box. How about going a different direction this time by choosing *extravagance?*

5 Click *extravagance* in the Meanings box and then click the Look Up button to see synonyms for this word.

Hmmm. These words don't look very good, either.

Shift+F7 is shortcut for opening Thesaurus

☑ Progress Check

If you can do the following, you've mastered this lesson:

❏ Open the Thesaurus dialog box to search for synonyms.

❏ Use the Meanings box, Replace with Synonym box, Look Up button, and other tools to search for a good synonym.

6 Click the Previous button to go back to the last word you looked up, *nonsense* in this case.

Besides clicking the down arrow on the Looked Up drop-down list, you can retrace your steps by clicking the Previous button. Try looking up one of the words in the Replace with Synonym box.

7 Click *balderdash* and then click the Look Up button.

Yet another set of synonyms appears in the Replace with Synonym box. There's a good one — *poppycock.*

8 Click *poppycock* to make it appear in the Replace with Synonym box.

9 Click the Replace button.

The Thesaurus dialog box closes and *poppycock,* a good synonym for *nonsense,* appears in your document where *nonsense* used to be.

You can't always find a perfect synonym in the Thesaurus dialog box, but the dialog box gives you many good tools for finding one. Happy hunting!

Lesson 14-3 — Finding and Replacing Words and Phrases

Suppose you are working on a 100-page report and know that somewhere between page 40 and 80 you misspelled the name of a very important person, the person who will read the report and judge whether you deserve a huge raise and a mighty promotion. How can you find that person's name? One way is to laboriously page through those 40 pages, but that might take hours. The other way, which takes all of five seconds, is to use the Edit⇨Find command.

Lesson 14-3 explains how to find words and phrases in a document. It also explains how to replace a word or phrase with the Edit⇨Replace command. If you were writing page 927 of a Russian novel and decided to change the main character's name from Oblonsky to Oblomov, you could do so in about a half a minute with the Edit⇨Replace command.

Finding words and phrases

on the disk

For this exercise in finding and replacing text, you will use a filed called Find and Replace in the Practice folder. Open that file now and follow these steps:

1 Choose Edit⇨Find to see the Find dialog box.

You can also choose the Find command by pressing Ctrl+F.

2 Type bow in the Find What box.

By entering **bow**, you tell Word 95 to search for all instances of those three letters, not just for the word *bow.* Your Find dialog box should look like Figure 14-4.

Ctrl+F is shortcut for finding text

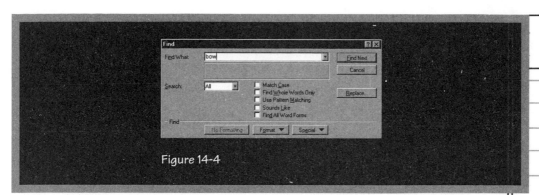

Figure 14-4: Finding text in a document.

Figure 14-4

Notes:

3 **Click the Find Next button and keep clicking it (or pressing F) until Word 95 tells you that it has finished searching the document. Then click OK.**

Notice how the program finds many instances of *bow*. Sometimes the word stands alone, and sometimes the three letters are part of a longer word, such as *elbow* or *bowler*. If this were a long document, you would want to click check boxes to narrow the search and not find every instance of *bow*.

4 **Choose the Find Whole Words Only check box, and then click the Find Next button. Keep clicking the Find Next button (or pressing F) until Word 95 finishes searching the document. Then click OK.**

This time, you don't land on *elbow, bowling,* or *bowler* because you told Word 95 to find whole words only.

5 **Type Bow (with an uppercase *B*) in the Find What box, click the Match Case check box, and click the Find Next button. Keep clicking this button (or pressing F) until Word 95 tells you that the document has been frisked. Then click OK.**

This time, Word 95 stops on only two words. By clicking check boxes, you can tell Word 95 exactly what you are looking for.

6 **Click the Sounds Like check box.**

If you vaguely know what you're looking for, you can always try your luck with this search option. Notice how the check marks disappear from the first two check boxes when you choose Sounds Like.

7 **Click the Find Next button and keep clicking it (or pressing F) until Word 95 tells you that it has finished searching the document. Then click OK.**

This time around, Word 95 stops on *be* and *beau* as well as *bow*.

You can search for more than just words in the Find dialog box, as the next six steps demonstrate.

8 **Click the Sounds Like check box to remove the check mark, and then click the Format button at the bottom of the dialog box.**

9 **Choose Font from the drop-down list.**

The Font dialog box appears. You can use this same dialog box to assign fonts and font sizes to text.

10 **Choose Italic from the Font Style list and click OK.**

Back in the Find dialog box, the words Format: Italic appear below the Find What box. Word 95 is all set to find an italicized *Bow*.

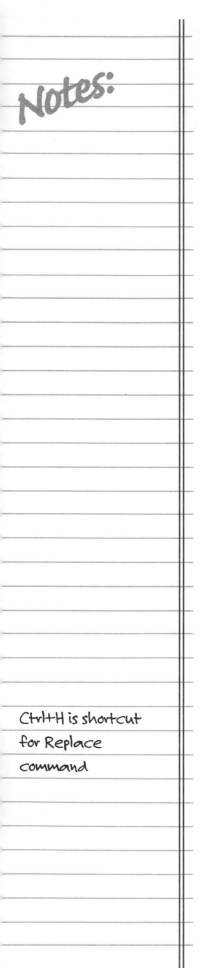

Notes:

11 Click the **F**ind Next button once, and then once again to find both instances of *Bow* in the document.

Searching for character styles such as italics is yet another way to narrow the confines of a search.

12 Click the **Spe**cial button at the bottom of the dialog box.

You can search for a number of things, including page breaks and tab characters.

13 Click the down arrow on the **S**earch drop-down list and choose Up.

If you are in the middle of a document and want to start searching, you don't have to go to the top and commence searching from there. You can choose a **S**earch option instead.

14 Click the **F**ind Next button.

Now you are back at the first *Bow*.

15 Click the **R**eplace button to get ready for the next exercise.

When you click the **R**eplace button, another text box called Replace With appears. Leave the Find and Replace file open for now.

By choosing options in the Find dialog box, you can tell Word 95 precisely what you're looking for. Then you can click the **F**ind Next button and find it quickly. In this exercise, you looked for a single word, but you can type as many words as you want in the Fi**n**d What box. In fact, typing several words that you know are in a document makes searches go faster, because the same several words don't often appear together more than once in a document.

Finding and replacing text

In the last exciting exercise, you clicked the **R**eplace button in the Find dialog box, and the Replace dialog box appeared. Notice that the dialog box is not called Find anymore. Now it is called Replace. When you choose the Edit⇨**R**eplace command, you see this very same dialog box. Follow these steps to practice finding and replacing text:

1 Click the Cancel button to close the Replace dialog box, and then press Ctrl+Home to go to the top of the document.

Maybe you didn't believe me when I said that you can choose Edit⇨**R**eplace to open the Replace dialog box.

2 Choose Edit⇨**R**eplace.

The Replace dialog box appears, as in Figure 14-5. You can also open this dialog box by pressing Ctrl+H.

Notice that the dialog box is all set to search for an italicized *Bow,* which is the search criteria you used before. The Find and Replace dialog boxes remember what you entered last time and show those settings again when you choose Edit⇨**F**ind or Edit⇨**R**eplace.

3 Click the No Forma**t**ting button to tell Word 95 that you do not want to find and replace text that has been formatted in a special way.

4 Type Smyth in the Fi**n**d What box.

For this exercise, suppose that *Smyth* should really be *Smith.*

Ctrl+H is shortcut
for Replace
command

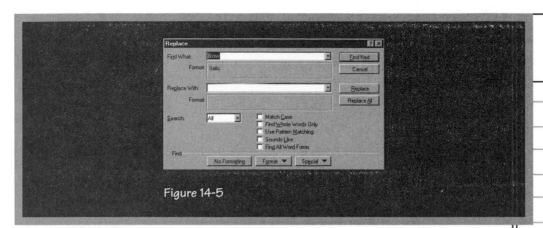

Figure 14-5

Figure 14-5: Replacing the text that you find with other text.

5 **Type** Smith **in the Replace With box.**

6 **Click the Search drop-down list and choose Down.**

7 **Click the Find Next button.**

Word 95 highlights the first *Smyth*. An apostrophe and an *s* follow this *Smyth*, but that's okay, because Word 95 will replace only the *Smyth* part of the name.

8 **Click the Replace button.**

Word 95 makes the replacement and moves to the next *Smyth*.

9 **Keep clicking Replace until Word 95 tells you that it has finished searching the document, and then click OK in the message box.**

If you *don't* want to replace text that Word 95 finds, you can bypass the text by clicking Find Next instead of Replace.

Now you are back at the top of the document. For the sake of practice, suppose that you were wrong about replacing *Smyth* with *Smith*. Suppose *Smyth* is the right name.

10 **Type** Smith **in the Find What box and** Smyth **in the Replace With box.**

You can click the Replace All button to replace all *Smith*s with *Smyth*s in one fell swoop (you will do that in step 12), but you have to do something very important first.

11 **Click the Find Whole Words Only check box.**

heads up

Before you click the Replace All button, always choose this option, because it lowers your chances of replacing something that shouldn't be replaced. For example, suppose the word *blacksmith* was in the Find and Replace file. If you replaced all the *Smith*s with *Smyth*s without clicking Find Whole Words Only first, you would end up with the word *blacksmyth* in your document.

12 **Click the Replace All button.**

This powerful button makes all the replacements in one fell swoop. This time around, Word 95 not only tells you that it has finished searching the document, but it also tells you how many replacements it made. You can be sure that no more *Smith*s are in your document, only *Smyth*s.

13 **Click Cancel to close the Replace dialog box and get on with your real life.**

heads up

The Replace All button is very powerful indeed, and some Word 95 philosophers say that you should save your document before you click Replace All. If you replace text that you shouldn't have replaced, you then can close your document without saving it, open your document again, and get your original document back.

☑ Progress Check

If you can do the following, you've mastered this lesson:

❑ Find text in a document.

❑ Find text that has been formatted a certain way.

❑ Replace the text that you find.

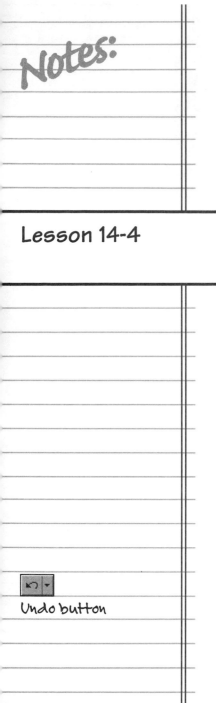

Recess

If you want to take a break now, I don't blame you in the least. You've just come off three difficult but very useful lessons — one in using the spell-checker, one in using the Thesaurus, and one in finding and replacing text. The Spelling, Thesaurus, Find, and Replace dialog boxes offer more options than most. How can you possibly remember them all? After you practice using these commands, knowing what the buttons do gets to be as easy as cake — I mean pie.

Lesson 14-4

Using the Undo and Redo Commands

In the first three lessons of Unit 3, I loaded you down with a lot of complicated instructions. To make it up to you, I'll make this lesson very short and sweet. What's more, this lesson explains something that previous lessons in this book already introduced you to: the Undo command and its twin brother, Redo.

You clicked the Undo button in earlier lessons, but you can do more than that. You can also pull down the Undo menu and click an option to undo your last one to six actions. By clicking the scroll bar on the Undo menu, you can undo as many as 99 of your last actions, although I'm not sure why anyone would do that. The Redo button redoes what you undid with the Undo command.

To do this exercise, open a new document and type some gibberish on-screen, press Enter, type some more gibberish, and then select your gibberish and move it somewhere else on-screen. Then follow these steps:

on the test

1 Click the down arrow beside the Undo button.

The Undo button is located on the Standard toolbar above the Font Size menu. When you click the down arrow, a record of what you did appears on the drop-down list. The list says *Move* and *Typing* followed by your gibberish. If you had done 99 things since opening this document, all 99 of them would be on the Undo menu.

2 Click the last item on the menu, *Typing* and your gibberish.

Everything disappears from the document window. To undo the last thing on the Undo menu, Word 95 has to undo everything that comes before it as well.

3 Click the down arrow beside the Redo button.

The Redo menu looks like the Undo menu did a moment ago, only in reverse. Redo records whatever you undo in the Undo menu, just as Undo records whatever you do in the document.

4 Click Move, the last item on the Redo menu.

Lo and behold, everything you undid in step 2 is back on-screen.

5 Click a line of gibberish and then click the Increase Indent button.

The Increase Indent Button is the second button from the right on the Formatting toolbar.

Undo button

Redo button

6 **Pull down the Undo menu.**

It says Increase Indent. The Undo menu records *all* your actions, not just key presses.

7 **Click Edit on the menu bar to see the Edit menu.**

Notice that the first command on the Edit menu is Undo Increase Indent. You can also undo actions by way of this menu command. If your last action had been to move text, the first command on the Edit menu would be Undo Move. If you had typed something, it would be Undo Typing.

8 **Choose Undo Increase Indent.**

So much for Undo and Redo. These commands can be very helpful; look to them when you make a mistake. Leave the practice file you just created open if you are the ambitious type and want to do the following Extra Credit assignment.

extra credit

Using the Repeat command

Another Edit menu command can be very helpful for doing tasks. With Edit⇨Repeat, the second command on the Edit menu, you can repeat your last action. To see how this command works, follow these steps:

1. Type **I will not talk in class** anywhere in your practice file, and then press Enter.

2. Choose Edit⇨Repeat Typing five or six times.

   Like Edit⇨Undo, this command changes names, depending on what you did last.

3. Copy the lines you just entered and paste them lower down in the document.

4. Pull down the Edit menu and choose Repeat Paste.

When doing repetitive tasks, as you so often have to do when you are word processing, by all means let the Edit⇨Repeat command do the work for you.

Ctrl+Z is shortcut for Edit⇨Undo

Ctrl+Y is shortcut for Edit⇨Repeat

☑ **Progress Check**

If you can do the following, you've mastered this lesson:

❑ Undo your last several actions.

❑ Redo what you undid with the Undo command.

❑ Choose Edit⇨Repeat to make repetitive tasks easier.

Entering "Automatic" Text   Lesson 14-5

No doubt you enter a few things time and time again in your documents — your address, for example, or the name of the company you work for. This lesson explains how you can store these things on a menu and simply choose them whenever you need to enter them in a document. Instead of typing your address at the start of every letter you write, you can insert your address with a few clicks of the mouse button.

Figure 14-6: The AutoText dialog box.

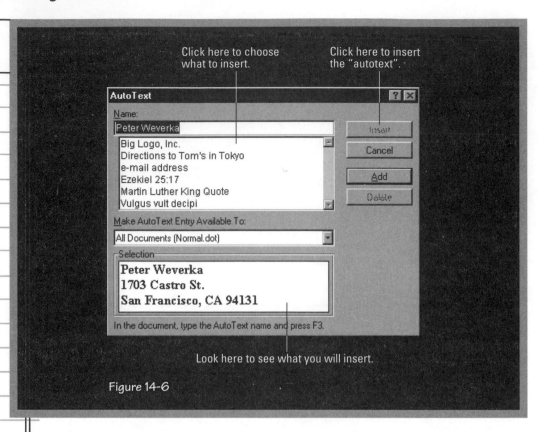

Figure 14-6

In this exercise, you will store your name and address so that you can insert it in documents whenever you want. Follow these steps:

1 Type your name and address.

Format your name and address while you're at it. Choose your favorite font and boldface everything if you want.

2 Select your name and address.

3 Choose Edit⇔AutoText.

The AutoText dialog box appears, as in Figure 14-6. Your name and address are in the Selection box.

4 In the Name box, enter a name like Address.

Whatever you enter appears as a selection in this dialog box the next time you open it. The name should be descriptive so that you'll know what you're choosing.

5 Click the Add button.

The AutoText dialog box closes. Now insert your address with the AutoText dialog box.

6 Place the cursor where you want to insert your address.

7 Choose Edit⇔AutoText.

The AutoText dialog box appears. The name you entered in step 4 is in the Name box.

8 **Click the name that you entered in step 4.**

The Preview box shows you what will be entered in your document if you click the Insert button. You see your address in the Preview box.

9 **Click the Insert button.**

The dialog box closes, and your address appears in the document.

It almost goes without saying that you can find a lot of good uses for the AutoText feature. I find it especially useful for e-mail and Internet addresses, which are hard to type. With the AutoText feature, you have to type these addresses only once.

☑ **Progress Check**

If you can do the following, you've mastered this lesson and are ready to move on to the Unit 14 quiz:

❑ Enter text in the AutoText dialog box.

❑ Insert an AutoText entry in a document.

Unit 14 Quiz

For the following questions, circle the letter of the correct answer or answers. You may find more than one right answer to each question.

1. **In which of the following sentences would the spell-checker *not* catch any spelling errors?**

   A. It's raining outseed.

   B. I'ts raining outside.

   C. It's raining ootside.

   D. It's saining outside.

2. **You can do which of the following to spell-check a document?**

   A. Choose Tools⇨Spelling.

   B. Press F7.

   C. Click the Spelling button.

   D. Right-click on a misspelled word and choose the correct spelling.

3. **You can use Word 95's Thesaurus to do which of the following tasks?**

   A. Find synonyms for words to help improve your writing.

   B. Find antonyms for words.

   C. Check the spelling of words.

   D. Learn to speak Greek.

4. **By using the Edit⇨Find command, you can find which of the following in a document?**

   A. A word

   B. Several words

   C. A word that has been formatted a special way

   D. A page break or tab stop

5. **Before you start finding and replacing text in a document, you should do which of the following tasks?**

   A. Burp the baby.

   B. Clean under the seats in your car.

   C. Save your document in case you need to abandon your changes and get the original document back.

   D. Return all overdue library books.

6. **Click this button when you want to do which tasks?**

   A. Redo what you just did by clicking the Undo button.

   B. Undo your last six actions.

   C. Undo your last 99 actions.

   D. Undo the last thing you did on-screen.

7. **Which of the following commands lets you insert gobs of text in a document all at once?**

   A. Insert➪AutoText

   B. Tools➪AutoCorrect

   C. Edit➪AutoText

   D. Auto➪Mobile

Unit 14 Exercise

on the disk

Open the Unit 14 Exercise file in the Practice folder and follow these steps to test yourself on what you learned in Unit 14:

1. Find and correct misspellings in the document. Use the spell-checker or shortcut menus as you please. Some of the words, such as the names of figures in history, you will ignore.

2. Find the following words, and then find synonyms for them: *breadbasket, powerhouse, abundance, roam.* If you can't find a synonym that is better than the original word, keep the original.

3. Use the Edit➪Replace command to find all instances of the word *winsome* and replace them with the word *charming.*

4. Undo what you did in step 3.

5. Redo what you undid in step 4.

6. Use the Edit➪Replace command to find instances of the word *charming* and replace them with the word *delightful.* You may decide not to change the word in some places.

7. Create an autotext entry that says, "I'm getting good at Word 95."

8. Insert the autotext entry that you created in step 7 in your document several times.

Some Neat Formatting Tricks

Objectives for This Unit

✓ Creating and manipulating a numbered list

✓ Creating and formatting a bulleted list

✓ Numbering the pages in a document

✓ Putting headers and footers on the tops and bottoms of pages

Prerequisites

▸ Finding your way around the screen (Lesson 1-6)

▸ Giving commands with buttons, menus, and shortcut keys (Unit 2)

▸ Filling in dialog boxes (Lesson 2-5)

▸ Selecting text (Lesson 3-2)

▸ Removing and adding tool-bars (Lesson 12-1)

on the disk

▸ Numbered List

▸ Bulleted List

▸ Page Numbers

▸ Header and Footer

▸ Journalism

Unit 15, a short one, explains a few formatting techniques that can save you hours of work. It begins with a discussion of entering and editing bulleted and numbered lists quickly. Whether you like it or not, Word 95 formats these lists for you as you enter the bulleted or numbered items. In this unit, you'll learn how to make the lists look the way you want them to look.

Unit 15 also explains how to number the pages of a document, which is pretty simple. You can start at 1 or choose another number. Finally, the last lesson in this unit tells you how to put headers and footers on pages. Headers and footers are a good way to help readers identify what they are reading. For example, the headers on the pages of this book tell you which part and unit you're in.

Creating a Numbered List

Lesson 15-1

Numbered lists are invaluable in manuals and books like this one that present a lot of step-by-step procedures. This book, for example, includes about 100 numbered lists that help you learn Word 95 tasks. "Doing it by the numbers" helps authors organize information — and readers learn things more quickly and thoroughly.

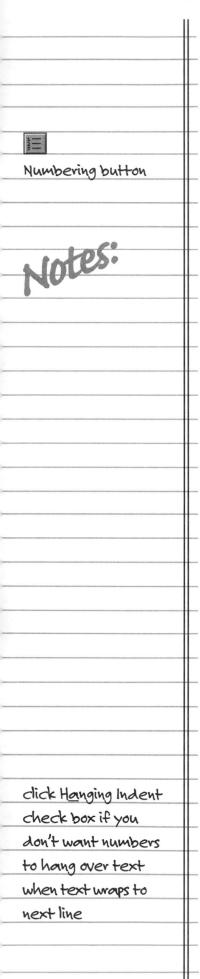

Numbering button

Notes:

click Hanging Indent
check box if you
don't want numbers
to hang over text
when text wraps to
next line

Lesson 15-1 explains how to create a numbered list. Just as important, it tells you how to interrupt and end a numbered list. For this lesson, you will use the Numbered List file in the Practice folder. Open that file and follow these steps to learn about numbered lists:

1 **Select the eight film titles in the list at the top of the screen, and then click the Numbering button.**

The Numbering button is the fifth button from the right on the Formatting toolbar.

Now the film titles are numbered 1 to 8. The fastest and easiest way to create a numbered list is to enter the items on the list without any concern for numbers. Just press Enter after each line. When you're done, select the list and click the Numbering button.

2 **Move the cursor to the end of the last line in the list and press Enter.**

Word puts a 9 on the next line on the assumption that you want to enter a ninth item on your list. But suppose that you want to end the numbered list. How do you tell Word 95 to quit numbering each new line?

3 **Right-click on the ninth line and choose Stop Numbering from the shortcut menu.**

Figure 15-1 shows the shortcut menu that appears when you right-click a numbered list. The 9 disappears, so you can type normal, unformatted text.

4 **Move the cursor to the end of the fourth item on the list, *The Magnificent Seven,* and press Enter.**

Word creates a new number 5 and bumps up the following numbers on the list. Now the list contains nine items instead of eight.

Suppose you want to interrupt the list and write some explanatory text (in the same way that I am interrupting my numbered list with this paragraph).

5 **Right-click on the fifth line and choose Stop Numbering like you did in step 3**.

Word ends the list and renumbers the second one. Now you have two lists, each numbered 1 to 4, with a blank line between each list. That's not what you wanted. You wanted to interrupt the list so that items 5 through 8 begin after a line of normal text.

6 **Click the Undo button to reverse what you did in step 5.**

7 **Right-click and choose Skip Numbering from the shortcut menu.**

Now the numbers are still intact, and you have a blank line on which to digress or write explanatory text, such as "What a great movie!" or "My personal favorite!" The explanatory text is formatted like a normal sentence and is not given a number.

8 **Select the second batch of movie titles on the lower half of the screen.**

9 **Choose Format⇨Bullets and Numbering to see the Bullets and Numbering dialog box.**

You can also get to this dialog box by right-clicking in the text and choosing Bullets and Numbering from the bottom of the shortcut menu.

10 **Click the Numbered tab.**

This tab offers other ways of numbering a list, as shown in Figure 15-2. You can choose Roman numerals or letters, Arabic numerals with parentheses, or the usual Arabic numerals with periods.

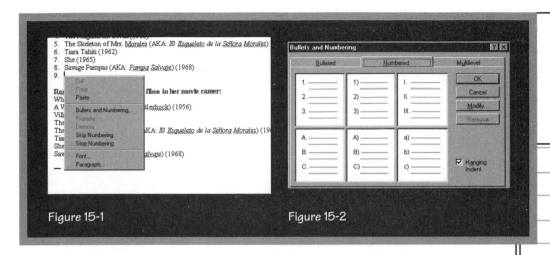

Figure 15-1

Figure 15-2

Figure 15-1: Right-click a numbered list, and you see this shortcut menu.

Figure 15-2: The Bullets and Numbering tab offers nonstandard ways to number a list.

11 **Click the numbered list style that tickles your fancy.**

A blue border appears around the style that you choose.

12 **Click OK to close the dialog box and see your numbered list in all its glory.**

In sum, you can get a numbered list in three ways: click the Numbering button, choose Format⇨Bullets and Numbering, or right-click and choose Bullets and Numbering from the shortcut menu. When completing the next lesson about creating bulleted lists, you will recognize many of the techniques that you learned in this lesson.

Note: To remove the numbers from a list, select the list and click the Numbering button.

✓ **Progress Check**

If you can do the following, you've mastered this lesson:

❑ Create a numbered list by selecting items first.

❑ Format and manipulate a numbered list with the shortcut menu.

❑ Create a numbered list with Roman numerals or other numeric schemes by way of the Bullets and Formatting dialog box.

Creating a Bulleted List

Lesson 15-2

In typesetting terminology, a *bullet* is a black, filled-in circle or other character. Use bulleted lists when you want to present alternatives to the reader or present a list in which the items are not ranked in any order.

Creating bulleted lists in Word 95 is pretty easy. If you completed the last lesson, creating bulleted lists will be especially easy for you because you are already familiar with the techniques for creating and manipulating lists. For this exercise, open the Bulleted List file in the Practice folder and follow these steps:

1 **Select the eight film titles in the list at the top of the screen.**

When order is not important, you can make a list a bulleted list. In the last lesson, you made a numbered list because the movies were listed by the dates on which they were made, and the list had a definite first-to-last order. In this list, using numbers might be redundant because the list is obviously in alphabetical order, so you will use bullets instead.

2 **Click the Bullets button.**

The Bullets button is the fourth from the right on the Formatting toolbar.

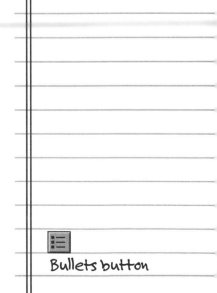

Bullets button

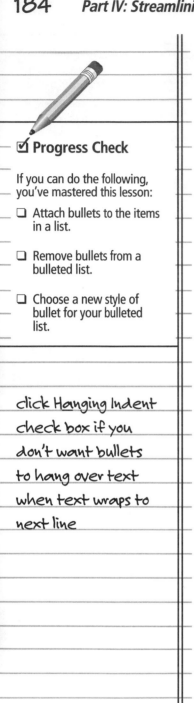

☑ Progress Check

If you can do the following, you've mastered this lesson:

❑ Attach bullets to the items in a list.

❑ Remove bullets from a bulleted list.

❑ Choose a new style of bullet for your bulleted list.

click Hanging Indent
check box if you
don't want bullets
to hang over text
when text wraps to
next line

Now each film title has a bullet next to its name. The fastest and easiest way to create a bulleted list is to enter the items on the list without any concern for bullets. Just press Enter after each line. When you're done, select the list and click the Bullets button.

3 Move the cursor to the end of the last line in the list and press Enter.

Word 95, assuming that you want to add an item to the list, puts a new bullet on the next line. Suppose, however, that you want to end the list.

4 Click the Bullets button.

That's pretty simple. By clicking the Bullets button when it is "pressed down," you "unpress" the button and make the bullets inactive.

5 Move the cursor the end of the fourth item on the list, *The Skeleton of Mrs. Morales,* **and press Enter.**

You want to write a normal sentence here, but Word 95 gives you a bullet. What to do?

6 Click the Bullets button on the Formatting toolbar.

When you click this button, you can type a normal sentence. Notice that the Bullets button on the Formatting toolbar is no longer pressed down.

7 Select the next batch of movie titles on the bottom half of the screen.

8 Choose Format➪Bullets and Numbering to see the Bullets and Numbering dialog box.

As the last lesson explained, you can also get this dialog box by right-clicking anywhere in a bulleted list and choosing Bullets and Numbering from the shortcut menu.

Figure 15-3 shows the Bulleted tab of the Bullets and Numbering dialog box. From here, you can choose diamond-shaped bullets, among other kinds of bullets, and even create bullet styles of your own, as the next step demonstrates.

9 Click the Modify button to see the Modify Bulleted List dialog box, click one of the bullet icons, click the up arrow in the Point Size box to make the bullet larger, and click OK.

The Modify Bulleted List dialog box is shown in Figure 15-4. You don't really have to go to all this trouble to create a new bullet, but I'm showing you anyway because a little challenge never hurt anyone.

10 Click OK to close the Bullets and Numbering dialog box and see your fancy new bullets.

on the test

To create a bulleted list, you can click the Bullets button, choose Format➪Bullets and Numbering, or right-click and choose Bullets and Numbering from the shortcut menu. Have fun with your bullets, and don't shoot them all in the same place.

Lesson 15-3

Numbering the Pages in a Document

In a document of any size, the pages need to be numbered. How else will readers know which page they are on or where to find the information they're looking for?

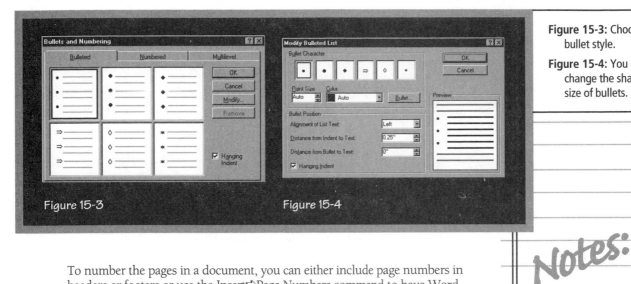

Figure 15-3

Figure 15-4

Figure 15-3: Choosing a bullet style.

Figure 15-4: You can change the shape and size of bullets.

To number the pages in a document, you can either include page numbers in headers or footers or use the Insert⇨Page Numbers command to have Word 95 do all the work of numbering the pages for you. This lesson describes how to number the pages of a document with the Insert⇨Page Numbers command. Lesson 15-4 explains how to include page numbers in headers or footers.

on the disk

For this exercise, you will use the Page Numbers file in the Practice folder. Open that file now and follow these steps to learn about page numbers:

1 **Choose Insert⇨Page Numbers to open the Page Numbers dialog box.**

The Page Numbers dialog box appears, as in Figure 15-5.

2 **From the Position drop-down list, choose on which end of the page you want the page number to appear: the top or the bottom.**

The page number can appear at the top of the page or at the bottom.

3 **From the Alignment drop-down list, choose where you want the page number to appear.**

The Left, Center, and Right options do exactly what they say they will do: put the page number in the left corner, center of the page, or right corner. Choose Inside or Outside if you are working on a double-sided document with text printed on both sides of the paper. On a double-sided document, Inside puts the page number close to the binding; Outside puts the page number away from the binding.

4 **Click OK to close the dialog box.**

Word 95 does not put a page number on the first page of a document. However, if you want it to do so, click the Show Number on First Page box in the Page Numbers dialog box.

Notes:

☑ Progress Check

If you can do the following, you've mastered this lesson:

❑ Put page numbers on the pages of a document.

❑ Tell Word 95 where on the pages the page numbers should go.

preview box shows where page number will go

Creating Headers and Footers   Lesson 15-4

A *header* is a little description that appears along the top of a page so that the reader knows what's what. Usually, headers include the page number and a title. A *footer* is the same thing as a header, except it appears along the bottom of the page, as befits its name.

Figure 15-5: Numbering the pages of a document.

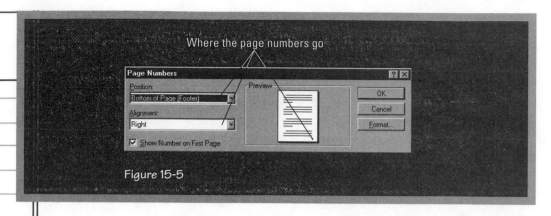

Figure 15-5

Headers and footers are often the same from page to page, except in double-sided documents, where even pages have one header and odd pages have another. In this book, for example, headers on even pages (the left side of the page spread) tell you which part you are in, and odd pages (on the right side of the page spread) say which unit you're working on. This lesson explains how to put headers and footers in documents, and you'll learn how to use the buttons on the Header and Footer toolbar, shown in Figure 15-6.

 on the disk

To learn how to enter a header or footer, open the Header and Footer file in the Practice folder and follow these steps:

1 Choose View➪Header and Footer.

Word 95 changes the view of your document to Page Layout view. You see the top of the screen, where a rectangle shows the outline of the header. In this document, I already put the title in the header.

Notice the Header and Footer toolbar. Throughout this exercise, you will click buttons on this toolbar to experiment with headers and footers.

By the way, you can see headers and footers in the main document window in Page Layout view. To edit a header or footer in Page Layout view, double-click it and start typing.

2 Type your name after the slash.

The author's name often appears in the header.

3 Type a few blank spaces and then click the Date button on the Header and Footer toolbar.

Clicking this button inserts the date. When you print a document, the date on which the document is printed appears in the header. The date in the header changes depending on when you print the document.

Date button

4 Enter a few spaces and type Page **and another space.**

5 Click the Page Numbers button on the Header and Footer toolbar.

Doing so inserts the page number in the header at the insertion point location.

6 Select the text in the header and change its font and font size.

In a header and footer, you can call on most Word 95 commands, including those on the Standard and Formatting toolbars. You can change the text's font and size, click an alignment button, or paste from the Clipboard, for example.

Page Numbers button

7 Click the Page Setup button, click the Margins tab of the Page Setup dialog box, click the up arrow in the Header box to make more room for the header, and click OK.

You didn't have to make more room for the header because your header isn't necessarily large and doesn't take up two lines. But you can make more room for a header and footer right away from the Headers and Footers toolbar.

Page Setup button

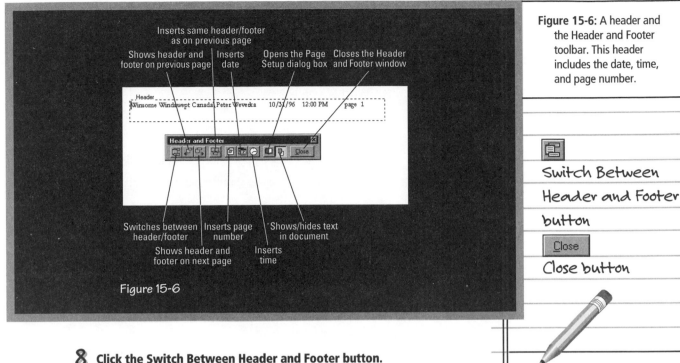

Figure 15-6

Figure 15-6: A header and the Header and Footer toolbar. This header includes the date, time, and page number.

Switch Between Header and Footer button

Close button

8 **Click the Switch Between Header and Footer button.**

This button takes you back and forth between the header and footer. Now you see a footer rectangle similar to the header rectangle.

9 **Enter a footer in the footer rectangle.**

I trust that you can think of something to put in this footer box. You might enter **Canada's flag has a maple leaf on it.**

10 **Click the Close button to get back to your document.**

The buttons on the Header and Footer toolbar look cryptic and uninviting at first, but when you start creating headers and footers, you soon find out how useful they are.

☑ **Progress Check**

If you can do the following, you've mastered this lesson and are ready to move on to the Unit 15 quiz:

❑ Enter a header in a document.

❑ Enter a footer in a document.

❑ Work with the buttons on the Header and Footer toolbar.

Unit 15 Quiz

For the following questions, circle the letter of the correct answer or answers. You may find more than one right answer to each question.

1. **This button does which of the following?**

   A. Creates a numbered list

   B. Creates a bulleted list

   C. Creates a table

   D. Plays a short song by Bing Crosby, America's favorite crooner

2. **To end a numbered list, you do which of the following:**

   A. Just stop counting.

   B. Right-click and choose Stop Numbering from the shortcut menu.

C. Click the Numbering button again.

D. Choose Format⇨End Numbering Now.

3. **What is a bullet?**

A. A kind of tab stop

B. A black, filled-in circle or other character

C. A ubiquitous prop in Sylvester Stallone movies

D. A Freudian projectile shot from the barrel of a gun

4. **To number the pages of a document, you do which of the following?**

A. Choose File⇨Page Setup.

B. Choose Insert⇨Page Numbers.

C. Click the Page Numbers button on the Header and Footer toolbar.

D. Choose View⇨Page Layout.

5. **What is a header?**

A. When you crash on your bike and go over the handlebars

B. A little description that appears along the top of a page

C. When you totally wipe out on your skateboard

D. The opposite of a footer

6. **This button does which of the following?**

A. Lets you play tic-tac-toe

B. Turns the page

C. Inserts the page number in a header or footer

D. Inserts the date in a header or footer

Unit 15 Exercise

on the disk

For this exercise on the formatting tricks in Unit 15, open the Rosenda Monteros Movies file in the Practice folder and do the following:

1. Number the pages of this document, and do so without including the numbers in a header or footer.

2. Click the Undo button to reverse what you did in step 2.

3. Number the pages by including a page number in the footer.

4. Create a long, elaborate header that includes the date and time as well as the first two lines of Elvis Presley's famous hit, "Jailhouse Rock." You may have to click the Page Setup button on the Header and Footer toolbar make more room for your header.

Part IV Review

Unit 12 Summary

▶ **Toolbars:** Right-click on a toolbar and click a toolbar name to remove it from or add it to the screen. You can also choose View⇨Toolbars to add or remove toolbars. You can drag toolbars to new places on-screen as well as resize them.

▶ **The ruler:** Choose View⇨Ruler to remove the ruler when you don't require it. Choose the command again to get the ruler back.

▶ **Full Screen view:** Choose View⇨Full Screen View to remove all but the ruler from the screen and be able to concentrate better on the text and layout of the document. To get back to Normal view, click the Full button or press Esc.

▶ **Page Layout view:** Click the Page Layout View button in the lower-left corner of the screen or choose View⇨Page Layout to get this view on-screen. In Page Layout view, you can see the borders of the page and also see precisely where the margins are.

Unit 13 Summary

▶ **Working with more than one document:** Choose Window⇨Arrange All to see all open documents on-screen at once. Each document appears in its own window. Choose options from the Control menu to minimize or maximize the windows. To switch windows, click in the window you want to work in.

▶ **Working two places in the same document:** To open a document in two different places, choose Window⇨Split or place the cursor above the vertical scroll bar, and when the split cursor appears, drag it onto the screen. Doing so splits the screen into north and south halves. You can also work in two places at once by choosing Window⇨New Window to create two outlooks on the same document. Choose different versions of the document from the Window menu.

▶ **Using bookmarks:** Choose Edit⇨Bookmark and create a bookmark in the dialog box to mark a place in the text to which you need to come back often. To get back to a place in the text where you have placed a bookmark, choose Edit⇨Bookmark, choose the bookmark name in the dialog box, and click OK.

▶ **Zooming in and out:** Pull down the Zoom Control menu and choose a new setting to make the text in your document look larger or smaller. You can also type a percentage setting directly into the Zoom Control text box.

▶ **Inserting a whole document:** Place the cursor where you want the document to go, and then choose Insert⇨File. In the File dialog box, find and choose the file you want to insert, and then click OK.

Part IV Review

Unit 14 Summary

▶ **Spell-checking:** Click the Spelling button, choose Tools⇨Spelling or press F7 to start a spell-check. The Spelling dialog box gives you many options for dealing with misspelled words. You can ignore them, change them, and even add them to Word 95's dictionary.

▶ **Using the Thesaurus:** Put the cursor in a word and choose Tools⇨Thesaurus or press Shift+F7 to find a synonym for the word. The Thesaurus dialog box offers several tools for searching for and maybe finding a good synonym.

▶ **Finding and replacing:** Press Ctrl+F or choose Edit⇨Find to find a word or phrase in a document. You can narrow your search by looking only for words that are upper- or lowercase or for whole words. Press Ctrl+H or choose Edit⇨Replace to replace words as well as find them. The Replace dialog box offers the same options for narrowing a search as the Find dialog box.

▶ **Undoing mistakes:** Click the Undo button on the Standard toolbar to undo your most recent mistake. You can also choose Edit⇨Undo or press Ctrl+Z. By pulling down the Undo menu, you can undo several of your most recent actions.

▶ **Entering "automatic" text:** With the Edit⇨AutoText command, you can store addresses and other things that you often type in documents.

Unit 15 Summary

▶ **Numbering lists:** To number a list, select it and click the Numbering button. You can also enter numbered items as you type them by clicking the Numbering button on the Formatting toolbar first. Each time you press Enter, Word 95 puts a number at the start of the new line.

▶ **Getting bulleted lists:** To create a bulleted list, either type the items in the list first, select them, and click the Bullets button; or click the Bullets button and type away. Each time you press Enter to start a new line, Word 95 puts a bullet at the start of the line.

▶ **Numbering document pages:** Choose Insert⇨Page Numbers and choose options in the Page Numbers dialog box to put numbers on the pages of a document.

▶ **Creating headers and footers:** Choose View⇨Header and Footer and enter the header in a header box, or else click the Switch Between Header and Footer button and enter a footer.

Part IV Test

This test will show you how much you learned in Part IV and what you need to review. In Part IV, you will find one "On the Test" icon for each question on this test. If you get a wrong answer, turn to the lesson for which you need more instruction and, using the "On the Test" icons as guides, find the paragraph or instruction list that tells you the answer to the question you missed. Read the paragraph or instruction list carefully to learn how to do the task. This test is not supposed to measure how well you learned Word 95. It is meant only to help you review what you learned and re-explore what you didn't get right the first time around.

By the way, the author of this test and this book — me — never did well on these kinds of tests. I shined on essay tests, where you get to deal with ambiguities and circle around and around a topic until you've explained it. On multiple-choice and true/false tests like this one, where every question has a definite answer, either all the answers seemed right to me or all of them seemed wrong. And I used to play a game with myself when I took multiple-choice tests. I would try to find patterns in the answers, so that if A was the right answer to question 10, for example, it couldn't be the right answer to question 11. On the other hand, if A hadn't been the right answer for a number of questions in a row, that meant A was due to be the right answer, so I would choose A. It wasn't a smart way to take multiple-choice tests.

Where I went to high school, you were allowed to get your confidential student records a year after you graduated. I got mine and learned that I was nearly a moron, according to the Hemet Unified School District. Somewhere along the line, I flunked a multiple-choice IQ test. That surprised me, because when I got my records, I was a sophomore in college and was doing very well in school.

The moral of this story is that there are many different kinds of intelligence and there are many different ways of measuring how smart a person is. If you do well on multiple-choice tests, don't let it go to your head. Don't let it bother your head if you do badly on these tests, either.

True/False

Circle T or F, depending on whether the statement is true or false.

T F	1. People who do well on multiple-choice tests are really, really smart.	
T F	2. Word 95 offers many different toolbars, and you can bring them on-screen if you want.	
T F	3. You can switch to Full Screen view by clicking a button.	
T F	4. You can have more than one document open at once.	
T F	5. The Zoom command enlarges the type size of text.	

T F	6. The spell-checker catches all spelling errors.
T F	7. You should save your document before you start finding and replacing text.
T F	8. If you select the third item on the Undo pull-down menu, you undo your last three actions.
T F	9. A bulleted list is a good way to present a list of equal alternatives in a document.
T F	10. You can include a page number in a header or footer.

Part IV Test

Multiple choice

Circle the right answer to the following questions. Some questions may have more than one right answer.

11. **To display a new toolbar on-screen, you do which of the following?**

    A. Right-click on a toolbar and choose the toolbar you want from the shortcut menu.

    B. Choose View⇨Toolbars and choose the toolbar from the dialog box.

    C. Choose View⇨Page Layout.

    D. Drag the toolbar onto the screen.

    E. Click on a toolbar and fill in the Toolbars dialog box.

12. **Which of these commands lets you import one complete file into another?**

    A. Edit⇨Paste

    B. Edit⇨Paste Special

    C. Insert⇨File

    D. File⇨Insert

    E. File⇨Recycle

13. **To search for a synonym for a word in a document, you use which of these commands?**

    A. Edit⇨Bookmark

    B. Format⇨Thesaurus

    C. Tools⇨Thesaurus

    D. Press Shift+F7

    E. Tools⇨Grammar

14. **You can create a numbered list by using which of these techniques?**

    A. Choose Format⇨Bullets and Numbering.

    B. Click the Numbering button on the Formatting toolbar.

    C. Right-click and choose Bullets and Numbering from the shortcut menu.

    D. Count the sheep as they go by in your dreams.

    E. Choose Insert⇨Page Numbers.

15. **To create a bulleted list, you use which of these techniques?**

    A. Right-click and choose Bullets and Numbering from the shortcut menu.

    B. Click the Bullets button.

    C. Choose Format⇨Bullets and Numbering.

    D. Take aim and fire.

    E. All of the above.

16. **Beatles fans circa 1969 knew that Paul was dead for which of the following reasons?**

    A. On the cover of the *Sgt. Pepper's Lonely Hearts Club Band* album, a hand can be seen directly over Paul's head.

    B. On the same album cover, you can see Paul's bass guitar lying on flowers over a coffin.

    C. At the end of "Strawberry Fields Forever," John says, "I buried Paul."

    D. Paul wears a black carnation in the *Magical Mystery Tour* movie.

    E. The lyrics of "Come Together" are "One and one and one is three." Three Beatles?

Matching

17. **Match the following views to their descriptions.**

    A. Page Layout view   1. The range of vision, understanding, or cognizance.

    B. Scenic view   2. Shows just the page and only one ruler.

    C. Full Screen view   3. Shows columns, graphics in text, and page borders.

    D. Purview   4. Shows the Grand Canyon.

    E. Normal view   5. Shows just text without the menu bar, scroll bars, or status bar.

Part IV Test

18. **Match each button in the Spelling dialog box with the description of what it does.**

A. Ignore All

1. Starts the spell-check after you go outside the Spelling dialog box.

B. Resume

2. Puts the word on the list of words that are fixed as you type them.

C. Change All

3. Changes all instances of the misspelled word in the document.

D. Add

4. Tells the spell checker to skip over the word throughout the document.

E. AutoCorrect

5. Puts the word in the spell-checker's dictionary.

19. **Match the button to the correct command name.**

A. 1. Undo

B. 2. Numbering

C. 3. Spelling

D. 4. Redo

E. 5. Bullets

20. **Match these buttons from the Header and Footer toolbar with the right names.**

A. 1. Page Setup

B. 2. Switch Between Header and Footer

C. 3. Close

D. 4. Date

E. 5. Time

Part IV Lab Assignment

As you surely know if you did the other three lab assignments in this book, lab assignments give you a chance to try out new word processing techniques in realistic situations. This lab assignment is not meant to make you sweat inordinately. Instead, it will give you practical experience with the techniques you learned in Part IV.

In the previous three lab assignments, you constructed documents for *Silver Screen* magazine. An editor at *Silver Screen* asked you, a famous journalist and movie star biographer, to write a "Where Are They Now?" article about Rosenda Monteros. Well, I have some bad news. You were not able to find anything about the extraordinary Hispanic actress — and neither was I. I've searched through newspaper and movie databases on the Internet, and I even called a movie buff acquaintance of mine who promised to get me word of her, but nobody can find Rosenda Monteros. Where did she go?

It looks as if you, the famous journalist, will have to do what any other journalist would do in this situation. Instead of a "Where Are They Now?" article, you have to write a "Tag Along with Me as I Search Fruitlessly for a Movie Star and Ruminate Out Loud the Whole Time about the State of the Movies, Politics, and Anything Else that Comes into My Empty Head" article. Don't worry — you don't actually have to write it because I wrote it for you.

Part IV Lab Assignment

For this lab assignment, open the Journalism file in the Practice folder and complete the following steps.

Step 1: Manipulating the screen

Experiment with different ways of seeing the article on-screen. Try out Full Screen view and Page Layout view. Remove the ruler. Which is the best way for you to work?

Step 2: Working with windows and other files

Go to the end of the article and insert the Print Preview file. You will find it on the Practice folder. Use the Zoom Control menu to choose the Zoom setting that suits you best.

Open a window on two different parts of the document, the start and the finish. You can do so by splitting the screen or by using the Window⇨New Window command. Scroll around in one of the windows and then close it.

Step 3: Clarity and writing

Spell-check the document and fix all spelling errors. The spell-checker will stop on a lot of names. You might tell it to ignore the one name, that of a famous actress, that keeps coming up.

Next, search for the following words, and when you've found them, open the Thesaurus to see whether you can find good synonyms for them: decadence, digress, passive.

Step 4: Formatting lists and pages

Go to the list of Monteros's movies near the start of the document (I've made it blue to help you find it) and make it either a numbered list or a bulleted list. Your call.

Next, number the pages of the document and create a footer with your name and the title of the article in it.

Appendixes

Part V

In this part . . .

In this part, the end of the book, are two appendixes. Appendix A gives you the answers to the questions in the part tests. It also tells you which lesson to review if you get an answer wrong. You can peek at Appendix A as you take the tests, but do so to the peril of your conscience and your immortal soul.

Appendix B is for people like me who can't remember what all those buttons in Word for Windows 95 do. It shows each button and offers a brief description of why you would click it.

How Did You Rate?

No matter how many questions you got wrong or right, you will always rate well with me.

Part I Answers

Question	Answer	If You Missed It, Try This
1.	False, absolutely	If you missed this one, ask yourself whether a computer ever had an original thought. Computers are machines and can do only what they have been told or programmed to do.
2.	True	Review Lesson 1-2.
3.	True	Review Lesson 1-3.
4.	False	Review Lesson 1-7.
5.	True	Review Lesson 3-2.
6.	False	Review Lesson 3-7.
7.	True	Review Lesson 4-1.
8.	True	Reviews Lessons 5-1, 5-2, and 5-3.
9.	True	Review Lesson 5-4.
10.	False	Review Lesson 5-5.
11.	B	Review Lesson 1-3.
12.	D	Review Lesson 1-5.
13.	A, D, E	Review Lessons 2-1 and 5-5.
14.	C	Not only are you naked, but you can't remember your locker combination or your locker number!
15.	D	Review Lesson 3-2.
16.	A	Review Lesson 3-4.

17.	D	Review Lesson 3-5.
18.	C	Review Lesson 5-5.
19.	A. 3	Review Lessons 1-2, 1-3, 1-5, 3-3, 3-4.
	B. 1	
	C. 4	
	D. 5	
	E. 2	
20.	A. 4	Review Lessons 1-2, 1-5, 2-1, 3-4.
	B. 5	
	C. 1	
	D. 2	
	E. 3	
21.	A. 3	
	B. 2	
	C. 5	
	D. 1	
	E. 4	
22.	A. 3	Review Lessons 1-3, 2-1, 3-3, 3-4.
	B. 1	
	C. 5	
	D. 4	
	E. 2	

Part II Answers

Question	Answer	If You Missed It, Try This
1.	False	A computer is a completely indifferent machine with no feelings whatsoever.
2.	True	Review Lesson 6-1.
3.	True	Review Lesson 6-2.
4.	False	Review Lesson 6-4.

5.	True	Review Lesson 7-1.
6.	True	Review Lesson 7-2.
7.	True	Review Lesson 8-1.
8.	False	Review Lesson 8-3.
9.	True	Review Lesson 8-3.
10.	True	Review Lesson 9-1.
11.	C, D	Review Lesson 6-1.
12.	D, E	Review Lesson 6-2.
13.	A, B, E	Review Lesson 7-1.
14.	B	Review Lesson 7-2.
15.	C	Review Lesson 8-3.
16.	A, C	Review Lessons 8-4, 9-2.
17.	C, D	Review Lesson 9-1.
18.	E, of course, but especially C	
19.	A. 3	Review Lessons 8-1 and 8-2.
	B. 5	
	C. 4	
	D. 1	
	E. 2	
20.	A. 5	Review Lessons 6-1, 6-2, 8-4.
	B. 2	
	C. 4	
	D. 1	
	E. 3	
21.	A. 2	Review Lessons 6-2, 8-1, 8-2, 8-4.
	B. 3	
	C. 5	
	D. 1	
	E. 4	

22.   A. 3   Ask your local grunge-rock video store
                       clerk about these movies.

           B. 4

           C. 5

           D. 1

           E. 2

Part III Answers

Question	Answer	If You Missed It, Try This
1.	False	Your creative abilities and talents, not to mention your superior intelligence, can never be replaced by a computer. Never.
2.	False	Review Lesson 10-1.
3.	True	Review Lesson 10-2.
4.	True	They say that the extra light encourages the seeds to sprout.
5.	True	Review Lesson 10-2.
6.	True	Review Lesson 11-1.
7.	True	Review Lesson 11-2.
8.	False	You could do it that way, but it is easier to tell Word to print more than one copy in the Print dialog box. See Lesson 11-2.
9.	True	Review Lesson 11-3.
10.	True	This rhyming couplet was spoken by the gypsy woman in *The Werewolf*.
11.	C	Review Lesson 10-2.
12.	B	Review Lesson 10-2.
13.	A, C, E	Review Lessons 10-2, 11-1.
14.	C	Review Lesson 11-2.
15.	B	Review Lessons 11-1, 11-2, 11-3.

16.   A. 3   Review Lesson 10-2.

        B. 2

        C. 4

        D. 1

        E. 5

17.   A. 4   Review Lessons 10-1, 11-1, Part I.

        B. 3

        C. 1

        D. 5

        E. 2

18.   A. 3   Review Lesson 11-2.

        B. 4

        C. 1

        D. 2

Part IV Answers

Question	Answer	If You Missed It, Try This
1.	False	Some of them are, maybe. But not all of them.
2.	True	Review Lesson 12-1.
3.	False	Review Lesson 12-3.
4.	True	Review Lesson 13-1.
5.	False	Review Lesson 13-3.
6.	False	Review Lesson 14-1.
7.	True	Review Lesson 14-3.
8.	True	Review Lesson 14-4.
9.	True	Review Lesson 15-2.
10.	True	Review Lessons 15-3, 15-4.
11.	A, B	Review Lesson 12-1.

12.	C	Review Lesson 13-4.
13.	C, E	Review Lesson 14-2.
14.	A, B, C	Review Lesson 15-1.
15.	A, B, C	Review Lesson 15-2.
16.	All of them. Trippy, *n'est-ce pas?*	

17.
A. 3   Review Lessons 12-3, 12-4.

B. 4

C. 5

D. 1

E. 2

18.
A. 4   Review Lesson 14-1.

B. 1

C. 3

D. 5

E. 2

19.
A. 3   Review Lesson 14-1.

B. 5   Review Lesson 15-2.

C. 1   Review Lesson 14-4.

D. 2   Review Lesson 15-1.

E. 4   Review Lesson 14-4.

20.
A. 5   Review Lesson 15-4.

B. 4

C. 3

D. 2

E. 1

The Toolbars

Appendix B is a quick reference that is designed to help you make sense of all the different buttons on the toolbars. Word 95 offers eight toolbars with the View⇨Toolbars command. All eight are described here.

To learn how to manipulate toolbars, see Lesson 12-1, "Removing and Adding Toolbars," in Part IV.

To find out the name of a button on a toolbar, point to it with the mouse cursor. The name appears below the button. (If it doesn't appear, choose View⇨Toolbars and click the Show ToolTips check box.) A brief explanation of what the button does shows up on the status bar when the mouse cursor is over a button.

Standard Toolbar

Button	What It Does
	Starts a new document
	Opens an existing document
	Saves the file in the document window
	Prints the document
	Opens a Preview window so that you can see documents before you print them
	Looks for spelling errors
	Removes text and places it on the Clipboard
	Copies text to the Clipboard
	Pastes text from the Clipboard
	Copies formatting so that you can paste it elsewhere with the Format Painter
	Reverses editorial changes
	Reverses something that you "undid" with the Undo command
	Automatically formats a document with the styles on the template
	Inserts an address from the Address Book

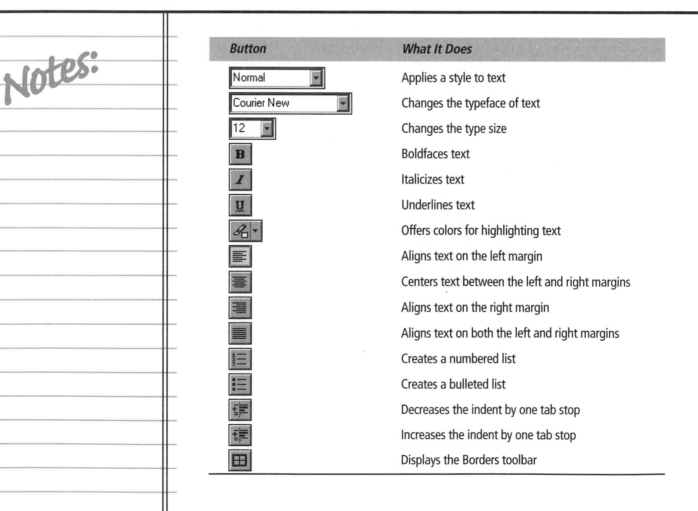

Button	What It Does
	Creates a table
	Inserts a Microsoft Excel worksheet in the document and opens Microsoft Excel
	Creates newspaper-style columns
	Displays the Drawing toolbar
¶	Shows formatting codes in the document
100%	Changes the size of text on-screen
	Shows or removes the Tip Wizard and its tip for using Word 95
▶?	Gives help on an area of the screen

Formatting Toolbar

Notes:

Button	What It Does
Normal	Applies a style to text
Courier New	Changes the typeface of text
12	Changes the type size
B	Boldfaces text
I	Italicizes text
U	Underlines text
	Offers colors for highlighting text
	Aligns text on the left margin
	Centers text between the left and right margins
	Aligns text on the right margin
	Aligns text on both the left and right margins
	Creates a numbered list
	Creates a bulleted list
	Decreases the indent by one tab stop
	Increases the indent by one tab stop
	Displays the Borders toolbar

Borders Toolbar

Button	What It Does
¾ pt ───────	Changes the line style of borders
	Changes the top border of table cells, paragraphs, and pictures
	Changes the bottom border
	Changes the left border
	Changes the right border
	Changes the inside border of table cells
	Changes the outside border of table cells, paragraphs, and pictures
	Removes borders
Clear	Changes the shading pattern of table cells, paragraphs, and pictures

Database Toolbar

Button	What It Does
	Changes how fields and records are separated
	Deletes, renames, or adds fields in the top row of the database
	Adds a record where the cursor is
	Deletes the record where the cursor is
	Sorts records in ascending order (A to Z, 1 to a zillion, oldest dates to more recent dates)
	Sorts records in descending order (Z to A, a zillion to 1, more recent dates to oldest dates)
	Inserts data into the document
	Updates records in a selected field
	Finds records in selected fields
	Switches to the main mail merge document

Drawing Toolbar

Notes:

Button	What It Does
	Draws a straight line
	Draws a rectangle
	Draws an oval
	Draws a bow-shaped arc
	Draws a squiggly, spidery line
	Draws a box inside which you can place a drawing or object
	Draws a label
	Formats a label you've drawn
	Pours color into a closed object you've drawn
	Lets you choose a color
¾ pt	Lets you choose a line width
	Lets you select or drag an object you've drawn
	Places an object in front of others in a drawing
	Places an object behind others
	Places an object in front of text
	Places an object behind text
	Makes several objects a single object so that you can move and resize them easily
	Breaks up a "grouped" object into its components
	Tips an object you've drawn onto its right side
	Turns an object upside-down
	Rotates an object by 90 degrees
	Pulls and tugs a freeform drawing into a different shape
	Lets you change the grid, which is used for aligning objects
	Aligns objects either with one another or with the page
	Opens a window so that you can create a picture
	Creates a frame so that you can insert or change the position of objects

Forms Toolbar

Button	What It Does
abl	Inserts a form field in which to type text
⊠	Inserts a box, or "multiple choice," form field
	Inserts a drop-down menu form field
	Changes the form field type
	Inserts a table
	Creates a frame to help position form fields
	Shows or hides gray shading where fields are
	Keeps users from changing the form

Microsoft Toolbar

Button	What It Does
	Switches to Excel
	Switches to PowerPoint
	Switches to Mail
	Switches to Access
	Switches to FoxPro
	Switches to Project
	Switches to Schedule+
	Switches to Publisher

Tip Wizard

 Frankly, I don't know why the Tip Wizard is considered a toolbar. The Tip Wizard offers a "Tip of the Day," which you can read and summarily remove from the screen by clicking the Tip Wizard button on the Standard toolbar. Lesson 5-4 explains how to use the Tip Wizard.

Index

•C•

◆D◆

◦*G*◦

•T•

Notes

Notes

10/31/95

The Internet For Macs® For Dummies® 2nd Edition	by Charles Seiter	ISBN: 1-56884-371-2	$19.99 USA/$26.99 Canada
The Internet For Macs® For Dummies® Starter Kit	by Charles Seiter	ISBN: 1-56884-244-9	$29.99 USA/$39.99 Canada
The Internet For Macs® For Dummies® Starter Kit Bestseller Edition	by Charles Seiter	ISBN: 1-56884-245-7	$39.99 USA/$54.99 Canada
The Internet For Windows® For Dummies® Starter Kit	by John R. Levine & Margaret Levine Young	ISBN: 1-56884-237-6	$34.99 USA/$44.99 Canada
The Internet For Windows® For Dummies® Starter Kit, Bestseller Edition	by John R. Levine & Margaret Levine Young	ISBN: 1-56884-246-5	$39.99 USA/$54.99 Canada

MACINTOSH

Mac® Programming For Dummies®	by Dan Parks Sydow	ISBN: 1-56884-173-6	$19.95 USA/$26.95 Canada
Macintosh® System 7.5 For Dummies®	by Bob LeVitus	ISBN: 1-56884-197-3	$19.95 USA/$26.95 Canada
MORE Macs® For Dummies®	by David Pogue	ISBN: 1-56884-087-X	$19.95 USA/$26.95 Canada
PageMaker 5 For Macs® For Dummies®	by Galen Gruman & Deke McClelland	ISBN: 1-56884-178-7	$19.95 USA/$26.95 Canada
QuarkXPress 3.3 For Dummies®	by Galen Gruman & Barbara Assadi	ISBN: 1-56884-217-1	$19.99 USA/$26.99 Canada
Upgrading and Fixing Macs® For Dummies®	by Kearney Rietmann & Frank Higgins	ISBN: 1-56884-189-2	$19.95 USA/$26.95 Canada

MULTIMEDIA

Multimedia & CD-ROMs For Dummies® 2nd Edition	by Andy Rathbone	ISBN: 1-56884-907-9	$19.99 USA/$26.99 Canada
Multimedia & CD-ROMs For Dummies® Interactive Multimedia Value Pack, 2nd Edition	by Andy Rathbone	ISBN: 1-56884-909-5	$29.99 USA/$39.99 Canada

OPERATING SYSTEMS:

DOS

MORE DOS For Dummies®	by Dan Gookin	ISBN: 1-56884-046-2	$19.95 USA/$26.95 Canada
OS/2® Warp For Dummies® 2nd Edition	by Andy Rathbone	ISBN: 1-56884-205-8	$19.99 USA/$26.99 Canada

UNIX

MORE UNIX® For Dummies®	by John R. Levine & Margaret Levine Young	ISBN: 1-56884-361-5	$19.99 USA/$26.99 Canada
UNIX® For Dummies®	by John R. Levine & Margaret Levine Young	ISBN: 1-878058-58-4	$19.95 USA/$26.95 Canada

WINDOWS

MORE Windows® For Dummies® 2nd Edition	by Andy Rathbone	ISBN: 1-56884-048-9	$19.95 USA/$26.95 Canada
Windows® 95 For Dummies®	by Andy Rathbone	ISBN: 1-56884-240-6	$19.99 USA/$26.99 Canada

PCS/HARDWARE

Illustrated Computer Dictionary For Dummies® 2nd Edition	by Dan Gookin & Wallace Wang	ISBN: 1-56884-218-X	$12.95 USA/$16.95 Canada
Upgrading and Fixing PCs For Dummies® 2nd Edition	by Andy Rathbone	ISBN: 1-56884-903-6	$19.99 USA/$26.99 Canada

PRESENTATION/AUTOCAD

AutoCAD For Dummies®	by Bud Smith	ISBN: 1-56884-191-4	$19.95 USA/$26.95 Canada
PowerPoint 4 For Windows® For Dummies®	by Doug Lowe	ISBN: 1-56884-161-2	$16.99 USA/$22.99 Canada

PROGRAMMING

Borland C++ For Dummies®	by Michael Hyman	ISBN: 1-56884-162-0	$19.95 USA/$26.95 Canada
C For Dummies® Volume 1	by Dan Gookin	ISBN: 1-878058-78-9	$19.95 USA/$26.95 Canada
C++ For Dummies®	by Stephen R. Davis	ISBN: 1-56884-163-9	$19.95 USA/$26.95 Canada
Delphi Programming For Dummies®	by Neil Rubenking	ISBN: 1-56884-200-7	$19.99 USA/$26.99 Canada
Mac® Programming For Dummies®	by Dan Parks Sydow	ISBN: 1-56884-173-6	$19.95 USA/$26.95 Canada
PowerBuilder 4 Programming For Dummies®	by Ted Coombs & Jason Coombs	ISBN: 1-56884-325-9	$19.99 USA/$26.99 Canada
QBasic Programming For Dummies®	by Douglas Hergert	ISBN: 1-56884-093-4	$19.95 USA/$26.95 Canada
Visual Basic 3 For Dummies®	by Wallace Wang	ISBN: 1-56884-076-4	$19.95 USA/$26.95 Canada
Visual Basic "X" For Dummies®	by Wallace Wang	ISBN: 1-56884-230-9	$19.99 USA/$26.99 Canada
Visual C++ 2 For Dummies®	by Michael Hyman & Bob Arnson	ISBN: 1-56884-328-3	$19.99 USA/$26.99 Canada
Windows® 95 Programming For Dummies®	by S. Randy Davis	ISBN: 1-56884-327-5	$19.99 USA/$26.99 Canada

SPREADSHEET

1-2-3 For Dummies®	by Greg Harvey	ISBN: 1-878058-60-6	$16.95 USA/$22.95 Canada
1-2-3 For Windows® 5 For Dummies® 2nd Edition	by John Walkenbach	ISBN: 1-56884-216-3	$16.95 USA/$22.95 Canada
Excel 5 For Macs® For Dummies®	by Greg Harvey	ISBN: 1-56884-186-8	$19.95 USA/$26.95 Canada
Excel For Dummies® 2nd Edition	by Greg Harvey	ISBN: 1-56884-050-0	$16.95 USA/$22.95 Canada
MORE 1-2-3 For DOS For Dummies®	by John Weingarten	ISBN: 1-56884-224-4	$19.99 USA/$26.99 Canada
MORE Excel 5 For Windows® For Dummies®	by Greg Harvey	ISBN: 1-56884-207-4	$19.95 USA/$26.95 Canada
Quattro Pro 6 For Windows® For Dummies®	by John Walkenbach	ISBN: 1-56884-174-4	$19.95 USA/$26.95 Canada
Quattro Pro For DOS For Dummies®	by John Walkenbach	ISBN: 1-56884-023-3	$16.95 USA/$22.95 Canada

UTILITIES

Norton Utilities 8 For Dummies®	by Beth Slick	ISBN: 1-56884-166-3	$19.95 USA/$26.95 Canada

VCRS/CAMCORDERS

VCRs & Camcorders For Dummies™	by Gordon McComb & Andy Rathbone	ISBN: 1-56884-229-5	$14.99 USA/$20.99 Canada

WORD PROCESSING

Ami Pro For Dummies®	by Jim Meade	ISBN: 1-56884-049-7	$19.95 USA/$26.95 Canada
MORE Word For Windows® 6 For Dummies®	by Doug Lowe	ISBN: 1-56884-165-5	$19.95 USA/$26.95 Canada
MORE WordPerfect® 6 For Windows® For Dummies®	by Margaret Levine Young & David C. Kay	ISBN: 1-56884-206-6	$19.95 USA/$26.95 Canada
MORE WordPerfect® 6 For DOS For Dummies®	by Wallace Wang, edited by Dan Gookin	ISBN: 1-56884-047-0	$19.95 USA/$26.95 Canada
Word 6 For Macs® For Dummies®	by Dan Gookin	ISBN: 1-56884-190-6	$19.95 USA/$26.95 Canada
Word For Windows® 6 For Dummies®	by Dan Gookin	ISBN: 1-56884-075-6	$16.95 USA/$22.95 Canada
Word For Windows® For Dummies®	by Dan Gookin & Ray Werner	ISBN: 1-878058-86-X	$16.95 USA/$22.95 Canada
WordPerfect® 6 For DOS For Dummies®	by Dan Gookin	ISBN: 1-878058-77-0	$16.95 USA/$22.95 Canada
WordPerfect® 6.1 For Windows® For Dummies® 2nd Edition	by Margaret Levine Young & David Kay	ISBN: 1-56884-243-0	$16.95 USA/$22.95 Canada
WordPerfect® For Dummies®	by Dan Gookin	ISBN: 1-878058-52-5	$16.95 USA/$22.95 Canada

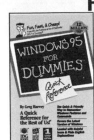

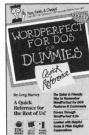

P C P R E S S

IDG BOOKS WORLDWIDE.

10/31/95

Official Hayes Modem Communications Companion
by Caroline M. Halliday

ISBN: 1-56884-072-1
$29.95 USA/$39.95 Canada
Includes software.

1,001 Komputer Answers from Kim Komando
by Kim Komando

ISBN: 1-56884-460-3
$29.99 USA/$39.99 Canada
Includes software.

PC World DOS 6 Handbook, 2nd Edition
by John Socha, Clint Hicks, & Devra Hall

ISBN: 1-878058-79-7
$34.95 USA/$44.95 Canada
Includes software.

BESTSELLER!

PC World Word For Windows® 6 Handbook
by Brent Heslop & David Angell

ISBN: 1-56884-054-3
$34.95 USA/$44.95 Canada
Includes software.

BESTSELLER!

PC World Microsoft® Access 2 Bible, 2nd Edition
by Cary N. Prague & Michael R. Irwin

ISBN: 1-56884-086-1
$39.95 USA/$52.95 Canada
Includes software.

PC World Excel 5 For Windows® Handbook, 2nd Edition
by John Walkenbach & Dave Maguiness

ISBN: 1-56884-056-X
$34.95 USA/$44.95 Canada
Includes software.

PC World WordPerfect® 6 Handbook
by Greg Harvey

ISBN: 1-878058-80-0
$34.95 USA/$44.95 Canada
Includes software.

QuarkXPress For Windows® Designer Handbook
by Barbara Assadi & Galen Gruman

ISBN: 1-878058-45-2
$29.95 USA/$39.95 Canada

NATIONAL BESTSELLER!

Official XTree Companion, 3rd Edition
by Beth Slick

ISBN: 1-878058-57-6
$19.95 USA/$26.95 Canada

NATIONAL BESTSELLER!

PC World DOS 6 Command Reference and Problem Solver
by John Socha & Devra Hall

ISBN: 1-56884-055-1
$24.95 USA/$32.95 Canada

SUPER STAR

Client/Server Strategies™: A Survival Guide for Corporate Reengineers
by David Vaskevitch

ISBN: 1-56884-064-0
$29.95 USA/$39.95 Canada

Microsoft and Windows are registered trademarks of Microsoft Corporation. WordPerfect is a registered trademark of Novell. ----STRATEGIES and the IDG Books Worldwide logos are trademarks under exclusive license to IDG Books Worldwide, Inc., from International Data Group, Inc.

PROFESSIONAL PUBLISHING GROUP

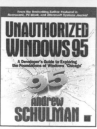

10/31/95

Unauthorized Windows® 95: A Developer's Guide to Exploring the Foundations of Windows "Chicago"
by Andrew Schulman
ISBN: 1-56884-169-8
$29.99 USA/$39.99 Canada

Unauthorized Windows® 95 Developer's Resource Kit
by Andrew Schulman
ISBN: 1-56884-305-4
$39.99 USA/$54.99 Canada

Best of the Net
by Seth Godin
ISBN: 1-56884-313-5
$22.99 USA/$32.99 Canada

Detour: The Truth About the Information Superhighway
by Michael Sullivan-Trainor
ISBN: 1-56884-307-0
$22.99 USA/$32.99 Canada

PowerPC Programming For Intel Programmers
by Kip McClanahan
ISBN: 1-56884-306-2
$49.99 USA/$64.99 Canada

Foundations™ of Visual C++ Programming For Windows® 95
by Paul Yao & Joseph Yao
ISBN: 1-56884-321-6
$39.99 USA/$54.99 Canada

Heavy Metal™ Visual C++ Programming
by Steve Holzner
ISBN: 1-56884-196-5
$39.95 USA/$54.95 Canada

Heavy Metal™ OLE 2.0 Programming
by Steve Holzner
ISBN: 1-56884-301-1
$39.95 USA/$54.95 Canada

Lotus Notes Application Development Handbook
by Erica Kerwien
ISBN: 1-56884-308-9
$39.99 USA/$54.99 Canada
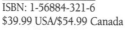

The Internet Direct Connect Kit
by Peter John Harrison
ISBN: 1-56884-135-3
$29.95 USA/$39.95 Canada

Macworld® Ultimate Mac® Programming
by Dave Mark
ISBN: 1-56884-195-7
$39.95 USA/$54.95 Canada

The UNIX®-Haters Handbook
by Simson Garfinkel, Daniel Weise, & Steven Strassmann
ISBN: 1-56884-203-1
$16.95 USA/$22.95 Canada

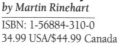

Learn C++ Today!
by Martin Rinehart
ISBN: 1-56884-310-0
34.99 USA/$44.99 Canada

Type & Learn™ C
by Tom Swan
ISBN: 1-56884-073-X
34.95 USA/$44.95 Canada

Type & Learn™ Windows® Programming
by Tom Swan
ISBN: 1-56884-071-3
34.95 USA/$44.95 Canada
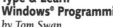

Windows is a registered trademark of Microsoft Corporation. Mac is a registered trademark of Apple Computer. UNIX is a registered trademark of AT&T. Macworld is a registered trademark of International Data Group, Inc. Foundations of ----, Heavy Metal, Type & Learn, and the IDG Books Worldwide logos are trademarks under exclusive license to IDG Books Worldwide, Inc., from International Data Group, Inc.

For scholastic requests & educational orders please call Educational Sales, at 1. 800. 434. 2086

FOR MORE INFO OR TO ORDER, PLEASE CALL ▶ 800. 762. 2974

For volume discounts & special orders please call Tony Real, Special Sales, at 415. 655. 3048

Order Center: **(800) 762-2974** *(8 a.m.–6 p.m., EST, weekdays)*

Quantity	ISBN	Title	Price	Total

Shipping & Handling Charges

	Description	First book	Each additional book	Total
Domestic	Normal	$4.50	$1.50	$
	Two Day Air	$8.50	$2.50	$
	Overnight	$18.00	$3.00	$
International	Surface	$8.00	$8.00	$
	Airmail	$16.00	$16.00	$
	DHL Air	$17.00	$17.00	$

*For large quantities call for shipping & handling charges.

**Prices are subject to change without notice.

Ship to:

Name _____

Company _____

Address _____

City/State/Zip_____

Daytime Phone _____

Payment: ☐ Check to IDG Books Worldwide (US Funds Only)

☐ VISA ☐ MasterCard ☐ American Express

Card #_____ Expires _____

Signature _____

Subtotal _____

CA residents add
applicable sales tax _____

IN, MA, and MD
residents add
5% sales tax _____

IL residents add
6.25% sales tax_____

RI residents add
7% sales tax_____

TX residents add
8.25% sales tax_____

Shipping_____

Total _____

Please send this order form to:

IDG Books Worldwide, Inc.
7260 Shadeland Station, Suite 100
Indianapolis, IN 46256

Allow up to 3 weeks for delivery.
Thank you!

IDG BOOKS WORLDWIDE LICENSE AGREEMENT

Important — read carefully before opening the software packet. This is a legal agreement between you (either an individual or an entity) and IDG Books Worldwide, Inc. (IDGB). By opening the accompanying sealed packet containing the software disk, you acknowledge that you have read and accept the following IDGB License Agreement. If you do not agree and do not want to be bound by the terms of this Agreement, promptly return the book and the unopened software packet(s) to the place you obtained them for a full refund.

1. **License.** This License Agreement (Agreement) permits you to use one copy of the enclosed Software program(s) on a single computer. The Software is in "use" on a computer when it is loaded into temporary memory (i.e., RAM) or installed into permanent memory (e.g., hard disk, CD-ROM, or other storage device) of that computer.

2. **Copyright.** The entire contents of this disk and the compilation of the Software are copyrighted and protected by both United States copyright laws and international treaty provisions. You may only (a) make one copy of the Software for backup or archival purposes, or (b) transfer the Software to a single hard disk, provided that you keep the original for backup or archival purposes. Do not use the software if you do not want to follow its Licensing Agreement. None of the material on this disk or listed in this Book may ever be distributed, in original or modified form, for commercial purposes.

3. **Other Restrictions.** You may not rent or lease the Software. You may transfer the Software and user documentation on a permanent basis provided you retain no copies and the recipient agrees to the terms of this Agreement. You may not reverse engineer, decompile, or disassemble the Software except to the extent that the foregoing restriction is expressly prohibited by applicable law. If the Software is an update or has been updated, any transfer must include the most recent update and all prior versions. By opening the package that contains the software disk, you will be agreeing to abide by the licenses and restrictions for the software. Do not open the software package unless you agree to be bound by the license agreements.

4. **Limited Warranty.** IDGB warrants that the Software and disk are free from defects in materials and workmanship for a period of sixty (60) days from the date of purchase of this Book. If IDGB receives notification within the warranty period of defects in material or workmanship, IDGB will replace the defective disk. IDGB's entire liability and your exclusive remedy shall be limited to replacement of the Software, which is returned to IDGB with a copy of your receipt. This Limited Warranty is void if failure of the Software has resulted from accident, abuse, or misapplication. Any replacement Software will be warranted for the remainder of the original warranty period or thirty (30) days, whichever is longer.

5. **No Other Warranties.** To the maximum extent permitted by applicable law, IDGB and the author disclaim all other warranties, express or implied, including but not limited to implied warranties of merchantability and fitness for a particular purpose, with respect to the Software, the programs, the source code contained therein, and/or the techniques described in this Book. This Limited Warranty gives you specific legal rights. You may have others that vary from state/jurisdiction to state/jurisdiction.

6. **No Liability For Consequential Damages.** To the extent permitted by applicable law, in no event shall IDGB or the author be liable for any damages whatsoever (including without limitation, damages for loss of business profits, business interruption, loss of business information, or any other pecuniary loss) arising out of the use of or inability to use the Book or the Software, even if IDGB has been advised of the possibility of such damages. Because some states/jurisdictions do not allow the exclusion or limitation of liability for consequential or incidental damages, the above limitation may not apply to you.

7. **U.S. Government Restricted Rights.** Use, duplication, or disclosure of the Software by the U.S. Government is subject to restrictions stated in paragraph (c) (1) (ii) of the Rights in Technical Data and Computer Software clause of DFARS 252.227-7013, and in subparagraphs (a) through (d) of the Commercial Computer—Restricted Rights clause at FAR 52.227-19, and in similar clauses in the NASA FAR supplement, when applicable.

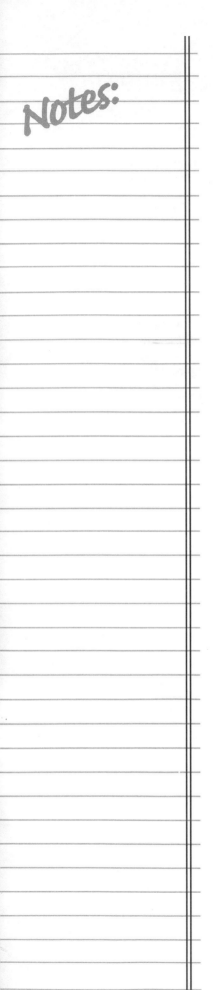
Notes:

Installing the Disk

Follow these instructions to install the files that you'll use throughout this book. Depending on your computer's setup, the installation program may have some difficulty installing the files. Try to go through the entire installation routine; then check to see whether the files were actually installed (you can see a listing of all the files on the Files at a Glance page in the beginning of this book). If they weren't, or if you have difficulty getting through the routine, call the IDG Books Customer Support number: 800-762-2974.

With Windows 95 running, follow these steps:

1. **Insert the Dummies 101 disk into your computer's 3¹/₂-inch floppy disk drive (the only drive in which it will fit).**

2. **Click the word Start at the bottom of the screen. A menu pops up.**

3. **Click Settings in that menu. Another menu pops up.**

4. **Click the Control Panel option. You see a group of icons.**

5. **Double-click the Add/Remove Programs icon. The Add/Remove Properties dialog box appears.**

6. **Click the Install button.**

7. **Click the Next button to ask Windows 95 to search for the installation program.**

8. **Click the Finish button to begin the installation program.**

9. **Follow the directions on-screen. You can press the Esc key at any time to exit the installation program.**

After you complete the installation process, all the files that you need for this book are ready and waiting for you on your hard drive. Store the disk where it will be free from harm — you'll need it later if you want to reinstall any of the files to your hard drive.

IDG BOOKS WORLDWIDE REGISTRATION CARD

RETURN THIS REGISTRATION CARD FOR FREE CATALOG

Title of this book: Dummies 101: Word For Windows 95

My overall rating of this book: ❑ Very good [1] ❑ Good [2] ❑ Satisfactory [3] ❑ Fair [4] ❑ Poor [5]

How I first heard about this book:

❑ Found in bookstore; name: [6] _____

❑ Advertisement: [8] _____

❑ Word of mouth; heard about book from friend, co-worker, etc.: [10] _____

❑ Book review: [7] _____

❑ Catalog: [9] _____

❑ Other: [11] _____

What I liked most about this book:

_____

_____

What I would change, add, delete, etc., in future editions of this book:

_____

_____

Other comments:

_____

_____

Number of computer books I purchase in a year: ❑ 1 [12] ❑ 2-5 [13] ❑ 6-10 [14] ❑ More than 10 [15]

I would characterize my computer skills as: ❑ Beginner [16] ❑ Intermediate [17] ❑ Advanced [18] ❑ Professional [19]

I use ❑ DOS [20] ❑ Windows [21] ❑ OS/2 [22] ❑ Unix [23] ❑ Macintosh [24] ❑ Other: [25]_____

(please specify)

I would be interested in new books on the following subjects:
(please check all that apply, and use the spaces provided to identify specific software)

❑ Word processing: [26] _____

❑ Data bases: [28] _____

❑ File Utilities: [30] _____

❑ Networking: [32] _____

❑ Other: [34] _____

❑ Spreadsheets: [27] _____

❑ Desktop publishing: [29] _____

❑ Money management: [31] _____

❑ Programming languages: [33] _____

I use a PC at (please check all that apply): ❑ home [35] ❑ work [36] ❑ school [37] ❑ other: [38] _____

The disks I prefer to use are ❑ 5.25 [39] ❑ 3.5 [40] ❑ other: [41]_____

I have a CD ROM: ❑ yes [42] ❑ no [43]

I plan to buy or upgrade computer hardware this year: ❑ yes [44] ❑ no [45]

I plan to buy or upgrade computer software this year: ❑ yes [46] ❑ no [47]

Name: _____ Business title: [48] _____ Type of Business: [49] _____

Address (❑ home [50] ❑ work [51]/Company name: _____)

Street/Suite# _____

City [52]/State [53]/Zipcode [54]: _____ Country [55] _____

❑ **I liked this book!** You may quote me by name in future
IDG Books Worldwide promotional materials.

My daytime phone number is _____

IDG BOOKS

THE WORLD OF COMPUTER KNOWLEDGE

❏ **YES!**

Please keep me informed about IDG's World of Computer Knowledge.
Send me the latest IDG Books catalog.